In their different careers in teaching and television **Penelope Middelboe, Donald Fry** and **Chris Grace** have enjoyed bringing other voices to a wider audience. This is the first book they have produced together. Penelope Middelboe's previous book was also based on diaries – the journals of her great great aunt Edith Olivier, 1924–48. She has worked with Chris Grace, former Director of Animation at S4C/Channel 4 Wales, producing and script editing award-winning adaptations of the Western canon including Oscar-nominated *The Canterbury Tales* and Shakespeare – *The Animated Tales*, the springboard for the charity, the Shakespeare Schools Festival, which they now run. Donald Fry taught for twenty years in secondary schools in Basildon, London and Coventry before becoming English Adviser for West Sussex. He has written a study of children reading, 'Children Talk About Books', and is now working on a book about children writing poetry.

WE SHALL
NEVER
SURRENDER

WARTIME DIARIES 1939–1945

Edited by
Penelope Middelboe, Donald Fry
and Christopher Grace

PAN BOOKS

First published 2011 by Macmillan

First published in paperback 2012 by Pan
an imprint of Pan Macmillan, a division of Macmillan Publishers Limited
Pan Macmillan, 20 New Wharf Road, London N1 9RR
Basingstoke and Oxford
Associated companies throughout the world
www.panmacmillan.com

ISBN 978-0-330-51134-6

The acknowledgements on page 375 constitute an
extension of this copyright page.

1 3 5 7 9 8 6 4 2

A CIP catalogue record for this book is available from
the British Library.

Typeset by SetSystems Ltd, Saffron Walden, Essex
Printed and bound by CPI Group (UK) Ltd, Croydon, CR0 4YY

Visit **www.panmacmillan.com** to read more about all our books
and to buy them. You will also find features, author interviews and
news of any author events, and you can sign up for e-newsletters
so that you're always first to hear about our new releases.

Contents

Introduction

The Second World War ended almost seventy years ago and for most of us it is hard to imagine what living through it was really like. Some of us might know about what older members of our families experienced, though we may wish we had listened more carefully or asked more when the opportunity was there. And of course, with continued fighting in Afghanistan and other parts of the world, war is still a reality for many British families today. But by and large those of us born after 1945 have not lived in close proximity to war, as our parents or grandparents did. For them, in their millions, it came into their lives: gas masks, rationing, blackouts, bomb shelters, the sending away of children, the conscription of men and women to battlefronts and factories and farms, the obliteration of homes, maiming and killing, the accumulation of atrocities, the persistent anxiety of separation, the spikes of fear, the dread of invasion and the longing, six years of it, for it all to be over.

Just two of our – the editors' – family members kept a diary, as far as we know. They were among the many who recorded the war, and we turned to them in our search to comprehend that period of our families' lives and our shared history. In all we chose nine diarists – five women, four men – all living in Britain when the war began in September 1939. We wanted more than entries that repeated the day's news, and we wanted writers who kept going for the duration. We looked for a range of viewpoints, and for people who wrote about their reactions and opinions. Events, yes, seen through different eyes, but we were also after accounts that would help us empathize with those we had not questioned enough – we wanted to understand how it felt.

They all wrote at length, and well. Perhaps they had future family readers in mind, but primarily they wrote for themselves. In their diaries they can complain without being thought negative, criticize others without being disloyal, predict events without being right, reveal their fears without being pathetic – howl or rage without being heard. Although, like us, you may find yourself shifting in and out of agreement and affinity with them, we hope you will end by being glad to have seen into their lives.

In 1939 **George Beardmore** (31) was living with his wife Jean and baby Victoria in North Harrow, not far from Jean's parents. He had been unemployed and was now a temporary insurance clerk. He had no love for the work, his ambition being to earn his living as a writer. Likely to lose his job, short of money and asthmatic, he worried about being able to provide for his family and keep them safe when the inevitable bombing began.

Vera Brittain (45) was married to George Catlin ('G.' in her diary), with a house in London and a cottage in the New Forest. She had served as a nurse in the First World War. The horror of that war, including the loss of her fiancé, her brother Edward and their two close friends, formed a large part of her best-selling book *Testament of Youth*, published in 1933. Two years later she lost more of those she loved: her father committed suicide and her long-standing friend Winifred Holtby died. By the time war was declared, Vera was a leading pacifist campaigner and member of the Peace Pledge Union. She feared that the new conflict would take yet more from her – her husband, her elderly mother, her two young children.

Alan Brooke (56), whose long military career stretched back to 1902, began his diary while on his way to take command of one of the three corps of the British army in France. He addressed it to Benita, his wife, as 'a record of my thoughts and impressions such as I would have discussed them with you had we been together'. She had saved him from the depression that had followed the death of his first wife after a car crash. He had been driving and blamed himself. He and Benita had two young children and lived in a house called Ferney Close in Hampshire. In 1939 neither of them could have known how Brooke's responsibilities would escalate and how much he would need the solace of his home and family.

Anne Garnett (30), originally from London, was known by her married name, Lee-Michell or Michell. Her teenage memoirs were eventually published under her maiden name; the extracts reproduced here are from her unpublished war diaries. She was married to Frank, a country lawyer who suffered from diabetes, then a life-threatening condition. They had two children, Sarah (6) and Caroline (3, also known as Toots), and were living in a detached modern house, Larks Lea, with a large garden in rural Somerset. She enjoyed reading and classical music, played the piano, and had studied art. Anne was an energetic member of her church and community but could also be outspoken and critical of established ways, and did not take well to the social duties of a solicitor's wife, preferring to have her friends round for a game of cards or tennis with drinks. How much of her world could the war destroy?

Clara Milburn (56) grew up in Coventry, married there in 1905 and made her first home a mile from the city centre and old cathedral. Since 1931 she and her husband Jack had lived in a village six miles from Coventry with their live-in helper Kate. Their only child Alan was 25 and back at home after university, having followed his father, now retired, into engineering. Gardening, church, walking the dog, shopping, village events – she had a peaceful routine. It would not last: Alan, as an officer in the Territorial Army, was likely to be among the first to be called up, and Coventry's engineering factories were bound to be a target for the Luftwaffe.

Naomi Mitchison (41) had published twenty works of fiction by 1939, and had given birth to six children, the eldest of whom had died of meningitis aged only 9.* She and her husband Dick were members of the Labour Party, and their London home, River Court in Hammersmith, was a meeting place for intellectuals of the left, including refugees from Europe with their grim news of race hatred. As war became certain, Naomi decided that Carradale, their estate in west Scotland, purchased recently as a holiday retreat, should become their new home, run-down though it was. Her family came from Scotland – her uncle still farmed in the east – and it would surely be safer than London.

Harold Nicolson (53), MP for West Leicester since 1935, had ended his diplomatic career at the embassy in Berlin, where he had got to know many now suffering under Hitler. When the foreign secretary, Anthony Eden, resigned in protest at the appeasement of Germany, Harold spoke in his support and joined the Eden Group of MPs critical of Prime Minister Neville Chamberlain. He knew that his home at Sissinghurst in Kent, where he and his wife Vita Sackville-West had created the garden that later became famous, would be in the path of a German invasion across the Channel. He knew too that his name would be on the list of those to be arrested.

---

* Geoff, who died, brothers Denny, Murdoch and Avrion, and sisters Lois and Valentine.

Hermione Ranfurly (25) 'lost' her parents when she was 16. Her mother, a manic depressive, was committed to a Swiss nursing home, and her father abandoned her with no money. Over the next year her remaining grandparents died and her adored brother was killed in a flying accident. Friends helped Hermione and her two younger sisters survive. She found work in London, from selling cookers to working in the War Office, which led to a posting in Australia. In Sydney she met Daniel Knox, the sixth Earl of Ranfurly, her future husband. At their wedding back in England there were twelve brides-maids and pages, one from each of the families which had shown her kindness. She and Dan settled in his Mayfair flat with no thought of ever being parted.

Charles Ritchie (32) was from Halifax in Canada. He had been in England before, studying for his MA at Oxford, and was now a diplomat at Canada House, his second posting. He arrived in January 1939, secured a bachelor flat and was beginning to enjoy mixing in upper-class literary circles. He had an affinity with the English, which became stronger through what he was to witness and endure during the Blitz and beyond.

Some of the nine were already in the habit of keeping a diary; the others began with the war, motivated by the momentous events. For the most part they wrote each day. When Clara Milburn began writing her thoughts in an exercise book in February 1940 she had no idea that she would fill another fourteen. As she finished the eleventh in 1944, she wrote, 'The only thing is to stick it and *stick it*, and STICK IT till the war is ended'. She could have been speaking for them all. Their thoughts often chime with our contemporary concerns – about the quality of political leadership, the ethics of war, the plight of refugees, control of information, changes in attitudes towards gender, class and race, and community cohesion. They tell us what happened, they put into words their feelings, and they also take us into their minds.

Most of the text is selected from our nine diarists' journals, but we have occasionally included extracts from their letters and books written at the time or from later memoirs, in order to complement the entries. We have also added at the end of each chapter some other voices in order to widen the picture of what people went through during the Second World War. For example, none of our principal diarists was interned or evacuated, or fought in the desert, or served in India or Singapore, or saw first-hand the horrors of the concentration camps. Again here we have not always confined ourselves to diaries, but most of these accounts are contemporary with the war.

'Writing all this,' noted George Beardmore at a low point in 1944, 'is perfectly useless except that it serves as an outlet for a mind oppressed with too many vivid images'. This 'outlet' is our insight – into the war we still want to know about and which is part of the history (often unspoken) of our families, and into the lives of people like us but under extreme stress. The diaries recreate for us the experience of familiar life becoming disrupted and distorted, of living with separation and loss, of fighting anxiety and fear. They are a form of resistance. That we read them now is part of their victory.

A note on the diary entries

Between them, our nine diarists wrote hundreds of thousands of words; Vera Brittain alone penned 150,000. Although we benefited hugely from the skill of the original editors of the published diaries, in putting this volume together we have had to be still more selective. We have visited the diaries at various points during the war, beginning with autumn 1939, ending in summer 1945. The selections cannot tell the full history of the war (a brief introduction to each chapter sketches in the major events) or cover the life of each diarist. But there are nine parallel stories here, often contrasting, providing individual viewpoints on the same public events, as well as what was only theirs to live through.

In making selections from the original material we have tried to keep diary entries intact and avoid too much explanation, but it has not always been possible to do one without the other. We have cut into some entries or left them before their end in order to keep the focus upon the selected subject matter or to get round the problem of presenting the reader with references to people and events that would require more editorial comment. Where names do appear, we have sometimes not explained who they are: for example, Naomi Mitchison's diary is full of names, but for the purposes of this book it suffices to know they are simply local people. Rather than pepper the text with three-dot ellipses to indicate the cuts, and risk interrupting the flow of the narrative, we have carried the sentence on after the omission. Nonetheless we have tried at all times not to misconstrue the sense of the original.

To retain the different characters of the diaries we have not standardized their presentation, so we have left the occasional spelling mistake without labouring the point with the traditional [*sic*], and kept Harold Nicolson's perfect and Alan Brooke's less-than-perfect punctuation, Vera Brittain's abbreviations and ampersands, and Naomi Mitchison's habit of writing o'clock as o'ck. The one exception to this is the date to each entry, which the diarists record differently but which we present as, for example, Sunday 3 September.

1. OUTBREAK

AUTUMN 1939

In September 1939 Neville Chamberlain had been British prime minister for just over two years. Even before he took office Germany was rearming and had moved forces into the Rhineland, the demilitarized area of the country adjacent to France. In May 1938 Germany annexed Austria and made it clear that the Sudetenland, in Czechoslovakia, would be next. All over Europe people became convinced that war was inevitable.

On 15 September Chamberlain flew to Germany to meet Hitler at his Alpine retreat. He promised to discuss the German claim to the Sudetenland with the French and the Czechs and return. But when he did so, mission accomplished, Hitler had changed his mind and mood. He wanted more, and he wanted it sooner.

Workmen began digging trenches in London's parks. Anti-aircraft guns were mounted. The Royal Navy was put on a war footing. 'How horrible, fantastic, incredible it is that we should be digging trenches and trying on gas masks here because of a quarrel in a faraway country between people of whom we know nothing', Chamberlain observed in a radio broadcast on the evening of 27 September, adding that war should only be embarked on if 'the great issues . . . are at stake'. After the broadcast Chamberlain flew to Munich for a meeting of Britain, France, Germany and Italy. The resulting agreement gave Germany everything Hitler desired but avoided a major European conflict.

Before flying home, Chamberlain asked Hitler to sign a peace treaty between Britain and Germany. He went to Hitler's modest Munich apartment and, once the Führer's interpreter had translated the document for him, he signed it. And so, on 30 September 1938, Chamberlain disembarked from his aeroplane at Heston Aerodrome waving a piece of paper bearing Hitler's signature. His car was mobbed as he left the airport and much of London turned out to sing 'For He's a Jolly Good Fellow' on his return to Downing Street, refusing to disperse until he'd appeared outside Number 10. 'I believe it is peace for our time', he told them.

Though the national mood was one of buoyant relief, Winston Churchill – out of office and an MP on the back benches – had a different view: 'England has been offered a choice between war and shame. She has chosen shame and will get war.'*

The Munich pact lasted barely six months. In March 1939 the Germans took over the rest of Czechoslovakia by force and later the same month rumours reached London of German plans to invade Poland. On 31 March Chamberlain told the House of Commons that Britain would go to Poland's aid in the event of a threat. 'And,' he added to resounding cheers, 'the French government . . . stand in the same position.'

Less than six months later, after months of tension and a growing certainty that war was inevitable, Germany invaded Poland in the early hours of 1 September. In London the evacuation of children began. There were steep rises in the number of weddings and pets being put down. Workmen painted white lines down the middle of roads in preparation for a blackout and the British government issued an ulti-matum to the Germans demanding that their troops with-

---

* Speech in the House of Commons, 3 October 1938.

draw from Poland. At 11.15 on the morning of 3 September the prime minister broadcast to the nation: 'I am speaking to you from the cabinet room of 10 Downing Street. This morning the British ambassador in Berlin handed the German government a final note stating that, unless we heard from them by 11 o'clock that they were prepared at once to withdraw their troops from Poland, a state of war would exist between us. I have to tell you now that no such undertaking has been received, and that consequently this country is at war with Germany.'

THE DIARISTS

GEORGE BEARDMORE

At the end of August George and his wife Jean were taking a short holiday at Love's Farm near Horsham, where they had spent part of their honeymoon in 1935. Now they also had with them their baby Victoria and Jean's mother (Mamma). George had travelled down separately on his motorbike.

Friday 1 September 1939 – Jean had been sleeping away from me all week so that the baby should not wake the Loves in the next room, but this morning she joined me after she had fed the baby, and we were glad and have been all day, for the comfort and communion it afforded us. We needed all the comfort we could get, for in the 10.30 a.m. wireless news we learned that Germany had invaded Poland and that therefore, because this country had 'guaranteed' Poland, both France and Britain had mobilised.

Big personal shocks at first leave me unmoved and their

force only makes itself felt after half an hour. So it was today. Jean wept a little. The whole scene is mixed up for us with a row in which Mamma became involved with Mrs Love. Mamma swore that she would sooner be bombed at home if she had to be bombed at all. The result was that I was given urgent instructions to find transport back to London for the three of them – Jean and her mother and the baby. My father-in-law is already at home: as Maintenance Engineer at Broadcasting House he has been working a fourteen-hour day and sometimes sleeping on the premises. As for me, I had the motor-bike.

Here I am at home in Harrow, therefore, waiting for the taxi to arrive with Jean and the baby in it. The whole of England is in total darkness, weird to experience, and I am more afraid for them now than ever I was while the baby was on its way into the world. The Guv'nor* has been down here helping to pin blackout paper over the kitchen and nursery windows. A watch-committee is patrolling the neighbourhood on the lookout for exposed lights. I saw Mrs Rendell defying them from her front doorstep as she would defy the Archangel Gabriel. One of the strangest sights encountered on the way home was a London double-decker bus speeding along between Guildford and Woking with a cargo of schoolchildren. The vast and elaborate plan for evacuating children, and for all I know the sick, aged, and crippled, from the country's industrial centres must be in progress. But the National Gallery, I wonder, the treasures of the British Museum, the Science Museum, the great libraries – what is being done to save them?

I want to be everywhere at once to witness and report.

Sunday 3 September – It would be impossible to convey the sense of utter panic with which we heard the first Air Raid

* Jean's father.

warning, ten minutes after the outbreak of war. We had all taken *The Shape of Things to Come** too much to heart, also the dire prophecies of scientists, journalists, and even politicians of the devastation and disease that would follow the first air raid. We pictured St Paul's in ruins and a hole in the ground where the Houses of Parliament had stood. But nothing happened.

Thursday 7 September – Apart from unemployment the general feeling is that we are engaged in a picnic. But then we are reminded that in August 1914 the war was thought to be a picnic but the imperishable retreat from Mons followed and with it the bitter winter of that year. Also, we cannot regard the 1914 war as a precedent. Now we are out to down a regime, not a nation. Now we know the full disaster of war and, more than this, we all know that we must fight or be dominated by a gang of bullies and liars. It's the lying I can't stand, any more than the Secret Police, the Concentration Camps, the rubber bludgeons, the plucking of Rabbis' beards, burning of synagogues, the lack of honour.

Sunday 10 September – This is one of the most mysterious wars through which I have ever lived. Mysterious because nobody knows what's happening. A paucity of news over the radio. Is anything happening? No cheering crowds, no drafts leaving Victoria, no indication indeed that we are to send an army abroad. But then, if we are leaving poor, battered Poland with the idea that we can somehow slide out of a major offensive, it's time we threw out the Peace Premier Chamberlain (71) and got someone more belligerent in his place.

Thursday 12 October – At the pictures on Tuesday we saw a newsreel of the troops in France. They seemed very old-

* By H. G. Wells, published in 1933.

fashioned, and one expected the film to grey over with speckles and flicker, like the old newsreels. Coming home in the pitch dark was an experience. All the streets were deserted as though plague had struck and the death-cart had made its daily collection. No children at play, no lovers up against lamp-posts, no sound, and only an occasional chink of light under a front door or the glow of a cigarette. It all seems very humiliating, this cowering down in expectation of death falling from the heavens. In fact, the plague years must have been very like this.

VERA BRITTAIN

On the day war was declared Vera was at home in the New Forest with John, aged 11, Shirley (9, known in the family as Poppy) and the family servants Mr and Mrs Burnett. Her husband George had left the day before to travel to Rochdale, where he hoped to be selected as the Labour Party candidate at the coming by-election. As part of her work for the Peace Pledge Union (PPU), Vera had proposed writing a regular personal Peace Letter.

It was the beginning of the new school year, and John returned to the Downs School while Shirley started at Oldfield School near Swanage. Both Vera and George had been offered work in the USA – Vera another lecture tour, and George another post at Cornell University in New York. Throughout the autumn Vera wrote articles and attended meetings in pursuit of peace. In November she gave talks in Birmingham, Glasgow, Reading, Exeter, Portsmouth and Liverpool, as well as in London. And in October the first issue of Vera's *Letter to Peace Lovers* was published by the PPU. It would appear weekly, then later fortnightly, throughout the war.

Sunday 3 September – First thing this morning the news was still indefinite & I half decided to go up to London to the PPU Hyde Park gathering organised for tonight. Then at 10.0

the BBC made the 'important announcement' that an ulti-
matum asking Germany to leave Poland would expire at 11
a.m. – and if no answer had been received, Mr Chamberlain
would speak at 11.15. At that time we turned on the wireless
again & heard his statement that from 11.0 this morning a
state of war existed between England & Germany. His voice
sounded old & trembled – and suddenly, as I sat on the camp
bed in the study listening between the two children, I found
that the tears were running down my cheeks – I suppose
from some subconscious realisation of the failure of my
efforts for peace over 20 years, for I had expected the
announcement. Poppy hugged me & all but licked my face
like a puppy. I rang up the PPU & Canon Morris* answered;
said they might want me to do my weekly letter, & also a
Pacifist Service Corps was going to be organised in wh. I
might take part. Went out in the forest; in the sunny quiet of
the gorse and heather it was impossible to take in the size
of the catastrophe. To comfort myself, wrote an article for
Peace News called 'Lift Up Your Hearts'. At night G. tele-
graphed from Rochdale that Morgan, not he, is selected.

Vera's article 'What Can We Do In Wartime?' was published on
9 September in *Forward*, a left-wing Scottish journal. What follows
is an extract from it.

To-day we who lost our friends and lovers between 1914 and
1919 are faced with the bitter fact that all the suffering and
service of those nightmare years failed completely in their
purpose. Far from smashing German militarism and making
the world safe for democracy, their long-range consequence
has been to smash German democracy and make the world
safe for militarism. The war to end war has resulted in a
greater fear of war than the world has ever known. The

---

* Stuart Morris, general secretary of the Peace Pledge Union.

attempt to smash militarism by force has led to more of it –
and not in Germany and Italy alone – than at any period of
history. The Europe that was to be made safe for democracy
has only 150 million people living under democratic governments, and 350 millions under different forms of despotism.

Tuesday 12 September – Took John back to Malvern by car.
Got caught in fleet of army lorries which exhausted our
diminishing supply of petrol – & Burnett had to get more
from a garage fortunately not too far away. John rather
subdued & quiet, but when we got to the Downs School he
said goodbye with equanimity & walked in with me quite
calmly loaded up with coat, suitcase, drawings & gas-mask.
Mr Hoyland* took me into his study for a talk. I mentioned
our possible service in America; he fully understood, &
undertook to be responsible for John in the Easter holidays if
I wished. We drove straight back stopping only for tea at
Cirencester. Burnett drove splendidly & did not even seem
very tired – but I felt cramped, dizzy & deaf after spending
the best part of 12 hours in an Austin 7.

Friday 22 September – Felt extraordinarily desolate all day
without the children. House very quiet. Answered letters all
day. Walked to Lyndhurst for stamps in morning, and after
lunch went to the children's 'submarine' – the big fallen tree
in the wooded glade over the brow of the nearest hill – and
pictured the children's small ghosts playing there. Have
decided it is just selfishness wh. makes me wish in these days
that they had never been born; it isn't so much the fear that
they will suffer, as reluctance to suffer more myself through
my love for them. Every dear human relationship which
makes one long for life turns one into a potential coward &
makes courage more difficult.

* The head teacher.

Sunday 24 September – Went for walk with G. Very quiet afternoon; no wind stirred the interlacing boughs of the beeches in the woods. Coming back, we passed the little group of cottages at the corner of the glade; a smell of peat-fires came from them, mingled with the scent of flowers & ripe red apples. In the corner garden was a riot of large dahlias – orange, crimson, yellow & scarlet. In the lane a little boy was twisting himself on a swing above a wood-pile. I remarked to G. how much more tragic the war seemed down here than in London; the contrast is so poignant between the lovely, serene, stable, civilised things which are the real essence of people's lives, and that cruel unnecessary violence, carnage & destruction that threatens their very existence.

Death of Sigmund Freud announced on wireless this morning.

Saturday 25 November – Came to Swanage from Portsmouth to see Shirley. Very wild blustery evening with cold heavy rain. Shirley looks quite well but lovely brown colour of the summer has gone.

Miss Hascroft of the WIL [Women's International League for Peace and Freedom] asked me to go to-day to the cremation of Mrs Swanwick,* who committed suicide last week by overdose of medinol owing to War. Could not bec. of seeing Shirley.

Monday 27 November – Spent afternoon in PPU office dictating answers to letters. Now have over 1,300 subscribers to Letter.

---

* Seventy-five-year-old feminist and pacifist, admired by Vera.

CHARLES RITCHIE

The Russo-German pact of 22 August 1939 had convinced Ritchie 'that a war to defend Poland with Russia benevolent to Germany would be suicide', since Germany's access to Russian raw materials would make it impossible to blockade her. On 26 August the British Foreign Office had suggested that the high commissioners of the Dominions (principally Ritchie's boss Mr Massey and the Australian HC) should encourage Mr Chamberlain to ask Poland to 'give in'. Ritchie was the messenger. 'As I walked back across the Horse Guards I thought, "Should I suppress this suggestion?" but I passed it on to Mr Massey. If I believed that nothing must be done to discourage the Poles I would not have passed it on. I knew that I had to make up my mind in a hurry. I suppose my feeling was that as a Canadian I should be right in doing anything, however small, in the direction of postponing war.'

On 8 September the *Athenia*, a British liner carrying women and children to Canada, was torpedoed by a German U-boat, with the loss of 112 lives. Ritchie shared the public's outrage.

Sunday 3 September – The war feeling is swelling. Believe it would sweep aside any compromise with Germany if the Government at the twelfth hour could secure one. This thing is a drug which alternately depresses and elates its victims and gives them release from the slow death of their daily lives. No one who has not felt this war-feeling inside him can know how it shakes the foundations and lets loose hate, generosity, lust, fear, courage, love – all the bag of human tricks. Some thought they had been analyzed away, but it was just that the right button had not been pressed.

At the doors of the houses in my neighbourhood stand cars laden with luggage. Little groups of Kensingtonians are evacuating their aunts, their canaries, and their small dogs.

Friday 8 September – The liner *Athenia* has been sunk by the Germans. The absurd folly of these utterly unwarlike people being drowned. This war has a quality which no other had. We do not approach it with our former innocence. We are in cold blood repeating a folly which belongs to the youth of mankind. We are driven to it by the force of sheer human stupidity, laziness, and error which we have been unable in the last twenty years to overcome.

NAOMI MITCHISON

At the beginning of September the Mitchison family were all at home in Carradale in Kintyre. There were also several visitors, including Denny's friend Robin and two of Naomi's women friends Joan and Tony. The first evacuees had arrived from Glasgow and were staying in the estate's farmhouse, known as Mains.

Naomi had been one of the founder members of the Carradale branch of the Labour Party, whose chairman was now Dick Galbraith, a fisherman known as Young Dick to distinguish him from her husband. She was critical of the Labour leadership over its support for the war, and, given her sympathy with the Soviet Union, felt 'like hell deep down because of the Russian news'.

Sunday 3 September – I listened to the 9 o'ck news, realising fairly clearly what the next was to be. The others were mostly not down, but I had not slept well. Valentine went off to Mains to look after the Glasgow children; Dick and I discussed what was to be done about the education of Avrion and Valentine; the latter can go to school here for a term, but the former would learn nothing. Tony said I'll start the war clean and went to wash her hair; a little later I did the same; it wasn't quite dry by 11.15. As we listened to Chamberlain speaking, sounding like a very old man, I kept wondering what the old Kaiser was thinking, whether he was old enough to see it all fully. The boys looked pale and worried, though Robin was laughing a little. At the end Joan said How could he ask God to bless us? As God Save the King started Denny turned it off and someone said Thank you.

The maids hadn't wanted to come through; I told Annie, who was wonderfully cheerful and said she remembered the Boer War, and Bella who said Isn't that heartbreaking. After a bit she began to cry, a saucepan in her hands, said Think of all our men going, then to me Of course you've got boys too. Dick said Think of the women in Germany all saying that too, but there was no response. Then she asked When will they send our men over? But none of us had much idea.

In the drawing room the big boys were writing and reading; I think perhaps writing poetry. I was feeling sick and I went over to Mains, but the teachers had just left – we followed them. Valentine had brought the Glasgow children over; they were talking happily but looked very white and thin and small. The village was empty; most people at church. It began to rain hard and we took shelter at the Galbraiths. Young Dick said So it's come.

At lunch Joan said she was on a small island of sand with everything cut off before and behind. I said I had been feeling the future cut off for some time. We all agreed it was queer to feel the past so cut-off, everything had a different meaning now.

Tuesday 26 September – I am beginning to wonder whether the point of a place like this may not be that it will keep alive certain ideas of freedom which might easily be destroyed in the course of this totalitarian war. There are increasing signs of totalitarianism in this country (for instance, decisions by local councils not to hold committees but to delegate things to chairmen) and democracy may most easily be kept alive in small communities. Meetings will not be possible in towns, but they will still be able to be held in the country. And again, here people will not be terrorised by darkness and regulations and this departure of the men, into accepting anything.

Friday 29 September – Came down, to finish my poem and write letters. Heard the 12 o'ck news with the new Russo-German treaty. In a way one had been expecting it, but not quite as definite. Of course one needn't make too much of protestations of friendship; and treaties are made to be broken. But it looks like a long, long war, involving even Avrion. And all the other children.

I set down, for future reading, that I think now, in three years, or five, I and mine will wish very deeply that we had made peace now; and this will be true of many millions. I only hope I am wrong.

In any case, none of us can do anything about it. Perhaps it is easier to be powerless.

The nightmare quality grows; one thinks one will wake up.

Saturday 7 October – I spent all the afternoon with Munro [the head forester], going round, looking at all the woods, deciding what trees to cut, what to prune, where to re-plant and what to re-plant. We walked for nearly three hours and never once mentioned the war.

I took him down to the wild garden to get his advice on the blue cedars and macrocarpas; he was so pleased with them, gasped with pleasure. And then we smelt a lovely smell, which neither of us could trace to any one plant or bush, but something balmy but pungent; the sun had been out for a bit, and brought it to the surface. We both wandered about smelling and touching; we found a lot of macrocarpa seedlings I hadn't known about in front of the house; and we ate brambles.

During these months Naomi worked on a long poem about the local fishing fleet and the community she was coming to love. In this extract she writes about returning to the harbour and home.

> At Airds I smell new bread; there is light in the
>   bakehouse.
> As I pass in the dawn the smell grows so rich that it
>   covers
> The smell of herring on my coat and hands.
> It dies along the road and instead I smell,
> As the first gold comes breaking through the grey,
> All the land things; earth, flowers, cattle, houses
> Where the goodwife begins to stir,
> And, under the high green arches between gate and
>   doorway,
> The essential sweetness of leaves.*

HERMIONE RANFURLY

On 30 August 1939 Hermione and Dan escaped the heat of their cramped London flat to take a short second honeymoon at the home of General Joe Laycock and his wife Ann in Ross-shire. Deer-stalking by the loch, arranged for their first day, was a welcome contrast to the talk of war in London, and Hermione caused much amusement crossing the peat bogs in her tennis shoes.

---

* From the ending of 'The Alban Goes Out: 1939', privately published later
  that year, reprinted in Naomi Mitchison, *The Cleansing of the Knife*.
  Canongate, 1978.

In early October Hermione joined Dan and his valet Whitaker in Wiltshire, where Dan was attending a machine-gun course. With thousands training on Salisbury Plain, accommodation to rent was scarce, but they eventually found a small cottage. There Hermione taught Whitaker to ride and he taught her to cook.

Thursday 31 August – Loch Torridon – Several times I slumped to the ground and looked back at the blue loch water below. I wondered if I was tired after the long drive from London yesterday – or am just lazy. How does one know the dif-ference? I counted three out loud to make myself get up.

When we came out of the wood and crossed the lawn it was dusk. Lights were on in the house. We opened the front door and were surprised to see suitcases in the hall. General Joe Laycock came out of his study and for a moment I thought he was going to be cross because we were nearly late for dinner. He looked tired, or older than he did at breakfast. 'Dear Dan and Hermione, welcome back,' he said. 'We are not changing for dinner.' He hesitated, then said very slowly – as if it hurt him – 'I want you to give me a lift in your car at day-break tomorrow. I must go south and so must you. Bob has telephoned from the War Office: the Germans are marching on Poland.'

No one spoke or ate much at dinner and immediately afterwards we went upstairs to pack and go to bed. Soon it will be dawn. Dan is fast asleep. I have counted sheep in vain – they are all turned into Germans.

Sunday 3 September – Melton Mowbray – Two days ago we left Torridon. It seems an age. As we stacked our guns, golf-clubs and fishing rods into the back of our Buick, fear pinched my heart: these are the toys of yesterday I thought; they belong to another world. General Laycock, Dan and I sat in front. We hardly spoke. No doubt the General was thinking of his sons, Bob, Peter and Michael, who will all have to go to war. Questions teemed through my mind: where will Dan's Yeomanry, the Notts Sherwood Rangers, go? Will I be able to see him? Mummy, ill in hospital in Switzerland – should I fetch her back to England? And Whitaker – our cook-butler – perhaps he is too old to be a soldier? It was raining. The windscreen wipers ticked to and fro' and it seemed as if each swipe brought a new and more horrifying thought to me. We had started on a journey – but to where? And for how long?

Dan left me here with Hilda, his Mother. She offered him her beautiful chestnut mare to be his second charger and he accepted gratefully. In twenty minutes, he and Whitaker were gone.

Thousands of children are being evacuated from London to the country. They, and their parents, must feel as desolate as me.

Wednesday 1 November – **East Chisenbury** – Mrs Sparrow forwarded our mail from London. One letter was from Monty Moore Montgomery (an amusing, sophisticated, travelled American who took me dining and dancing during my week in New York on my way back from Australia):

Wall Street, New York 10 October 1939

The feeling here is intense against involvement although sentiment is pro-Ally. Americans, you know, revere sagacity – and there are some of us who think Hitler has the finest brain in Europe, if not in the world today – and that with such a leader Germany is sufficiently powerful to do a lot of unpleasant things if you insist. It would seem foolish to me to go on, killing hundreds of thousands and squandering pounds sterling to the ultimate end of fostering communism in all Europe.

If England doesn't negotiate a peace within six months, I shall be both surprised and shocked. False pride and foolish alliances are no reason for a war – and when it comes to broken promises, well, Hitler may have the high score but England and France are close seconds.

CLARA MILBURN

As war began to seem inevitable, Clara and Jack knew that their son Alan would be called up. On 1 September he was told to report to Coventry. Clara was a leading member of the team organizing accommodation for the children and teachers being evacuated from Coventry, and much of Sunday was spent allocating them to their new homes.

Saturday 2 September – Saturday was full, with going round to billets early in the morning and then driving into Coventry, meeting Alan at the solicitors for him to make his will, and doing a little hasty shopping with the thought of two evacuee teachers being billeted upon us next day. Jack was busy all day making the dining-room gas-proof, and he did it in his usual thorough and effective manner. The blackout was already done – we'd gone to Leamington the week before to buy the blackout curtain material, and when they said 'How much do you want? There are 26 yards in this roll,' I said I'd take the roll. But two large bay windows and two smaller windows in the living and dining-room ate a huge piece of the black Italian cloth, and by the time all the windows in little Burleigh had been draped, curtains made and re-made till I was nearly weeping with sewing black seams, undoing and restitching, the roll was entirely finished and a few more yards were needed. Then came a careful shading of lights, for the broadcast message was insistent as to the extent of the blackout required.

Sunday 3 September – It was bright and sunny and a really hot day by 10 a.m., when all billeting wardens were to be in their appointed places in the school playground to receive the teachers and children arriving from Coventry by bus. Before that time one room at Burleigh had to be entirely re-arranged – Alan's room had to be put ready for the two teachers we had promised to accommodate.

A second bed was set up, drawers emptied, and Alan's own intimate things stuffed hurriedly away for two strange women to take possession. It was too much! Out went his desk into the spare room, his numberless ties taken out of their special drawer, the wardrobe cleared, tankards won in many motor trials parked away for the duration, photographs removed, and at last the room was ready. It was not Alan's room now, and I brimmed over – and felt relieved.

But there was no time for moaning. There was work to be done and I got off to the school. The sun worked wonders, and with an effort the tears were forced back and the business in hand took all one's attention. At last the buses came and queue after queue of clean and tidy children filed into the playground accompanied by many teachers.

During the week we were called up by the air raid warden, who found our blackout insufficient, and still more curtains had to be made. By now the price of the material had gone up from 2s 6d to 3s 11d a yard, and the quality was decidedly inferior. But a very definite blackout was obtained at the bay windows by covering the whole bay, from the top of the pelmet to a foot from the floor, with a great black pall reminiscent of a first class French funeral! These had to be hung every evening at blackout time and not removed before a specified time in the morning. The lack of ventilation was stifling in hot weather, but it is wonderful how one can conform to an order when it is absolutely necessary to do so.

By the end of November many of the evacuees had returned home and the two teachers went too. Alan was at a training camp in Swindon, prior to joining the British Expeditionary Force (BEF) in the new year.

ALAN BROOKE

Brooke arrived in France on 29 September to take command of II Corps of the BEF, with two divisional commanders, Montgomery and Johnson. His old colleague and friend John Dill commanded I Corps. Commander-in-chief was John Gort. All had served with distinction in the First World War and now found themselves revisiting old territory.

The BEF was preparing to defend the Franco-Belgian border where the Maginot Line stopped. The Germans were expected to invade Holland and Belgium before winter set in.

Tom, Brooke's son from his first marriage, was with an artillery regiment in I Corps.

Wednesday 4 October – I was unable to write during the last 3 days as I went forward to look at the front we are to take over. I stopped with Dill in his temporary HQ for both nights, and had long talks with him. Found him still very depressed about the general state of unpreparedness for war. We condoled with each other on the lack of equipment and shortage of training of many components. I feel however that his disappointment at having missed both CIGS* and C-in-C jobs has coloured his life, and that he is looking at his own situation possibly with slightly over-pessimistic outlook. I feel desperately sorry for him as he is in the depths of gloom.

Tuesday 17 October – Spent the morning in the office. Amongst other jobs trying to write a letter to the King as Gort had told us he was rather hurt that we had not yet written to

---

*   Chief of the Imperial General Staff.

him. In the afternoon looked up Tom whom I found very
well and cheerful. His Colonel says he is doing well.

Sunday 22 October – Fairly hard frost this morning. Went out
with Johnson to look at the Reserve Front he is preparing.
Started at 10 am and walked most of the day returning about
5.30 pm. They have been doing great work in spite of the
very inclement weather, and the defences are making rapid
strides. The position will soon be fairly strong but requires
far more troops than we have got to hold it against a
determined attack. Still very short of sandbags; when one
remembers the lavish use made of sandbags at home in
localities that will never see a bomb it makes one's blood boil
to be so short of them out here.

Saturday 11 November, Armistice Day – **Vimy Ridge*** – I felt
throughout the ceremony as if I were in a dream. The white
tall pillars of the monument standing out against the ashy
grey sky seemed entirely detached from this earth, whilst the
two red wreaths of poppies looked like two small drops of
blood on that vast monument. They served as a vivid
reminder of the floods of blood that had already been spilt
on the very ground [on which] we were standing, and of the
futility of again causing such bloodshed. I suppose that it is
through such punishments that we shall eventually learn to
'love our neighbours as ourselves'.

Monday 13 November – We are still being kept in suspense –
still no move of the Germans into Holland or Belgium!
    Dill came to see me and tell me results of his talk with
Gort which he asked for to draw attention to our weakness
on the proposed line. I gather that he failed to make Gort
realize the risks he was taking with the BEF. I am afraid Dill

---

*   Site of the First World War battle, April 1917.

feels the situation acutely, his astute military knowledge makes him see clearly that with such strung-out forces, even behind a river, serious resistance is impossible. He feels it his duty to inform Gort who has not quite the same breadth of vision, and Dill feels that Gort has the impression that he suffers from 'cold feet' and is an alarmist. It is a very sad situation; he is torn between loyalty to his commander and loyalty to his Corps.

Thursday 23 November – Started the day by having to 'tell off' Monty for having issued a circular to his troops on the prevention of venereal disease worded in such obscene language that both the C of E and RC senior chaplains had complained to the Adjutant General.

I had already seen the circular and told Monty what I thought of it, namely that [by] the issue of such a document he had inevitably undermined the respect and esteem of the division for him, and thus seriously affected his position as commander. I also informed him that I had a very high opinion of his military capabilities and an equally low one of his literary ones! He took it wonderfully well, and I think it ought to have done him good. It is a great pity that he spoils his very high military ability by a mad desire to talk or write nonsense.

Tuesday 28 November – It is a great relief and a load off my mind that the 2 Corps has not been subjected to active operations yet, and has had this additional time to complete its preparations and training. On arrival in this country and for the first 2 months the Corps was quite unfit for war, practically in every aspect. Even now our anti-tank gunners are untrained and a large proportion of our artillery have never fired either their equipment or type of smoke shell that they are armed with. To send untrained troops into modern war is courting disaster such as befell the Poles. I only hope that we may now be left in peace for the next 2 to 3 months to complete the required readiness for war of the 2nd Corps including its new division the 5th.

HAROLD NICOLSON

On the morning of 3 September Harold Nicolson was in Westminster with the Eden Group. They listened to the prime minister's broadcast together. 'He is quite good and tells us that war has begun'. A planned stroll down to the House of Commons became a hurried lift in a car when an air-raid warning sounded. After a brief stay in the shelter, where there were 'all manner of people from Cabinet Ministers to cooks', he attended the debate, during which Chamberlain 'makes a speech which is restrained and therefore effective' but 'looks very ill'.

Sunday 3 September – At 1.50 I motor down with Victor Cazalet* to Sissinghurst. There are many army lorries passing along the road and a few pathetic trucks evacuating East End refugees. In one of those there is an elderly woman who shakes her fist at us and shouts that it is all the fault of the rich. The Labour Party will be hard put to it to prevent this war degenerating into class warfare.

When I reach Sissinghurst I find that the flag has been pulled down.

Monday 11 September – How odd one's feelings are at this moment! I hate this war and dread its consequences. I know that whatever happens it will destroy everything I care for. Thus there is a little timid selfish side of myself that tempts me by still murmurings to hope that we shall reach a form of appeasement after the Germans have conquered Poland.

*   Fellow MP and near neighbour in Kent.

Yet the real thing in me loathes and detests any such capitulation.

Tuesday 26 September – The Prime Minister gets up to make his statement. He is dressed in deep mourning relieved only by a white handkerchief and a large gold watch-chain. One feels the confidence and spirits of the House dropping inch by inch. When he sits there is scarcely any applause. During the whole speech Winston Churchill had sat hunched beside him looking like the Chinese god of plenty suffering from acute indigestion. He just sits there, lowering, hunched and circular, and then he gets up.

The effect of Winston's speech was infinitely greater than could be derived from any reading of the text. His delivery was really amazing and he sounded every note from deep preoccupation to flippancy, from resolution to sheer boyishness. One could feel the spirits of the House rising with every word. It was quite obvious afterwards that the Prime Minister's inadequacy and lack of inspiration had been demonstrated even to his warmest supporters. In those twenty minutes Churchill brought himself nearer the post of Prime Minister than he had ever been before. In the Lobbies afterwards even Chamberlainites were saying, 'We have now found our leader'. Old Parliamentary hands confessed that never in their experience had they seen a single speech so change the temper of the House.

In early November, after intensive work, Harold's *Why Britain Is at War* was published by Penguin. The following is an extract.

Are we aware even now of the actual cruelty of the Nazi system?

I have met a man who was sent to a German concentration camp and thereafter released. He managed to escape into Switzerland and I saw him later in Paris. He was an elderly man of short stature and great girth. On arrival at the camp he was made to take off all his clothes and to creep on all fours around the room. The youths of the S.S. who were in control of the camp amused themselves by flicking with wet towels at his naked frame. They then told him to urinate into the mouth of an elderly Jew, who was also stripped naked. When he refused to do so, they were both flogged until they were unconscious. I did not believe this story at the time. Since then I have heard other stories which confirm it in every detail. I cannot conceive that, in any circumstances which could possibly arise, could youths of my own race either wish, or be allowed by their elders, to behave with such obscenity.

Harold's elder son Ben was now a private in an anti-aircraft battery commanded by Victor Cazalet not far from their home in Kent, while the younger, Nigel, was at the Royal Military Academy at Sandhurst.

Saturday 25 November – How curious are the moods through which one passes! I sit here in my room at Sissinghurst thinking back on the days since 3 September. The acute depression and misery of the first weeks has passed. I have accepted the fact that we are at war, and I suppose I am physically relieved by the fact that there are not likely to be any raids during the winter upon London and that the Germans have not made a dash through Holland. Yet the fact that this war is costing us six million pounds a day and that I am not really certain that we shall win it, fills me with acute sadness at times. We all keep up a brave face and refuse to admit that defeat is possible. But my heart aches with apprehension.

Then Victor Cazalet rings up to say that Ben has got his stripe and is now a Bombardier. We are absurdly pleased by this. A windy night with a scudding moon. I think of the people at sea and all those devils in Germany and Rome plotting, plotting, plotting our destruction in the spring.

CHILD EVACUEES FROM CZECHOSLOVAKIA

In December 1938 Stanley Baldwin made a radio appeal on behalf of Jewish refugees from Nazi Germany: 'I ask you to come to the aid of victims not of any catastrophe in the natural world, not of earthquake, not of flood, not of famine, but of an explosion of Man's inhumanity to Man'. As a result of this broadcast between 3 December 1938 and 14 May 1940 ten thousand Jewish children were rescued in Operation Kindertransport. Czechoslovakia, however, had no organization to help Jewish children.

Just before Christmas 1938 Nicholas Winton, an unmarried 29-year-old merchant banker working in the City, cancelled the skiing holiday he'd planned with a fellow Peace Pledge Union member. Instead they both travelled to Prague to offer their assistance. Under the auspices of the British Committee for Refugees from Czechoslovakia (BCRC), Winton and his friend set themselves up in an office in Wenceslas Square and did what they could.

NICHOLAS WINTON

Christmas 1938 – There were thousands of children needing help.

My day usually started with interviews in my bedroom whilst I was shaving (sometimes at 6.00 a.m.). Some parents said that they would willingly take the risk of staying in the country if we could only find some way of getting their children to safety. A few had plenty of money, others not the price of a meal. Many required clothing as it was bitterly cold.

Some of their questions were unanswerable. If Doreen* [head of the BCRC] told the parents that she could get them to safety, but not the children, there was weeping and there was also weeping when we had to say that, at the moment, we could help neither parents nor children. And there was more weeping when we told the parents that if the children were found places in England, we could not guarantee if, or when, they would be reunited. It was all quite overwhelming. Some of the mothers were already on the 'streets' to get money to buy food for themselves and their families. I felt quite dazed. What suffering there is when armies start to march!†

Winton's first group of children left on 14 March 1939, the day before German troops entered Prague. For each child he had to supply proof that the foster-family was willing to pay for the child's keep and provide a fifty-pound deposit to cover the eventual cost of repatriation.

The last 'Winton' transport, on 2 August 1939, brought sixty-eight children to Britain. A larger transport of more than 250 children was scheduled for 1 September, but Hitler invaded Poland that day and the borders were closed. The train was not allowed to leave the station and, as far as is known, all these children were later deported to concentration camps.‡

---

* Doreen Warriner.
† Muriel Emanuel and Vera Gissing, *Nicholas Winton and the Rescued Generation*. Vallentine Mitchell, 2002.
‡ Of the 6,000 who applied, 699 children were rescued. Winton had pinned his hopes on sending many to the United States, but Congress rejected the legislation which would have made this possible in February 1939.

VERA GISSING

Vera Gissing and her sister Eva were rescued. Their mother went behind her husband's back to add her daughters' names to Winton's list. Vera, aged 10, and Eva, 15, were booked on a transport for the end of June; their cousins Tommy and Honza would leave in September. Upon hearing the news, their father covered his face with his hands 'whilst we all waited in silence. Then he lifted his head, smiled at us with tears in his eyes, sighed and said, "All right, let them go"'.

In the diary her father gave her, Vera recorded the journey via Germany, Holland and the English Channel. The girls were separated upon arrival in London, and Vera was the last to be collected. However, their foster-families – Eva's in Dorset, and Vera's in Liverpool – took great pains to see that the sisters remained in contact and visited each other. Letters and parcels to and from home were exchanged regularly during the first months of the war. But a letter from their mother dated 21 November 1939 would be the last they ever received.

End of June – **Prague station** – The station platform was filled with anxious parents, the train packed with excited children. There were tears, last words of advice, last words of encouragement, last words of love, the last embrace. 'See you in a free Czechoslovakia!' I cried impulsively as the whistle blew. My parents looked scared, and so did other people, as there were Gestapo men about. And as the train slowly pulled out of the station, in the sea of people I saw only the beloved figures of mother and father, their brave smiles vainly trying to hide their anguish.*

---

* Vera Gissing, *Pearls of Childhood*, Robson Books, 1994. Exact date is not specified.

Early July – **London** – I was led into an empty room to await the arrival of my English foster-parent. Before very long the door opened and there stood a little lady, barely taller than I was. Her hat sat askew on her head and her mackintosh was buttoned up all wrong. She ran towards me then, laughing and crying at the same time, and hugged me tightly, talking to me with words I could not understand. I was slightly baffled, not a little embarrassed and somewhat over-whelmed, but greatly relieved to be met by such a warm and jolly person.*

MRS RAINFORD
('Mummy', Vera's foster-mother from Liverpool)

I was taken to a house in Bloomsbury and shown into a big room. It was quite empty, there wasn't a stick of furniture in it, not even a chair. In the middle of the room was a little rucksack and a little jacket, and next to them a forlorn little girl. It was such a pitiful sight! I flung my arms around the girl and said, 'You shall be loved!'†

CHILD EVACUEES FROM LONDON

From 31 August 1939 thousands of children were evacuated from the capital. They went with their schoolteachers, with labels around their necks and a single change of clothing. When parents saw their children onto the trains, they generally had no idea of

---

* Vera Gissing, *Pearls of Childhood*.
† Gissing, *Pearls of Childhood*.

their destination and no guarantee that brothers and sisters would be billeted together. Cards would be posted from their eventual host families so that luggage could be forwarded and letters written, but the loss of sons and daughters was harrowing.

Two of these young children had no difficulty recalling the experience as adults. Their accounts reflect the dependency of evacuees on the good nature or otherwise of their host family.

ANITA GREENBERG

Anita, aged eight, was evacuated to Windsor with her 6-year-old brother Arnold.

On 31 August my father came home early and brought with him two white canvas haversacks (something like the ones sailors use). My mother put a few items of clothing in the haversacks for my brother and me. They had a list of the things they had to pack. Everything was ready and then my father remembered that he had forgotten to buy an 'indelible pencil' (what on earth could that be?) he went out and came back a little later with the pencil. He wet the point in his mouth and proceeded to write our names on the haversacks – Anita Greenberg, Arnold Greenberg. It came out a mauve colour.

We were all up early the next morning because it was the day Arnold and I were going to be evacuated. It all sounded wonderful. We were going into the 'country'. We would see cows and sheep and trees and flowers. These things weren't exactly in abundance in London's East End.

At about nine o'clock we all started off on foot for Stepney Green Station. On the way we saw lots of other little family groups going in the same direction.

The station itself was really crowded and we had to queue

to get in. We were given buff-coloured name tags to tie on to our coats. Some of the teachers were waiting for us on the platform and this is where we said our 'good-byes' to our mummies and daddies. There wasn't a lot of time because we were ushered onto the waiting train by our teachers. I wasn't sad or unhappy – in fact I was quite looking forward to the adventure. Someone must have done a wonderful job of brainwashing me.

We didn't know, and neither did any of the parents, where we were going. My mother and father had drummed it into me that my brother and I must not be separated. My brother was six years old and I was the big sister.

The train finally arrived at a place called Windsor. We were taken to a church hall and there we were given brown carrier bags with string handles. Inside we found sandwiches, a cold drink and a bar of chocolate. We were in a big hall and there were lots of children.

After we had rested and eaten we were all taken on a march down a very long road. I think it was called St Leonard's Road. Along this road there were rows and rows of houses and outside each house stood the housewife. As we walked along, the housewife would say 'I'll have a girl', or 'I'll have two little boys', etc. It was a long walk down St Leonard's Road. All the children in front of my brother and I had been swallowed up and were already in various houses. Now it was our turn. Mrs Taylor said, 'I'll have the little girl.' When I heard that, I grabbed my brother's hand and refused to go. I said, 'My mummy said that we must stay together,' and Mrs Taylor agreed to take both of us, Arnold and me. She had only one spare bed, but that didn't matter – we were only little children and could both sleep in the one bed. And so we took on our new status – we were now Evacuees.

I realise now how very vulnerable we little children were. My brother and I were lucky. We didn't come across any unkindness, but I know that this was not so in the case of many evacuees.*

When Arnold fell ill in February 1940 both children returned home. 'After all, nothing terrible was happening in London.' As a result both children, like so many others, were back in London when the Blitz began.

BARBARA BIRCHALL

Aged three, Barbara was evacuated to Reading in Berkshire with her 4-year-old sister. They were housed with a shoe mender and his wife and daughter who, after a couple of years, allowed their dissatisfaction with the situation to turn into cruelty. Their father was in the army as a cook and used to send them sweets, though they never got any.

One night we were so hungry and thirsty that we crept downstairs to find something to eat and drink. We couldn't find anything. We were desperate, so I saw the tap was dripping and it had made a pool of water in the bottom of the bowl, my sister pulled up a chair to the sink and helped me up. She was one year older than me. Then I bent my head down and got some of the water in my hand to drink. Then we heard footsteps coming and the woman caught us. She opened the coal cupboard and pushed us in and locked the door. We had to stay there till the morning and it was very dark, cold and spiders! Horrible, we were very scared.

Bathtime used to be four inches of COLD water in front of the fire. If she was cross with us, she used to lock us in

---

* Anita Truman in Pam Schweitzer (ed.), *Goodnight Children Everywhere. Memories of Evacuation in World War II*, Age Exchange, 1990.

the garden shed at the bottom of the garden all night. It was really a nightmare.

When the billet worker used to come to see if we were well and happy the woman and her husband used to put on a big spread of cakes and sandwiches, and always cuddled us in front of her to make it look good.

My sister had irons up her legs and couldn't walk very well, so I used to take her to school and we were so hungry and sick that we used to sit by the pig swill bins and wait for the rubbish to be thrown away. Then we used to eat as much as we could out of the bins. One day we had a big harvest festival and in the front row was fruit and vegetables and these big tomatoes. We were all sitting on the floor quiet when my sister made a mad dash and took a big bite out of the tomato. The teacher took her and spanked her on the knuckles with a ruler. When I explained that we were very hungry she called us liars and got the woman round and she denied that we were not fed. When we got home she beat us and her husband beat us and we were very afraid that we would die if we didn't get out of there.*

Somehow they survived their stay in Reading until the end of the war; but the experience caused Barbara 'a lot of unhappiness' in later years.

---

*   Barbara Birchall, in Pam Schweitzer (ed.), *Goodnight Children Everywhere*. ibid.

2. THREAT OF INVASION

SPRING 1940

It was not the Home Front but a cold front that dominated the months that bridged 1939 and 1940, bringing the frostiest winter for forty-five years. Around Teddington an eight-mile stretch of the Thames froze solid. The freeze affected the whole of Europe and German advances into France were delayed as a result.

Evacuation was not a universal success. By January many of the official evacuees (a further two million had moved voluntarily and under their own auspices) had gone home. Mothers had new worries: the extension of the call-up to the age of 41 meant that husbands as well as sons were going to war. And rationing began. From 8 January 1940 each adult was allowed four ounces (115 grams) of ham, bacon and cheese per week and twelve ounces of sugar. From March meat was rationed to just over one pound (460 grams) per person per week.

The business of fortifying the country against attack had begun in earnest. The British public had been told that Germany's opening air attack would last sixty days and almost certainly result in the deaths of 600,000 people, leaving more than a million injured. For months every man, woman and child had possessed a square cardboard box containing their personal gas mask. Two million household gardens had also been furnished with six curved pieces of corrugated iron bolted together, half buried and with earth piled on top. These were known as Anderson Shelters after Home Secretary Sir John Anderson, who had been responsible for devising air raid precautions (ARP) the previous year and who had commissioned them.

The blackout kept people busy as they sought to eliminate the slightest chink of light escaping from their homes. An unforeseen consequence was that twice as many were killed on the roads in September 1939 than the previous September.

Though Chamberlain now spoke of the 'Twilight War', the public had already opted for 'Bore War' and would soon adopt the phrase 'Phoney War'. But despite the apparent lack of action, some 160,000 men and over 23,000 vehicles were already in France. Commander of the 3rd Division Major General Montgomery recalled, 'Much of the transport consisted of civilian vans and lorries from England; they were in bad repair and, when my division moved up to the French frontier, the countryside of France was strewn with broken-down vehicles'.*

In November 1939 Russia had invaded Finland, and though public opinion sympathized with the Finns, British assistance might have led to war with Russia as well as Germany. Britain nevertheless agreed to send military aid to the Finns, via Sweden, but the decision was overtaken by events when Finland and Russia signed a peace treaty.

At the beginning of April 1940 Chamberlain, convinced that the German delay in initiating offensive action had given Britain time to prepare fully for war, gave a speech in which he said that 'Hitler had missed the bus'.† Just five days later, on 9 April, Germany invaded Denmark and Norway. Within twenty-four hours Denmark had surrendered.

---

*   Bernard Law Montgomery, *The Memoirs of Field Marshal Montgomery*, Collins, 1958.
†   Speech at Central Hall, Westminster, 4 April 1940.

Prompted by Churchill, now first lord of the Admiralty, positive reports began to appear in the press: BERGEN CAP-TURED BY THE BRITISH, NORWEGIANS RETAKE TRONDHEIM, BRITISH FLEET COMMANDS ENTRANCE TO OSLO. In truth, two battalions, poorly equipped, without anti-aircraft guns, fighter cover or field artillery, had landed in Norway. After four days' fighting, half were in retreat with the rest killed, wounded or captured. 'We've simply been massacred', said an unnamed officer.*

By the beginning of May public opinion had turned against Chamberlain. After a two-day debate in the House of Commons during which he was greeted with jeers of 'He missed the bus', he resigned. Churchill became prime minister on 10 May, the same day that Germany invaded Belgium, Holland and Luxembourg.

On 14 May recruiting began for the Local Defence Vol-unteers, later known as the Home Guard, confirming what many people suspected: such was the speed of the German advance that invasion had moved from theory to real threat. The next day Churchill sent a telegram to President Roose-velt: 'We expect to be attacked here ourselves, both from the air and by parachute and airborne troops, in the near future'.†
The order went out that church bells should only be rung to warn that the German invasion had begun.

The German army continued its blitzkrieg – 'lightning war' – advancing into France and forcing the British, French and Belgian armies back towards the coast. By 23 May German forces had reached the Channel ports, trapping the

---

* Dispatch from American correspondent Leland Stowe reported in UK newspapers 26 April 1940 and quoted in Lawrence Thompson, *1940 Year of Legend, Year of History*. Fontana, 1968.
† Francis L. Loewenheim, Harold D. Langley and Manfred Jonas, *Roosevelt and Churchill. Their Secret Wartime Correspondence*. Saturday Review Press/E. P. Dutton & Co. Inc., New York, 1975.

Allies. Three days later the evacuation of the BEF at Dunkirk began. The best official estimate was that 40,000 troops
– a tiny fraction of the total number – could be ferried
home.

THE DIARISTS

HAROLD NICOLSON

Throughout the winter Harold had continued going to meetings
of the Eden Group. They were all convinced that Chamberlain
could not last and that their group would play a decisive role in
his going. However, Harold was not sure that Churchill was the
man to replace him.

Thursday 11 April 1940 – To the House. It is packed. Winston
comes in. He is not looking well and sits there hunched as
usual with his papers in his hand. When he rises to speak it
is obvious that he is very tired. He starts off by giving an
imitation of himself making a speech, and he indulges in
vague oratory coupled with tired gibes. I have seldom seen
him to less advantage. The majority of the House were
expecting tales of victory and triumph, and when he tells
them that the news of our reoccupation of Bergen, Trondheim and Oslo is untrue, a cold wave of disappointment
passes through the House. He hesitates, gets his notes in the
wrong order, puts on the wrong pair of spectacles, fumbles
for the right pair, keeps on saying 'Sweden' when he means
'Denmark', and one way and another makes a lamentable
performance. It is a feeble, tired speech and it leaves the
House in a mood of grave anxiety.

Tuesday 7 May – Down to the House for the Norwegian debate. [Chamberlain] makes a very feeble speech and is only applauded by the Yes-men. He makes some reference to the complacency of the country, at which the whole House cheers vociferously and ironically, inducing him to make a little, rather feminine, gesture of irritation.

Wednesday 8 May – [Winston] has an almost impossible task [concluding the debate for the Government]. On the one hand he has to defend the Services; on the other, he has to be loyal to the Prime Minister. One felt that it would be impossible to do this after the debate without losing some of his own prestige, but he manages with extraordinary force of personality to do both these things with absolute loyalty and apparent sincerity, while demonstrating by his brilliance that he really has nothing to do with this confused and timid gang.

Friday 10 May – I go down to Sissinghurst. Met by Vita and Gwen.* It is all looking too beautiful to be believed, but a sort of film has obtruded itself between my appreciation of nature and my terror of real life. It is like a tooth-ache. We dine alone together chatting about indifferent things. Just before nine, we turn on the wireless and it begins to buzz as the juice comes through and then we hear the bells. Then the pips sound 9.0, and the announcer begins: 'This is the Home Service. Here is the Right Honourable Neville Chamberlain M.P., who will make a statement.' I am puzzled by this for a moment, and then realise that he has resigned.

He begins by saying that recent events in Parliament and elsewhere have shown that the country wants a Coalition Government. He has since understood that the only obstacle to such a Coalition is himself. Therefore he has tendered his resignation, and Churchill is Prime Minister. For the moment,

* His sister.

acting Ministers will carry on. He will agree to serve under Churchill. He ends with a fierce denunciation of the Germans for invading Holland and Belgium. It is a magnificent statement, and all the hatred that I have felt for Chamberlain subsides as if a piece of bread were dropped into a glass of champagne.

Friday 17 May – At 12.40 the telephone rings. I lift the receiver and wait without hearing anything. Then after about two minutes' silence, a voice says, 'Mr. Nicolson?' I say, 'Yes.' 'Please hold on. The Prime Minister wishes to speak to you.' Another long pause and then Winston's voice: 'Harold, I think it would be very nice if you joined the Government and helped Duff at the Ministry of Information.' 'There is nothing I should like better.' 'Well, fall in tomorrow. The list will be out tonight. That all right?' 'Very much all right.' 'O.K.,' says Winston, and rings off.

Come up from Sissinghurst. Ring up Duff Cooper* who welcomes me warmly.

Letter to his wife Vita from his apartment at Kings Bench Walk, London EC4.

Sunday 26 May – What a grim interlude in our lives! The Government may decide to evacuate Kent and Sussex of all civilians. If, as I hope, they give orders instead of advice, then those orders will be either 'Go' or 'Stay'. If the former, then you know what to do. If the latter, we are faced with a great predicament. I don't think that even if the Germans occupied Sissinghurst they would harm you, in spite of the horrified dislike which they feel for me. But to be quite sure that you

---

* Minister of Information, who had resigned from the previous government following the Munich agreement and had voted against Chamberlain on 8 May after what Harold described as a 'devastating speech'.

are not put to any humiliation, I think you really ought to have a 'bare bodkin' so that you can take your quietus when necessary. I shall have one also. I am not in the least afraid of such sudden and honourable death. What I dread is being tortured and humiliated. But how can we find a bodkin which will give us our quietus quickly and which is easily portable? I shall ask my doctor friends.

My dearest, I felt so close to you yesterday. We never need to put it all in words. If I believe in anything surviving, I believe in a love like ours surviving: it is all so completely unmaterial in every way.

CHARLES RITCHIE

As private secretary to the Canadian high commissioner, Vincent Massey, Ritchie dined regularly with those in high society, among them the PM's private secretary Jock Colville, the wealthy art collector and Conservative MP Victor Cazalet and former prime minister Stanley Baldwin.

Wednesday 13 March – Mr Massey wanted me to include in my dispatch something to contradict the illusion that England is a class-ridden society. Why illusion?

Lunched with John Tweedsmuir.* He does not agree that England will be much changed after the war. 'People who hunt six days a week will only hunt four days and when things pick up again they will hunt six days again.'

Everyone is stunned by the Finnish surrender. The Foreign Office only a week ago had no idea of Finland suing for

---

* Ritchie was friends with John, William and Alistair, sons of John Buchan, first Lord Tweedsmuir, author of *The Thirty-Nine Steps* and former governor general of Canada. John had inherited the title from his father in February 1940.

peace with German connivance. The Foreign Office has had more disagreeable surprises in the last twelve months than ever before in its history. The dictatorship countries move suddenly, boldly, and secretly. We carry on our fumblings in an irritating half-light of partial censorship.

Monday 8 April – Went to the House of Commons to the last day of the great debate on the conduct of the war. There they sat on the front bench – the three of them – Chamberlain, Simon [Sir John Simon, chancellor of the exchequer], and Hoare [Samuel Hoare, lord privy seal], the old-fashioned, solid, upper-middle-class Englishmen, methodical, respectable, immovable men who cannot be hurried or bullied, shrewd in short-term bargaining or political manipulation, but with no understanding of this age – of its despair, its violence, and its gropings, blinkered in solid comfort, shut off from poverty and risk. Their confidence comes from their certainties. They are the old England. When Chamberlain goes, that goes and it will not return.

Sunday 19 May – When Haines, the valet who works in all these service flats, came to see me this morning he was in a state of high excitement. 'The news this morning is awful. We have got the men and the spirit, but we have not got the planes. Somebody is responsible for this.'

Michael Vyvyan* said today at lunch, 'How absurd to blame a liberal social democracy for not being organized to deal with war. It is like blaming a fine flower garden for not moving at sixty miles an hour'.

Meanwhile two French journalists who attended a lunch in Lord Athlone's honour the other day returned in a state bordering on nervous hysteria. They found all the Blimps at the luncheon discussing sports for the British troops behind

---

* A friend currently at the British Foreign Office but keen to join the army.

the lines. 'Men must have some rugger and cricket. Keep them fit,' etc.

Refugees are beginning to arrive from the Continent – tough-looking Norwegian seamen with shocks of coarse blond hair, dressed in blue serge suits, lunching at Garland's Hotel – Dutch peasant girls in native costume like coloured photographs in the *Geographical Magazine* – walking down Cockspur Street carrying their worldly possessions tied up in bundles. A group of Dutch soldiers in the street in German-looking uniforms gives one a turn. (Shall we see German soldiers in London streets?)

My brother Roley has cabled asking me to do my best to get him a commission in the British Army to get him over here quicker than he could with the Canadians. Why should he be hurled into that hell in France? Why can't he wait until his turn comes to come over with the Canadians? It is not his England. It would be more appropriate if I went, as I have always been so bloody English.

Wednesday 22 May – Last night I wrote a speech for Mr Massey to deliver to Canada on the general theme of 'the darkest hour before the dawn', 'British spirit is unbreakable', 'the nightmare of horror and destruction that hangs heavy in the air in these lovely days of English spring'.

Before the war I used to say that I could not understand how any man of conscience could write propaganda, and in my mind I was always critical of my father for the recruiting speeches he made in the first war and he, unlike me, was trying to go to war himself.

Poor old Franckenstein* came to see me today. He wants now to get out to Canada. He is usually so suave and

---

* George Franckenstein, Austrian first minister plenipotentiary in London until the *Anschluss* in 1938. The former embassy building at 18 Belgrave Square was now under the protection of the Swiss legation.

mannered but today he looked shattered. He is partly Jewish and he knows that if the Germans come he will be shot at once. N* says, 'Well, he has had a pretty good time all his life. Now he is old – why shouldn't he be knocked on the head? Look at all the chaps who are being killed in France'.

HERMIONE RANFURLY

Dan had been posted to Palestine. Whitaker had gone with him, but the War Office had forbidden the wives of 'non-regular' (non-career) soldiers from going overseas. However, Hermione and a fellow non-regular wife named Toby had joined their husbands in Palestine. Crossing the Channel, she feared being bombed and sunk, and at every point of embarkation – Marseilles, Malta, Cairo – she expected either to be caught and returned to England or, at the very least, to lose her firearms: Dan's shotguns in her suitcase and a revolver hidden in her elastic girdle. Remarkably, she reached Palestine after fourteen days with very few hitches and luggage intact. Dan was there to meet her.

Saturday 2 March – I saw him a long way down the train looking up at the carriages. All bronzed by the sun, wearing khaki shorts and tunic, marvellously good-looking . . . I stood and watched him spellbound. I thought my heart would burst . . .† Heaven is being together.

Wednesday 13 March – The Sherwood Rangers are moving north to Karkur which consists of a few Arab houses, a little Jewish settlement of box-like bungalows, a water tower and a small agricultural school. Except for the view over the plain beyond, where the Yeomanry will camp, it is a dreary place.

* Unidentified in the original.
† Hermione's original punctuation.

Hermione rented a tiny bungalow from someone called Elsa, who spoke only German and Hebrew. There was just room for the upright 'honky tonk' piano Whitaker had hired in Tel Aviv.

Saturday 16 March – The Sherwood Rangers had a terrible two days getting here. Now Dan and Whitaker are gone to their tents in camp and I am alone – stitching curtains and listening to the night serenade of frogs and cricket, and the eerie howls of pye dogs.

Dan said it was a fine sight – seeing the Regiment parade by squadrons and file away across the plain. Each man carried a forage net, a noose bag, and rations for two days. They rode all morning, plagued by flies and halted at noon for lunch in a narrow lane with a hedge on one side and a line of trees on the other. Dan had dismounted and given his troops the order to take bits out and prepare to water when suddenly without the slightest warning, two squadrons of horses, which were standing in a rise beyond him, charged down the track at full gallop. Dan flung himself into a ditch. They swept by like an avalanche; some of them crashed headlong into two army trucks which were parked in the lane, others hit the telegraph poles which fell like nine-pins and, as they passed, Dan's troop broke loose and went with them. When the dust cleared Dan saw an incredible scene of destruction – injured men, dead horses and a tangle of equipment lay everywhere and, far away, a moving trail of dust showed the horses were still racing madly on.

Dan found his chestnut mare covered with blood – all the skin torn off her shoulders and flanks. She had galloped through a barbed-wire fence. But many other horses were worse and several had to be shot. To add to their anxiety, storks, which are in migration, kept landing on the nearby power cables and burning in blue flames. Dan put his bed two hundred yards from the horse lines and went to sleep. He was woken by the thunder of hooves. It was terrifying –

in the dark he couldn't see which way they were coming till one horse crashed into the cook-house tent and sent it up in flames.

No-one knows what caused these stampedes. Some think there may be a mad horse which is the ring-leader. The Cheshire Yeomanry, who are right up at Acre in the north, have had the same trouble, some of their horses stampeded and plunged over a cliff into the sea. Whitaker says this is all caused by the Holy Ghost.

Monday 13 May – Dan had three days' leave for Whitsun so we set off for Beirut at the Baby Austin's maximum speed of forty-five miles per hour.

When we were dancing happily on the moonlit terrace of a night club by the sea, a Frenchman told us that Germany has invaded Holland, Belgium and Luxembourg and that Mr Churchill has taken over from Mr Chamberlain as Prime Minister. Dan thought perhaps he was drunk.

Thursday 16 May – The size and speed of the German thrust grows hourly more apparent and more horrifying. Standing, sweating, behind the big urns in the Rest Camp Canteen I felt so sorry for the soldiers; no one whistled, laughed or even talked much; the books, games and the gramophone stayed in the cupboard today. On our way home, I wondered how Elsa and our neighbours think; they never comment on the news and, of course, we can't understand their Hebrew and German conversations. Toby is so near to tears she can hardly speak – she is so worried for her children. Each day, with shaky hands, we mark and re-mark our maps of Europe.

Monday 20 May – Winston Churchill, now Prime Minister, has made another broadcast. It gave us a clear understanding of the gravity of the hour and of his absolute belief in the British people – that we will never surrender. His news was petrifying but I felt braver for his words. Whitaker came up to the bungalow. He, too, had taken courage from Mr Churchill. We had a chat before his bath and he looked over the top of his spectacles and said, 'My Lady, the likes of me believe we will win this war, somehow, someday. I think it would help all our "hesprits du corpses" if you and His Lordship gave a Ball in this bungalow – just like they did before Waterloo'. I agreed. When he'd gone back to camp I locked the doors, pulled the curtains and wept till I fell asleep.

ALAN BROOKE

Brooke managed to go home from France for a week's leave at the beginning of April despite his fear that 'something might yet crop up at the eleventh hour to stop me'.

Returning to his base in Phalempin village near Lille in northern France, he resumed the hectic work of preparation for a German attack and for the possibility of a British advance into Belgium.

Tuesday 16 April – Still no move on the part of Germany into either Holland or Belgium! This evening a move into Luxembourg seems more probable, though I fail to see why he should try such a move. Italy on the other hand is definitely looking more aggressive again, and likely to come in with Germany.

This morning I went to a demonstration of booby traps prepared by the 4th Div. Blunt (commanding RAF contingent with BEF) came to lunch. He is not very inspiring.

In the afternoon I went for a walk in the woods nearby and imagined you were at my side. We discussed the lovely carpet of anemones, and all the nice green young shoots. In the garden M. Rosette has found a blackbird's nest that I am watching. I wish I could take photographs of it.

Thursday 18 April – Today the BEF sustained the most serious loss that it has had since the beginning of the war. Dill was ordered home to take up the appointment of DCIGS [deputy chief of the Imperial General Staff]. I only hope that this may be a preliminary step to his replacing Tiny Ironside as CIGS. That would be the wisest step we had taken since the start of hostilities. Meanwhile he leaves a terrible blank behind him, and I have a horrid lonely feeling knowing that he is gone. During those trying early months of October and November when an attack seemed imminent and there was little to meet it with, it was the greatest comfort to me to be able to discuss it with him and to obtain from him his valuable advice. Gort asked me to lunch with him at a farewell lunch party for Dill. Adam* was there also. We then went to the aerodrome to see him off. He departed in a deluge of rain and was soon lost in a bank of black clouds. I felt very sad at seeing him go, he is quite one of the finest men I have ever known.

Thursday 25 April – Ronnie told me that Mackie (Tom's colonel) had written a note saying that Tom had been evacuated to No. 8 Rouvroy with acute appendicitis. Meanwhile Ronnie had phoned up the hospital and found out that Tom had arrived there at 3 am and had been operated on by 8 am. He was a very serious case as his appendix had burst, was gangrenous, and peritonitis had developed. I had an appointment with Eves, the painter, for 3 pm in Arras, so after sitting for my portrait went on to Rouvroy to find out how Tom was. I saw the surgeon, who said that the operation was quite successful, but in view of the peritonitis the next few days must necessarily be very critical.

Friday 10 May – It was hard to believe on a most glorious spring day with all nature looking quite its best, that we were

---

*   General Sir Ronald Adam, commander of III Corps, an old friend of Brooke.

taking the first step towards what must become one of the greatest battles of history! All day long planes have been droning overhead and many have been brought down, one not very far from the Corps HQ. I spent the day checking over the orders for the move. Everything so far has been running like clockwork and with less interference from bombing than I had anticipated.

I move up tomorrow. Had time to look up Tom in the morning and found him holding his own well, I thought rather more cheerful about himself.

This finishes 7 months of war spent at Phalempin!

Eight days later II Corps was forced to withdraw, as the Germans penetrated both the Belgian and French fronts to the north and south and began to encircle the British. Brooke received a telegram that Tom was 'just holding his own' but heard nothing more. 'It was an additional burden to bear throughout those very dark days.'

Thursday 23 May – Nothing but a miracle can save the BEF now and the end cannot be very far off!

We carried out our withdrawal successfully last night back to the old frontier defences, and by this evening were established in the defences we spent the winter preparing. But where the danger lies is on our right rear; the German armoured divisions have penetrated to the coast, Abbeville, Boulogne and Calais have been rendered useless. We are therefore cut off from our sea communications, beginning to be short of ammunition, supplies still all right for 3 days but after that scanty.

It is a fortnight since the German advance started and the success they have achieved is nothing short of phenomenal. There is no doubt they are most wonderful soldiers.

Over the next week Brooke travelled between a shifting general headquarters and his retreating divisions – a hectic, perilous and exhausting time. The role of the 5th Division at Ypres was crucial.

Sunday 26 May – Went early to see 5th Div in Plugstreet [Ploegsteert] Wood, found that they had been getting into position on Ypres–Comines Canal during the night. Motored on to Ypres to find out whether Belgians were defending this place. Found nothing on our left except the Postal Service of the 1st French Motorized Div! Then examined canal and railway to see what defences were like. Only just escaped being locked out by the blowing of the bridge owing to the arrival of the Germans.

Attended GHQ conference where we were informed of instructions received from home for evacuation of the BEF. We discussed plans for this operation and I spent the rest of the day in conference finishing off plans for this withdrawal. It is going to be a very hazardous enterprise and we shall be lucky if we save 25% of the BEF! We are bound to suffer heavily from bombing. I have already been put into the ditch 3 times today to avoid bombing attacks.

On 27 May Brooke issued instructions for the withdrawal of the 3rd and 4th Divisions. The 5th Division was under heavy shelling at Ypres, and news came that the Germans had broken through their front. Brooke moved battalions and tanks to strengthen the defence, but the German advance was relentless.

Tuesday 28 May – Visited 5th Div to find out situation which is not satisfactory at junction with 50th Div. Germans still pressing on. Gave verbal instructions for further withdrawal (tonight).

Proceeded north to see Martel* who was covering Ypres

---

* Commander of 50th Division.

and to find out what touch he had on his right south of Ypres with 5th Div. Saw Haydon commanding 150th Brigade who said he had no contact on his right and that he had thrown back his right flank. Told Martel to send 4th Northumberland Fusiliers to clear up this situation. Then proceeded north to see whether Monty had reached his front along canal north of Ypres. Found he had as usual accomplished almost the impossible and had marched from Roubaix to north of Ypres, a flank march past front of attack, and was firmly established in the line with French Division to his north.

Down again to 5th Div HQ to find situation of hard day's fighting. Division had held on by its eyelids, 17th and 13th Brigades greatly reduced by casualties. I Corps artillery which had been left behind to help had fired 5,000 rounds of medium artillery in 36 hours! Line had held thank God otherwise 5th and 4th Divisions were lost and II Corps would have been rolled up!

Despite his worst fears, the BEF was not lost.

On 29 May Brooke was ordered to hand over his corps and return home so that he could lead the task of re-forming the army. His request to stay was turned down.

Thursday 30 May – There is no doubt that the 5th Div in its fight on the Ypres–Comines Canal saved the BEF.

I can hardly believe that I have succeeded in pulling the 4 divisions out of the mess we were in, with allies giving way on all flanks. Now remains the task of embarking which will be a difficult one. Went to see how embarkation was proceeding and found the whole thing at a standstill owing to lack of boats!! Went to see Gort and got little satisfaction.

Returned to Gort to get him to telephone to 1st Sea Lord to press for marines, more ships and boats. Went down to beach at 7.15 p.m., was carried out to open boat, and with

Ronnie Stanyforth and Barney Charlesworth* we paddled out to the destroyer and got aboard. There I found Adam, to my great joy. We have been waiting till 10 pm before starting, rather nerve wracking as the Germans are continually flying round and being shot at, and after seeing the ease with which a few bombs can sink a destroyer, it is an unpleasant feeling.

Later – We never started until 12.15 am, at 3 am we were brought up short with a crash. I felt certain that we had hit a mine or been torpedoed. But she remained on an even keel and after some shuffling about proceeded on slowly. I heard later from the commander that he had 3 routes to select from, one was under gun fire from the coast, one had a submarine and mines reported in it, and the other was very shallow at low water. He chose the latter and hit the bottom, damaging a propeller slightly. Finally arrived in Dover at 7.15 am. Wonderful feeling of peace after the last 3 weeks.

CLARA MILBURN

In early January Clara's son Alan went to France to join the BEF. Cheerful letters arrived nearly every fortnight, and Clara sent off parcels of cakes and biscuits. His MG was returned home from the Swindon training camp in February, and on 13 April his regular letter home announced his promotion to lieutenant.

The bitterly cold winter, a prolonged bout of gastric flu followed by food poisoning ('tinned tongue') and missing her son all encouraged Clara to take a break and visit her friend Joyce on the Hampshire coast.

Monday 29 April – **Milford** – A soft, grey day and warm, with the nightingale singing at the corner of the garden. We saw

---

* His aides-de-camp.

him sitting on the topmost branch of the crab tree as we came back from shopping in the village this morning. We took with us little curly-headed David, an evacuee baby, whose voice is heard in this house – which is strange indeed to me. Then, after lunch, came one of those unforgettable times we store in our memory as Wordsworth did.

Joyce took the nice little wife of the doctor, and me, to a primrose wood not far away. With baskets and our tea, we set off in the car. Wellingtons on our feet ready for the boggy, sloshy patches we were to come across. The car was parked at the edge of the wood and off we went, first along a path, coming out into a clearing, next through brown, oily mud splashes, under branches, over brambles, with tufts of primroses here and there. But the best was yet to be, and soon we came to masses of huge primroses, and setting down our baskets, began to pick. Chatting and picking, we tied up bunches from time to time with wool brought by Joyce.

The plovers were calling in a field close by, a chaffinch singing the old song, and the chiffchaff repeating his monotonous call. Tea was very welcome, and we sat and enjoyed every sip and every crumb. Then we picked more pale primroses, bunch after bunch.

After she returned home, Clara and Jack followed the news closely, wondering where Alan was. Her diary notes the change of prime minister although makes no comment about Churchill, only noting that Chamberlain was 'a great man'.

Friday 17 May – The war news is grave. The Germans have turned the salient into a bulge on the Western Front and great strength will be needed to flatten it again. The RAF are doing magnificent work in preventing easy advance by bombing roads, railways, key points, etc. On the whole they are clever and, having done their work, the announcer says: 'All our aeroplanes returned safely'. Sometimes it is 'One of our

aeroplanes failed to return'. In a tremendous effort on a key
position today, 'Eleven of our aeroplanes failed to return'.

Last night, just as I was in the half-dreamy stage of
dropping off to sleep, I suddenly saw a face, rather white,
against the dark background of my closed lids, and tried to
keep it long enough to see whose face it was. As it faded
away, it seemed to be Alan, calmly asleep.

Tuesday 28 May – Up and round the household jobs so as to
be ready to leave for Berkswell Rectory at 10 a.m., where we
all worked hard making triangular bandages – nine dozen
today – as well as an operation garment. We talk and work
and the machines clatter too till at 12.45 we stopped for lunch
(sandwiches), and then took a little breather outside. I bought
a few toffees at the village shop, but on hearing the sad news
of Belgium's capitulation through Leopold, their King, I
forgot to eat them. This is indeed bad news and we were all
rather overcome at first, but settled to work again, discussing
parachutes and parashooters, etc., till 4 p.m.

The news at 9 p.m. was still very grave: the Belgian
capitulation has increased the difficulties of the BEF, and the
thought of Alan being with them in Belgium is almost more
than one can bear tonight. It has been a hard day for us,
though we do not say a great deal to each other, for one
must keep up.

On 1 June, as the evacuation from Dunkirk continued, the war
reached Clara on a more personal level. News came of the death
of two local men, 'the first of the men we really know'. But there
was no news of Alan.

VERA BRITTAIN

In April Vera and George returned from America, where he had been teaching and she had completed a lecture tour. They had left the children first with her mother and then at their boarding schools and the separation weighed heavily on her conscience.

Thursday 23 May – Germans up to Channel ports; fighting round Boulogne. Saw Mother off to Bournemouth by the 9.30 from Waterloo. Went at midday to George Lansbury's* Memorial Service at Westminster Abbey – 'Memorial Service for the Human Race' it might have been. Strange irony of service for a pacifist on such a day, especially as at same moment Dr Wood, Stuart Morris & Maurice Rowntree were being tried at Bow Street for the poster: 'Wars will cease when men refuse to fight. What are You going to do about it?' Many wet eyes & strained faces at Westminster Abbey – especially during singing of 'From death's dread sting' and 'Jerusalem'.

Gerald Bailey[†] joined us for lunch & told us Cyril Joad[‡] had written a virtual recantation in yesterday's 'News Chronicle' saying that nothing now mattered but victory. Went to PPU & discussed trial with Maurice Rowntree, Stuart and Dr Rutherford; the magistrate (Sir Robert Dummett) has apparently made up his mind adversely in advance.

Later, Vera described the trial in more detail in her memoir of the first two years of the war *England's Hour*, published in 1941.

---

[*] Leader of the Labour Party 1931–5, prominent pacifist.
[†] Secretary of the National Peace Council.
[‡] Philosopher, who joined the *Brains Trust* on BBC radio in January 1940, member of PPU.

Long before the trial has ended, it becomes clear that the Attorney General does not wish to press the case for the police. In giving judgment, the Chief Magistrate maintains that the failure to withdraw the poster is an infringement of the present defence regulations, but he merely binds over the defendants under the Probation of Offenders Act after they have undertaken that the poster will be discontinued owing to its liability to misinterpretation in time of war. This technical sentence is less significant than the arguments of the young defending counsel, Mr J F Platts Mills, who is taking his last case before joining the Air Force, and their acceptance by the magistrate in spite of his obvious objection to the opinions of the defendants.

'Those views,' quotes Mr Platts Mills from a recent decision, 'which are only held by a few, which are unpopular, and which run counter to the great majority of views of mankind, particularly in times of emotional crisis, as in times of war, are views which this Court is particularly jealous to preserve.'

From his carved chair between two bookcases filled with leather-bound legal volumes, the old magistrate grimly agrees.*

Friday 31 May – Tens of thousands from BEF getting back across the Channel hungry, tired, half-clad, and in any kind of boat that will take them, bombed all the time. Thank God I don't know anyone with the Army this time.

Unprofitable morning; then went to PPU & worked on Pacifist Ambulance Scheme. On to a meeting arranged by the NPC to examine position of pacifists under Defence Regulations.

Both [of us] felt jaded, tired, chaotic, so after tea at the Euston Hotel walked in Regent's Park amid shaded mauve

---

* *England's Hour*, Futura, 1981, first published in January 1941.

pansies and lupins in many delicate colours. Desertedness of everything gave impression of Sunday. Since most of the iron railings had gone for conversion into armaments, the Park looked like a vast green field, very fresh & vivid. A few elderly people were sitting in chairs, a few young people sailing in boats with striped sails. Such an illusion of peace. I felt as though I were watching the funeral of civilisation elegantly conducted. So the Roman Empire must have appeared just before the barbarians marched in.

NAOMI MITCHISON

In Carradale, Naomi was expecting her seventh child – due in July. Denny, her eldest, was in London training to be a doctor, and the others were all back at school in England. Dick was now working at the Ministry of Labour with William Beveridge, who was carrying out a survey of wartime manpower. (A year later Beveridge would chair the inquiry for the Ministry of Health which would lead to his famous report and the birth of the welfare state.)

Monday 20 May – In the morning Dick went back to London; we would both have liked some assurance that we would be seeing one another again: and in at least tolerable circumstances. It was less dramatic, less moving perhaps, than when he went back to London from Glasgow Central the Wednesday of Munich, or when he went back from Campbeltown by air last September. But it was more depressing. I am alone now for the first time for some weeks; the last time I was alone, in March, none of this had happened. One hardly listened in; one could forget for hours. I feel sick this evening; I have a kind of pressure at the back of my head, the same I used to get as a child after [a] frightening nightmare. The rats are making a lot of noise under the drawing room floor: not that I mind them.

Thursday 23 May – Nightmares. Almost inevitable. And the baby wriggling terrifically all night. I am thinking much less about this baby than I ever did about the others; I haven't made little she-plans about it as I did with the others; the future is black-fogged ahead of this one; all one can cultivate is acceptance.

The 6 o'ck news, with the fighting at Boulogne and capture of Abbeville, was a bit of a shock. I remember so well going through Abbeville when Dick was wounded and I went out as next of kin. I began to worry a lot about him and Denny in London and the others at school. Winchester is very near Southampton. I looked at the map, to see just how far all the children's schools were from Boulogne. They might easily drop parachutists in Surrey. Also worrying about possible suppressing of CP [Communist Party] with all one's friends. I do hope Denny will be sensible and just work and not try to make 'contacts' in London; he isn't old enough to know who's trustworthy, and he's pretty good at putting his foot in it from the highest motives.

Saturday 25 May – Dick says in his letter 'We might all have to bolt for Australia, if indeed we could get there. I wonder if any of the fishermen would risk an Atlantic crossing.' Of course we've both got bad political records, if the Gestapo did come over – But it seems so fantastic. He half thinks so and half not. I should like just to have a taste of the London atmosphere; it is too safe here to understand. Funny, I suppose I would be in London but for this baby. I can't say I'd like an Atlantic crossing at the moment, in a herring boat; one wouldn't be able to take much, because most of the space would be needed for the diesel oil. Yet I feel guilty to have been so little involved.

Despite her efforts, the local Labour Party was becoming inactive. Naomi 'felt pretty depressed about the whole thing'.

Thursday 30 May – Remains of the Carradale [Labour] Party turned up tonight, mostly the committee, except Mairi who had gone to the pictures. We decided to go on but only to meet once or twice a year.

Discussed rumours; several sinister people have been seen; one, who was deliberately mis-directed by our woodcutters, was the net-man from Campbeltown! He was later seen on the golf course, making notes – presumably about nets. Angus found a bit of an aeroplane on the warren and took it over to show MacKillop the joiner; they decided whoever the tradesman who had worked on it, it was grand work. The next day this had got round to Campbeltown and a Govt official came to see the bit of wood. The milkman is one of the main rumour culprits. We also talked about the amount of scrap iron lying about and the stupidity of the new rails they are putting up round the housing estate.

We discussed Germans in disguise; Archie said he had often noticed what big feet nuns had, and probably the half of them were men; the conversation, as Scottish Presbyterian conversations do, then became extremely ribald. We also tried to think what it would be like here supposing the Nazis won; I have a nasty feeling that I should get into a concentration camp; I wish this baby were due a month sooner. It is a damned awkward time.

Then all came into the other room to hear the 9 o'ck news. All were thinking in terms of the men, especially those who had been in the last war. All these folk with fishing connections are particularly upset at naval disasters, such as the loss of these destroyers.

I notice I have bitten my nails very badly, a thing I have not done for months.

GEORGE BEARDMORE

George was now working at the BBC as an assistant store-keeper, and each day travelled into town from Harrow either by train or on his Royal Enfield motorbike. He sold his third novel for a one-off sum in order to get it published, enough to pay the rates and buy Jean some new stockings, and was now working on *The Spy Who Died in Bed*, managing 500 words a day in the storeroom.

Wednesday 15 May – Incredible that one should be living in such times. I find myself shaking my head to bring back reality. Dreadful, unthinkable visions enter my head of what would happen if they won and crossed the Channel. Mentally I have already sent Jean and Victoria to Canada, and seen Harrow bombed, and parachutists seize Broadcasting House. The imagination makes these fantastic notions so real, but of course they are purely mischievous. To counter them, we heard the new War Minister [Eden] last night appeal for Local Defence Volunteers to deal with parachutists. That at least is something I can do.

Wednesday 22 May – Last night at about 9.10 p.m. one had the impression of all England bent over its wireless-sets as we learned that German advance troops had taken Arras and Amiens, names familiar from the previous war, only a short distance from Abbeville and the coast. Reynaud, the French Premier, gave out the news in the afternoon, alleging that the enemy's speed was due to failure to blow up the Meuse bridges. One waits for a counter-attack which Duff Cooper promised last night would be 'formidable'. One imagines that when the objective of the coast towns is attained, the troop-carrying bombers will be diverted to landing in this country, laying Canterbury waste and its cathedral a crumbling grey ruin such as Rheims cathedral was left twenty-five years ago, besieging places like Manchester, turning our own selves into refugees trudging down English roads and lanes that have suddenly become hostile. All these horrors are possibilities at this moment. Although the rumour is that my department will be evacuated to Droitwich, Jean has decided to stay at home, although she might take the baby to Freda's (my sister-in-law's)* near Wetherby in Yorkshire. Even so, Droitwich and Wetherby are only fifteen minutes or so away by bomber.

No hard news about the British Expeditionary Force. How many of our men does it muster, and where are they now?

The general mood I should say is one of growing anger. I felt it last night when I went to Kenton to collect a cot for Victoria, who is now standing up. By then Reynaud's news had sunk in. First there was Marsh, now in the Ministry of Supply and while there an Air Raid Warden. He said that twenty-three years ago almost to the day he had been one of those who had cleared Arras of the Germans. I saw tears in the eyes of this homely fellow, living three doors away, when he said he recalled the friends he had lost there. Hetty, whose cot I was borrowing for the next three years, said that she and her 4-year-old Christine were staying in their home, come what may. Her husband, Alfred, came home about 8 p.m. He is employed by Stoke Newington Boro' Council in Food Supply. They are taking in a Belgian refugee, a woman of thirty. On the way home I was helped by a tall, sturdy, and very grubby young man who said he was due soon to be called up and was meanwhile making all he bloody well could (as an electrician) by dint of working twelve hours a day and at week-ends so that he would have something to leave with his wife. Finally George Edgar

* Explanation added by George in preparation for publication.

said that the situation was as bloody as it could be, speaking as an old soldier, and he had switched the wireless off and was taking his missis to the pub, even with beer at 11d the pint.

The worry was enough to wake me at 4.30 a.m. As torrents of rain had fallen, breaking a three-week drought, I couldn't use the Enfield to get to work and took a Workman's ticket at 1½d instead of 2/8d and arrived at Baker Street at 8 a.m.

A Bible outside a church in Baker Street was open at the passage: 'I will lift up mine eyes unto the hills from whence cometh my help.' Very apt, I daresay, but the psalmist didn't specify which hills and whether he had a German blitzkrieg followed by invasion in mind. Still, it comforted because it took one's mind back to invasions long ago.

I forgot to say that should the Alert go at night we have decided that while Jean picks up the baby and her mattress I should (1) fill the bath, (2) empty the pantry of its mops and mangle and black it out by means of the moveable shutter I have fabricated, (3) get the wireless going, and (4) run a lamp and lead from the hall light to the pantry. Somehow, I don't see all this happening, not at once anyway. We consider the pantry safest because it is under the stairs which will shed descending rubble and because its window has very little glass, and is shielded by next door.

Sunday 9 June – A week ago I watched a street cinema, contained in a van of which the engine charged the batteries for a projector, in aid of National Savings. It was a film of the Dunkirk operation, that is, the rescue of a large part of our army and some French from the sands of Dunkirk. Among those Yiddish tailors and foremen and button-makers (this was in Margaret Street) I became aware of a common anger: those muddied and exhausted men stumbling off gangplanks were the chaps one usually meets in pubs or walking the street with their girls. One hears accounts of sergeants swimming with wounded on their backs, a fisher-boy making the cross-Channel trip three times in a boat that had been holed by shrapnel and plugged with waste, of a 'once round the lighthouse' motor launch sunk by shellfire apparently in mid-Channel and finding itself in only five feet of water. Oddly enough, while cutting the front hedge at North Harrow I had heard the drumming of guns which could only have come from Dunkirk (as it turned out later) and called Amos from next door to listen. His comment was: 'Our turn next.'

REFUGEES

From 17 May, the date the Germans announced the fall of Brussels, Belgian refugees began arriving in England in whatever sailing craft they could find. Bombing raids had been so intensive that a Belgian commander told the *Daily Express* correspondent Geoffrey Cox, one of the last to leave Brussels, that 'It was as if the very sky fell on us'.

F. Tennyson Jesse, an English criminologist, author and one of the few women journalists to report from the front during the First World War, and her secretary, Miss Moira Tighe, referred to as 'Tiger', were working in London as French-speaking interpreters receiving refugees. On their first day, 17 May, they began at Charing Cross station, moving on to Victoria in the afternoon.

F. TENNYSON JESSE*

Monday 27 May – **Letter to friends the Hoveys, Hubbles and Balderstons in California** – Everywhere the story is the same: refugees deliberately machine-gunned up and down the roads. Two men who had been twelve days walking from Lille to the coast said that the road was covered with cars that had been machine-gunned all full of civilians escaping. They opened the door of one car and looked in – to see three young girls all dead.

One woman within a month of having a baby had with her two little children of three and four, a boy and a girl. I picked the children up and sat them on a luggage trolley and we cleared a space for the woman and made her sit down. She was Flemish and understood no French, so Mrs. P (a Dutch translator) again came into play while Tiger and I fed the children with bananas and cups of milk. They seemed extraordinarily untouched by what they had gone through and smiled confidingly at us though you would have thought, when you had heard the woman's story, that they would be shell-shocked for life.

They were the nephew and niece of the woman, and she let lodgings in Ostend in the summer and her husband had a boat. She and her husband, their two children, her sister, her sister's husband and the two little children we saw, and fourteen other members of the family got away in his fishing-boat. They were bombed when out at sea, her husband, her children, her sister, her sister's husband and all the family excepting herself and the little nephew and niece were killed. The last thing she remembers seeing was her little girl of

---

* F. Tennyson Jesse and H. M. Harwood, *London Front – Letters written to America August 1939–July 1940*, Constable & Co., 1940.

fourteen hit by an incendiary bomb, throw up her arms and go up like a blazing torch.

She herself and the little nephew and niece were thrown into the water which was covered with oil, and she was in it about half an hour. She managed to scramble back into what was left of the boat and she heard 'Tante Louise, Tante Louise!' and the little boy of four and the little girl of three who had been hanging on to a rope the other side of the boat climbed in, the boy first, then he helped his baby sister. These children were so small that I could pick them up and carry them quite easily. They saved themselves as instinctively as drowning kittens. The boat drifted along and at last all three were rescued by a British vessel.

I think all of us at the station were almost sick with rage and anger as the poor woman sat there; we tried to coax her to drink a little hot tea and she stared out in front of her. A young policeman said to Tiger: 'Why, Miss, but this is really serious!' in accents of surprise. And Tiger said: 'How do you mean serious?' and he said: 'Why, this may happen to *us*.' Which, you must admit, is a very good definition of something being really serious.

The speed with which Germany overran the Low Countries and France gave rise to the rumour that this was due to the help of German spies masquerading as refugees. On 12 May the order went out for the arrest of over 2,000 male 'enemy aliens' – 'aged sixteen to sixty, from Hampshire to Nairn'. Between then and 15 July another 28,000 were to follow. Jewish refugees often found themselves interned alongside Nazi sympathizers. The three largest internment camps were on the Isle of Man, at Huyton in Liverpool and at Wharf Mills at Bury in Lancashire. Holloway and Brixton prisons were also used, as was Kempton Park Racecourse.

The composer Hans Gál, 50, and his 18-year-old son Franz, who had fled Vienna after the *Anschluss*, were among those arrested that Sunday, at their home in Edinburgh. His wife, Hanna, remained free 'for the time being', as did his younger son Peter, at boarding school in Yorkshire.

HANS GÁL*

Monday 13 May – **Donaldson Hospital, Edinburgh** – We have now been stuck here for 24 hours, guarded by grim-looking soldiers with rifles and bayonets; they must think we are very dangerous fellows.

Almost all of us who come from Edinburgh know one another. There is not a single one among all of these for whom I would not stake my life that he is as harmless as I am. And now we are imprisoned because we have been mistaken for the enemy – our enemy! And we are put into a building – this is like a grim mockery – in which a few hundred German civilian prisoners from captured ships are interned. These have already settled in quite comfortably, manage the kitchen and dish out the food to us, who have to line up in turn with our tin bowls. The flaxen-haired Hamburg type predominates who greet us with sneering grins and evident satisfaction.

Franz comes running. This evening he will be taken away, along with the whole group of young men under eighteen, to a special camp in the south of England.[†] I tried unsuccessfully to protest; boys are not allowed to stay here with the adults, that is a rule that admits no exception. The boy, who is otherwise a rough diamond, is gentle and almost tender at our parting. I share with him the small amount of money that I've been allowed to keep [bank-notes were taken away, together

---

* Hans Gál, *Musik hinter Stacheldraht. Tagebuchblaetter aus dem Sommer 1940*, Peter Lang (Bern), 2003. Unpublished diary translated into English by Eva Fox-Gál and Anthony Fox.
† Franz was interned at Lingfield, near London.

with all knives, scissors and other suspicious articles, e.g. books], then he is chased away by a non-commissioned officer, as he was naturally not allowed on our floor, with the adults.

Thursday 16 May – Yesterday people came who are hungry for music. There are about a dozen of the best people from my Edinburgh Refugee Orchestra here. We could quite easily form a small string orchestra, if we had the instruments.

Friday 17 May – Nothing has come of our music plans. Marching orders! We are to leave tomorrow, supposedly for the Liverpool area. That hit us like a bolt from the blue.

In the afternoon Hansi* was here. I hardly recognised her, she looked so pale, tearful and run down. She was very unhappy about the removal of the boy. I could at least give her his address, which I had obtained in the meantime.

We talk little. She strokes my hand and would most like to cry. So would I.

The soldier looks at the clock.

Never again will I let anyone visit me as a prisoner! Never again!!!

Sunday 19 May – **Huyton, near Liverpool** – We were led into a hut with long tables and benches and were given tea, bread and cheese, and a burly captain made a speech of welcome in which he appealed for our good behaviour. We shall be able to arrange our lives as we wish. Anyone who wants to can take part in 'digging for peace'. He paused slightly before the last word: the slogan 'digging for victory' evidently seemed to him to be tactless when addressing German prisoners. How difficult it must be to understand what a refugee is!!

By 23 May there were moves to imprison women, with a *Times* leader invoking Rudyard Kipling's 'The female of the species is

* His wife.

often more deadly than the male'. Fortunately Gál's wife remained
at liberty.

Tuesday 4 June – Strange how it happened.

I had slept wonderfully well yesterday – the first time for
three weeks – I had sung duets with [dentist] Schneider,
argued with [zoologist] Gross, allowed myself, in spite of
valiant opposition, to be pressed into cleaning by [laryngolo-
gist] Sugar, and then I sat down and started a quite decent
piece of music. A flute and two violins, these are the only
available instruments that are seriously worth considering. A
problem to create a trio out of them!

Thursday 13 June – We will no longer play my 'Huyton Suite'
(this is what I have called my trio) here, and who knows
whether and where we shall ever play it. Tomorrow we are
off, we are going to the Isle of Man.

Sunday 16 June – **Central Promenade Camp, Douglas, Isle of
Man** – We are enclosed in a barbed-wire rectangle like in a
zoo. Inside this enclosure, which is about a hundred paces
long in one direction and seventy in the other, lies a block of
thirty-four small hotels of the London middle-class boarding-
house type, divided by a road running at right angles.

The view of the sea is certainly magnificent, and Douglas
Bay, which can be seen on both sides, is enchantingly
beautiful. The air is pure and wonderful. The accommodation
itself – well, I have always had a violent hatred of boarding-
houses, and I won't rid myself of it here.

Every house has to take an exact quota, albeit one that is
sometimes calculated according to unfathomable criteria. In
our house, No. 2, the second house on the sea-front, seventy-
two inmates are crammed together like sardines in a tin.

Hans shared a bed with Schneider and a room with Gross and
Sugar. Though their room looked into a dank little courtyard, the

sea was tantalizingly near. Ingredients for cooking (chiefly oats) were thrown over the fence, and each house was responsible for its own meals. There were no sheets, only rough sacking, no hot water and no implements for washing dishes or pans. The camp held 2,000.

On 30 June all unmarried men under 30 were told to be ready to travel to Canada.

Tuesday 2 July – My young baritone Hans Mayer with his two Dutch friends has just flitted past me in full travel outfit. 'We've had enough with *one* German invasion,' he says, 'we have no desire to experience that again.'

Friday 5 July – One of the bits of news that has been brought in has got me agitated: a ship called *Andorra Star*, filled with prisoners and internees and sailing without a convoy, was torpedoed and sunk last week in the Irish Sea. Seven hundred prisoners are said to have drowned. There were apparently wild scenes, as there were no life-saving facilities. This news immediately went right through me, as a letter from my wife contained the news that Franz is no longer in Lingfield and his whereabouts are unknown.

One of the cellists has at last had his instrument sent. He is called Dr Ball and was a distinguished law-officer in Berlin and must have been an excellent cellist. His right hand became almost useless in a German concentration-camp through frost-bite, the fingers are crooked and incapable of gripping anything. It is a mystery to me how he can use the bow, but he manages it, although he is somewhat restricted and technical things can easily go wrong.

Friday 26 July – Still no news of Franz. I am in complete despair. I no longer know what peaceful sleep is. And I shall probably even give up eating.

Music can sometimes still make me forget, and there is

always plenty of that. Now a concert on a grand scale is being planned. Over in the Palace Hotel. There is a large, beautiful theatre that holds about 2,000 spectators. We have got permission to organise a concert there for the camp occupants.

Saturday 27 July – I have just behaved like a hysterical old maid. On the promenade, in front of all the people, in the presence of Gross, I had a crying fit, when I opened the telegram, Hanna's telegram. God be praised, the boy is in Canada! No details, no explanation. But he is safe!!!

The first fifty men were released from the Isle of Man on 5 August. During his internment Hans developed eczema on his face and scalp. It had begun as a nervous itch, but had spread and was now both untreatable and unbearable. Nonetheless his release on grounds of medical hardship seemed slow in coming.

Thursday 15 August – In the morning I noticed that I couldn't see out of my eyes. My face must have been swollen and distorted. In response to my question as to how I looked, Sugar replied in a friendly way: 'Like a monkey's behind, my dear friend.' He is always kindly, but he does not mince his words. He then went straight to the hospital and arranged for a room to be made available for me.

Monday 19 August – Höllering [a film-maker] was [here] again, burning with a new idea. He wants to produce a review, a real piece of theatre. With music. And naturally with my music!

I laughed. I am supposed to make music here in the hospital! The music for what? Where is the script? There is no script yet. He still has to write it. But the title is already there: 'What a life!' It is to be a sort of photo-montage of our life in the camp, a series of short, lively scenes taken from everyday life.

Hans embraced the idea as the perfect PR exercise. 'Of course we want to present the best forces of our camp in as effective a way as possible, if only because [British Army] officers will probably be present.'

Tuesday 3 September – The curtain rises, one sees a barbed-wire fence, *our* barbed-wire, our cage. And *we ourselves*, people like us, enter, poor wretched internees with their little suitcases. Resounding laughter! Two refugees tell each other about their experiences, how they fled from Berlin to Vienna, Vienna to Prague, Warsaw, Amsterdam, Paris and London. 'Join the refugees, and you will see the world!' Resounding laughter! How fortunate that with tragi-comic things it is above all the latter component that the spectators are conscious of. This morning one of the patients in the house who was at the performance told me how pricelessly he had enjoyed himself, and how he then cried half the night because it was so dreadful.

Friday 27 September – **Finally released, and on the crossing to Liverpool** – The beautiful moments of last night's performance keep going around in my thoughts. After the performance there was a celebration in [the] house with the usual speeches and replies. None of us said what we were really thinking: that through the community our life here had acquired a new, nobler meaning; that all of us, family men as well as single men, have discovered something new and beautiful; that there is something more general and higher that transcends family and individual existence. And all of us have felt enriched by it, have enjoyed the warmth, the atmosphere of friendship and comradeship such as we have never known before.

The island has long since disappeared below the horizon. 'What a Life!' Draw a thick line under it, it is over.

What will Hansi say when she sees my face?

3. THE BATTLE OF BRITAIN

AUTUMN 1940

The British public had been kept in the dark about Dunkirk until the evening of 30 May, the fifth day of the evacuation, when the BBC announced that it was proceeding. By the time it had been completed, on 4 June, 68,000 members of the BEF were presumed killed or had been taken prisoner and were being force-marched to Germany and Poland. Of the 861 vessels that had taken part, 243 had been sunk, and the RAF had lost at least 100 aircraft. Nonetheless it was nothing short of miraculous that 338,226 troops (198,229 British and 139,997 French, Polish and Belgian) had been lifted safely off the beaches, with a further 220,000 rescued from other French ports.

At the end of the operation Churchill reminded the country that 'wars are not won by evacuations' and used the phrase 'we shall fight' no less than seven times in six lines.* But for the moment there was little to fight with. Three years' worth of rearmament (880 field guns, 700 tanks and 40,000 other vehicles) now littered the lanes of northern France.

Italy declared war on Britain and France on 10 June. Germany took Paris two days later and by 18 June France had surrendered. Churchill addressed the House of Com-

---

* Speech in House of Commons, 4 June 1940.

mons: 'The Battle for France is over. I expect that the Battle
of Britain is about to begin. Upon this battle depends the
survival of Christian civilisation ... If we fail, then the whole
world, including the United States ... will sink into the abyss
of a new Dark Age ... Let us therefore brace ourselves to
our duties and so bear ourselves that if the British Empire
and its Commonwealth last for a thousand years, men will
still say, "This was their finest hour"'.

The first test of Churchill's resolve involved the French
navy. If Germany was able to take control of the French fleet
British command of the sea would be severely compromised.
On 3 July all French ships in British ports were seized and
eighteen British warships proceeded to Mers-el-Kébir on the
Algerian coast, where much of the French fleet was based,
and delivered an ultimatum: join the fight against Germany,
surrender, scuttle your ships or be sunk. The French refused
and the British vessels opened fire. The bombardment lasted
ten minutes and over 1,200 French sailors died. In America
they were impressed: this was a fearless and determined
nation. Relations with France, until a month earlier Britain's
primary ally, took many years to recover.

For an invasion of Britain to succeed, Germany had to
gain air supremacy over south-east England. The Luftwaffe
sought to eliminate the RAF by destroying British fighters
either in the air or at their aerodromes, by making airfields
unusable and by disabling factories producing new planes,
which were leaving the production line at a phenomenal
rate. The British had developed a sophisticated radar air
defence system which was able to detect attacking German
formations at a considerable distance so their speed and
direction could be plotted and their probable destination
guessed at. British fighters were then sent up to intercept.
Their task was to disperse the escorting fighters in order to
destroy or divert the vulnerable bombers from their destination.

Hitler had specifically put London off limits for the Luftwaffe but on 24 August, more by accident than design, bombs fell on the capital. Churchill ordered reprisal raids on Berlin for the next two nights, and Hitler, who had promised the Germans that Berlin would not be attacked, retaliated, declaring that British cities should be razed to the ground. The Blitz had begun.

By 2 November London had suffered fifty-seven days of continuous bombing, and though a short respite followed, the attacks soon resumed and would continue until mid-May 1941. Other cities of military or industrial importance were targeted – Coventry, Plymouth, Liverpool, Swansea, Birmingham, Bristol were all heavily bombed. Undisturbed nights became a rarity and four hours' sleep a night the norm. The last major daytime attack took place on 30 September, but by then Hitler had indefinitely postponed the invasion of Britain. His plan to destroy the RAF before winter set in had failed, and he now diverted German resources east for the planned invasion of Russia, while his Italian allies sought to control the Mediterranean.

THE DIARISTS

VERA BRITTAIN

Vera's entry for 26 June 1940 simply states, 'Children sailed from Liverpool'. Their good friends in the USA the Colbys had urged Vera and George to send the children to them to escape the dreadful consequences of a German invasion. At the beginning of September, confident that they would be reunited soon, as Vera had a new invitation to tour America, George also left to resume his teaching at Cornell. Lonely, Vera went to stay with her mother, now back in London in Edwardes Square off Kensington High Street.

As the Blitz gathered momentum, she collected material for her book *England's Hour* and continued to produce a pacifist newsletter, which had made her extremely unpopular with the authorities. In February a question had been asked in Parliament about her first lecture tour of America, and it now seemed that there was a move to restrict her travel. The government knew that the war could only be won if the USA joined the fight against Germany, and it was feared that Vera's lectures might influence American public opinion towards isolationism. Might she be prevented from seeing her children because of her pacifist views?

Saturday 7 September – Wrote all morning. PPU Council meeting in afternoon. Didn't hear siren just before I left; strolled calmly through Hyde Park wondering why people were standing about in groups; by the time I got to Hyde Park Corner whole city was shaken by roar of guns and I saw about 12 German 'planes in the sky above the docks with shrapnel bursting all round them. After watching a minute or two took a taxi; from top of Edwardes Square, which I reached safely, saw columns of smoke rising into sky from direction of docks.

Decided not to go to bed too early after supper but work despite siren, when suddenly it went. Had just taken dress off & was going downstairs in dressing gown when Vera Z* called Mother & me to look at the glow of fire over the City. We had just gone into the drawing-room when suddenly there was a terrific roar & a crash; the house shook like a ship in a rough sea. We turned to rush downstairs when there was a second & louder crash, & we were practically <u>blown</u> down into basement – where we sat all looking very

---

* Her mother's maid.

green, & listening to tinkle of falling glass. I 'phoned the
police who came in later & said that the bomb had fallen –
not on us, as I imagined, but on 29 Warwick Gardens [two
streets away], which lost its roof & is practically in ruins
down to ground floor. We had several panes of glass damaged by bomb splinters but most escaped thro' being open.

Church bells rang as if for invasion.

As a result of this, Vera and her mother moved out of their
'unsubstantial eighteenth century houses'. Her mother went to
stay with friends near Woking, and Vera took a flat in a modern
block near Portland Place W1.

Saturday 14 September – Spent morning trying to fix up
American visit. At passport office, after long wait, found
passport safely there but still polite uncertainty about exit
permit – though this virtually promised. Felt sick & tired –
as G. wouldn't have gone without me if he had thought any
doubt about it.

Wrote a chapter of book. Evening raid started about 8.15
& never let up till 4.30 a.m.

Tuesday 17 September – Still no news of exit permit – passport
office just stone-walling.

Wednesday 18 September – Seemed to spend all day trying to
telephone, but still no decision from passport office.

Thursday 19 September – Back in town; visited passport office;
saw the man I had hitherto spoken to on 'phone; usual polite
stone-walling.

Walked back from Piccadilly to Langham Place & structure blackened; in one antique furniture store whole plate-
glass window was smashed but two elegant yellow porcelain
vases stood untouched on their stands. Street ankle-deep in

glass; air filled with smell of burning wood. Passers-by moving aghast beneath dangerous walls with glass falling round them in showers as they moved. Weary policeman repeating in kind of helpless resignation: 'Naw then, show a little commonsense, cawn't yer?'

News came of the sinking of the *City of Benares*, which was carrying evacuee children, most of whom died. Vera had been working voluntarily for the Children's Overseas Reception Board (CORB), where there was much distress at this news. Days later CORB learned that a lifeboat had been found, containing six boys and their escort. Vera had met the escort when interviewing back in the summer.

Wednesday 25 September – In afternoon Passport Office rang up to say my exit permit to USA refused. No explanation.

Thursday 3 October – Huge mail, which included definite refusal from Passport Office of both my applications for exit permits, and a cable from G. to say he was writing Morrison (who is now Home Sec.) about it.

Friday 4 October – Met mother in Kensington; went on to 37 Edwardes Square – really very grim; bomb had fallen exactly opposite, just inside square railings; windows & doors gone; ceilings down; fire in front hall had destroyed curtains & carpet. Real desolation; structure and furniture mostly intact. If Mother had been there, the shock [would] have killed her.

On 11 October her mother went to stay in Devon. At the end of the month Vera received an invitation to a conference in India. Friends and organizations in England and America were using their influence to have Vera's travel ban lifted, but on 3 December her application for a permit was again refused. 'They really object to

my opinions – and to the question asked about me in the House
– but won't admit it.'

Friday 6 December – Got back to find cable from George to say
he was taking early December Cunard sailing immediately.
Long to have him but do wish he hadn't decided to come at
this dangerous time – after my cables saying he wasn't to
come immediately.

On 15 December Vera read that the liner *Western Prince* had
been sunk on its way back to England. It was not a Cunarder, but
Vera discovered that Cunard had taken over all civilian sailings
and that George had been on board.

ALAN BROOKE

By the middle of June 1940 Brooke was back in France as overall
commander and managed to extricate the remainder of the army
after the French surrendered. In July he was appointed commander-in-chief Home Forces. He then began a hectic schedule
of meeting (and assessing) his senior staff, inspecting defences
throughout Britain and preparing for the invasion.

Tuesday 3 September – First day of the second year of the war!
It is just a year ago that I drove over from Salisbury to
Aldershot to see Dill to find out from him what the BEF
would be required to do. I arrived just before 11am and
watched the war start with him! This evening instead I spent
1½ hours with him in the WO discussing how we are to run
the 2nd year of the war, and how we are to meet the German
invasion if it comes within the next few days.

Sunday 8 September – Heavy bombing of London throughout
the night, the whole sky being lit up by the glow of fires in

London docks. Went to the office in the morning where I found further indications of impending invasion. Everything pointing to Kent and E. Anglia as the two main threatened points.

Sunday 15 September – Still no move on the part of the Germans! Everything remains keyed up for an early invasion, and the air war goes on unabated. The coming week must remain a critical one, and it is hard to see how Hitler can now retrace his steps and stop the invasion. The suspense of waiting is very trying especially when one is familiar with the weakness of our defence!

I wish I could have 6 months now to finish equipping and training the force under my command. A responsibility such as that of defence of this country under the existing conditions is one that weighs on one like a ton of bricks, and it is hard at times to retain the hopeful, confident exterior which is so essential to retain the confidence of those under one, and to guard against their having any doubts as regards final success.

Thursday 19 October – Another day gone and thank God for it! Every day that passes must at least be one day less of this war. But there are times when the madness and folly of war choke one. And yet through all its destruction, uselessness and havoc I can see some progress. Progress that could never be achieved without the upheaval of war. Long standing institutions and social distinctions are shattered by war and make room for more modern methods of life. Those that would never release what they hold in peace, are forced to do so in war, to the benefit of the multitude.

Ultimately I suppose that human beings from much suffering will become wiser and will appreciate that greater happiness can be found in this world by preferring their neighbours to themselves!

Meanwhile for all my philosophy I am very tired of this war and long for peace. A peace that will allow us to spend the remaining years of our life quietly together in a small cottage with a garden to work in, some trees to look after and perhaps a stream close by where I can watch the fish even if I don't catch them! And above all somewhere where I can bask in the sublime happiness of the sunshine of your company. But even if I can't be with you at present I still thank God for having allowed me to know you and for all the wonderful happiness of seeing you once a week. I am now counting the hours till tomorrow when I hope to start for my Sunday with you.

Saturday 16 November – A real unpleasant night, and from midnight to close on 5 am there was almost incessant bombing. I got up to look out of the window, it was a weird sight looking east to see the end of the street one blaze of flames and made it hard to realize this was London in 1940!

Friday 22 November – Left home at 9.30 for the Staff College where I ran exercise from 10 am to 5 pm. It was very well attended and on the whole a success. Should form a good basis for further exercises in other Commands. Finally drove back in Dill's car. He confided to me that his wife is now very ill having had a stroke and is paralysed on one side and unable to speak properly. It is pathetic, he is urgently in need of a rest, cannot I think face going home for a week's leave, and if he goes elsewhere he feels he must go visiting troops as he can't bear doing nothing and being left with his thoughts! He finds the PM very difficult to deal with and I feel that he is having a miserable life and do wish that I could think of somehow providing a rest for him.

HAROLD NICOLSON

The summer had been full of activity for Nicolson in his new post at the Ministry of Information, housed in London University's Senate House. He enjoyed the work, even though the ministry was widely criticized for censoring the news. At Sissinghurst, where he spent most weekends, he often saw fighters battling overhead.

Sunday 15 September – A slack morning with the usual raid going on overhead. After luncheon there is a terrific dog-fight above us. Two 'planes come down near Sissinghurst village and one crashes in flames at Frittenden. We see a parachute descending slowly with the man below it wriggling as if on a pendulum. They take four German prisoners. The station at Staplehurst has been laid flat by a Spitfire which crashed upon its roof. A Spitfire comes down in Victor Cazalet's park, only a hundred yards from Swift's. In the evening we have the news. They say we have brought down 185 of the enemy against 30 of ours. They have again bombed Buckingham Palace. We are told that Göring is directing this campaign. If so, he must be a stupider man than I thought. There is another raid at night. Poor Vita worries about my going up tomorrow. As Priestley said tonight, London is in effect in the front line. Thank God they have got the delayed bomb out from under St Paul's.

Thursday 19 September – We all refuse to face the fact that unless we can invent an antidote to night-bombing, London will suffer very severely and the spirit of our people may be broken. Already the Communists are getting people in shelters to sign a peace-petition to Churchill. One cannot expect the population of a great city to sit up all night in shelters week after week without losing their spirit. The only solution

I can see at present are reprisals, which we are both unable and unwilling to exert.

Tuesday 24 September – I detect in myself a certain area of claustrophobia. I do not mind being blown up. What I dread is being buried under huge piles of masonry and hearing the water drip slowly, smelling the gas creeping towards me and hearing the faint cries of colleagues condemned to a slow and ungainly death. Always as I write this diary the guns boom. One writes that phrase, yet it means nothing. There is the distant drum-fire of the outer batteries. There is the nearer crum-crum of the Regent's Park guns. Then there is the drone of aeroplanes and the sharp impertinent notes of some nearer batteries. FF-oopb! they shout. And then in the middle distance there is the rocket sound of the heavy guns in Hyde Park. One gets to love them, these angry London guns. And when they drop into silence, one hears above them, irritating and undeterred, the dentist's drill of the German aeroplanes, seeming always overhead, appearing always to circle round and round, ready always to drop three bombs, flaming, and then . . . crump, crump, crump, somewhere . . . I feel no fear or anger. Hum and boom. Always I write my nightly diary to that accompaniment.

Thursday 17 October – I go to the smoking-room [in the House of Commons]. Winston is at the next table. He sits there sipping a glass of port and welcoming anyone who comes in. 'How are you?' he calls gaily to the most obscure Member. It is not a pose. It is just that for a few moments he likes to get away from being Prime Minister and feel himself back in the smoking-room. His very presence gives us all gaiety and courage. People gather round his table completely unawed. They ask him questions. Robert Cary* makes a long disserta-

* Conservative MP for Eccles for the past fifteen years.

tion about how the public demand the unrestricted bombardment of Germany as reprisals for the raids on London.
Winston takes a long sip at his port gazing over the glass at
Cary. 'My dear sir,' he says, 'this is a military not a civilian
war. You and others may desire to kill women and children.
We desire (and have succeeded in our desire) to destroy
German military objectives. I quite appreciate your point. But
my motto is "Business before Pleasure."' We all drift out of
the room thinking, 'That was a man!'

On the evening of 7 November Nicolson returned to Senate
House to continue working on the draft of a paper he had been
commissioned to write explaining the aims of the war. He was in
good spirits. The election of Roosevelt the day before was 'the
best thing that has happened to us since the outbreak of the war',
and he was pleased that the Foreign Office had reacted well to
his paper.

Friday 8 November – I was busy last night drafting away as if I
were back in the Foreign Office twenty years ago. Then I got
to bed and curled up on my rubber mattresses and went fast
asleep. Splaaassh! Craash! Tinkle! Tinkle! Oh, I was no longer
in my bed, but on the floor. Charles Peake* burst in. 'Are
you all right, Harold?' 'Yes,' I said. 'We've had another direct
hit: a bad one this time.' Well, up I got, and into my trousers
I got, and into my British-warm† I got. The passage outside
was filled with a red fog which was just dust. There were
air-raid wardens rushing about in steel helmets. And would
you believe it? We really had been struck on the boko by
the Luftwaffe. Not a single soul was hurt. I went round the
shelters on a tour of inspection. I brought one or two of the
paler people up to my room and gave them sherry which

---

*   Chief press adviser to the Ministry of Information.
†   A short thick overcoat, originally worn by officers in the First World War.

Miss Niggeman had thoughtfully provided. And then I went to sleep again and did not wake up till my alarm clock went off at 7.30. A bomb had hit us just on the shoulder. It had broken through one floor and exploded on the floor below. It had done in the University library. Our windows on the courtyard side had been twisted out into shreds. The court-yard is full of masonry. But not a single soul even scratched. It was all great fun and I enjoyed it. This is not a pose. I was exhilarated. I am odd about that. I have no nerves about this sort of thing. Mentally I am like the people who stick daggers into their flesh.

I think we have managed to avoid losing this war. But when I think how on earth we are going to win it, my imagination quails.

CHARLES RITCHIE

At the Canadian embassy Ritchie was promoted to second sec-retary in June. For British and refugee Jews with money to travel to Canada, his office became 'the door of escape from hell'. The endless queues outside his door caused him to comment, 'the sense of dissolution of civilised society is overpowering'. On 26 June Ritchie noted that, in addition to Canadians and New Zealanders (among them many Maoris), London 'thronged with the remains of the shattered continental armies, Dutch, French and Norwegians'. And 'English men and women of differ-ent classes, localities, sets, and tastes [were] for the first time talking to each other'.

Wednesday 9 to Friday 11 October – How much does this con-tinual danger to our lives make us forget our smaller fears? Do we still suffer from shyness, or feel that a cold in the throat may turn into pneumonia?

We are accustomed to our familiar fears; in the same way even in the midst of a bombardment with planes droning overhead and the noise of the barrage I can sleep quite comfortably, but if through this monstrous uproar I hear the still, small voice of a dripping tap, I get out of bed unable to sleep until the sound is stopped.

The random bombing of central London is like an act of nature, like a volcano erupting nightly. The bombers are like the agents of some blindly destructive force. Their bombs fall, like rain, on the just and the unjust. They do not hate me nor I hate them. We are caught in a fated mechanistic duel of forces which maims and kills bombers and bombed. This is a war fought in cold blood. That is my feeling about it, but I often hear people say, 'Why don't we give them hell in Berlin?' I sense a lack of conviction, a sort of nervous irritability in this question as though those who asked it knew the futility of the query.

Saturday 12 October – Hart [Vincent Massey's second son, then 22] and I went to an American movie. We sat there lapped in a feeling of false security while the cinema shook from the explosion of bombs outside. As we came out it seemed as though all Piccadilly were on fire. Tongues of flames were licking the colonnade at the top of the London Pavilion. We drove to the Dorchester Hotel through bombs and shrapnel – there seemed to be fire everywhere. For once London had a catastrophic appearance worthy of American newspaper accounts. At the Dorchester we found the Masseys pacing the floor nervously. In our elation Hart and I seemed childishly excited in telling them what was going on. Mr Massey lost his temper, and, his voice rising to a peak of exasperation, he said, 'You seem to be pleased at what is happening. I do not understand you. These places that are being destroyed are irreplaceable – to me it is like a personal loss.' We looked somewhat shamefaced. Then he led the way on to the Dorchester roof. We could see fires in all directions. A bomb came whistling down and we all ran for shelter except Hart.

I was annoyed with myself for taking shelter not because I was afraid but because the others had run for shelter and I had instinctively imitated them.

I noticed that when Mr Massey came down from the roof he was in the same exalted state that we had been in when we arrived. There is an exhilaration in this orgy of destruction and in the danger, but next day was the morning after the debauch. I was awakened by the sound of shovelling glass.

Ritchie's old Oxford friend Frank Ziegler and his wife Margery were living in World's End in Chelsea. One evening after dinner in town, Ritchie spent the night with them.

Saturday 26 October – Their house, like the others, is a little square box of bricks of the type that falls down when a bomb comes anywhere near it. On this occasion the bomb fell in the next street. We all rushed out and I found myself helping to remove the people from the remains of three bombed houses. There was a large crater where one house had been, and in the centre of the crater were Margery and a doctor, trying by the aid of a torch to see who was injured and how badly. People were being pulled and pushed up the sides of the crater, to be taken off to the nearest pub to wait for the ambulance to come.

Margery called in imperious tones from her crater, 'Hot water.' I rushed panting through the dark and empty streets to the nearest police station then to the nearest public house in search of water. By now the sky was an ugly 'fire pink' glow from a row of houses burning noisily in a street nearby. Bombs were steadily falling and the members of the Air Raid Precautions and Rescue Squad whom I encountered in the streets cowered in carefully restrained attitudes against walls as the bombs came down. In the end when I came back with the hot water it was only to find that full supplies had been brought up already.

Wednesday 6 November – Things one will forget when this is over – fumbling in the dark of the blackout for one's front door key while bits of shrapnel fall on the pavement beside one – the way the shrapnel seems to drift – almost like snowflakes through the air in an aimless, leisurely way, and the clink of it landing on the pavement.

Saturday 16 November – I came back from spending the night at Aldershot to find my flat a heap of rubble from a direct hit, and I have lost everything I own . . .

Last week when I wrote this diary I was sitting on my sofa in front of my electric fire in my perfectly real and solid flat with my books at arm's length – the furniture had that false air of permanence which chairs and tables take on so readily – the drawn curtains shut out the weather. Now all that is a pile of dirty rubble, with bits of my suits, wet and blackened, visible among the bricks.

GEORGE BEARDMORE

In July George was informed that his job no longer exempted him from conscription. He registered for military service but was refused because of his chronic asthma. He had already joined the Local Defence Volunteers and found he was a good shot but useless at drill. He was also taking turns on night watch at the BBC. In August bombs destroyed much of the local high street. George took great care to make the family home safe from blasts and tried to make it possible for them all to get some sleep at night.

Tuesday 10 September – The greatest devastation that I saw was at Chiltern Court which now looks like an East End tenement, its windows blown out, its middle ravaged by one bomb whose twin had landed plumb on Tussaud's Cinema, scattering masonry over the Euston Road, causing Tussaud's itself to collapse, turning the adjoining mews into a shambles of bricks, coping-stones, furniture, glass, and human and wax flesh. Even the large Crown Estate residences in the Outer Circle of Regent's Park, a whole arc of them, had spewed out their glass as far as the gardens. But complete, almost matter-of-fact calm in the way the police steered traffic round the debris, the firemen stood by, the Civil Defence in steel helmets stood round a WVS mobile canteen, the blue-clad heavy-mob (Heavy Rescue) were rigging up block and tackle. This was the after-the-party scene. What sort of hell it must have been a few hours before is anyone's guess.

Jean and I have now finally come to rest on camp-bed and couch in the drawing-room (at the back) while Victoria lies snug in her carry-cot behind the chimney breast and protected by a book-case. As a result we spent a good night last night, heedless of the planes which were ranging up and down the Thames Valley. I am to hang wire-netting over the French windows and meanwhile I push the single mattress against them, backed by another book-case, backed by an arm-chair.

Saturday 21 September – I daresay that I ought, like Pepys, to be 'much terrified i' the nights, nowadays, with dreams of fire, and falling down of houses', but in fact we have all slept well these last two nights. This morning I spliced a new shaft on a broken spade, cut the privet-hedge for the last time this year and wired up a frame for the honeysuckle, tidied up the front garden and side passage, found a new foot-rest for the Enfield, and am now at my desk working out plot. Very quiet here last night but the wrecking of London continues.

The BBC decided to evacuate the engineering departments to Droitwich, between Worcester and Birmingham.

Monday 7 October – Jean said: 'All the same, we've got to think of Victoria,' and I said: 'I'm rather stuck with the job. It's a tram I can't get off. They won't let me.' Jean said: 'Try it for a bit and if things get too bad here I'll join you.' I said: 'I don't want to leave you,' and she said: 'I don't especially want you away from me either, but that's how it would have been if you had been called up.'

That's roughly how the conversation went although no true record of any conversation can ever be made (unless by Henry James) because the subtleties are lost. Shall bike it to Droitwich and not use the BBC's one-way ticket. With a motor-bike I feel less of a prisoner.

Once he was settled at work, George started cycling round the area house-hunting.

Monday 14 October – Jean's temperament remains true. She appeared to take my departure calmly, saying that she had Victoria to look after and her mother not far away, but I had a tearful letter on Saturday complaining that these meant very little without her husband.

The cycle rides have brought me to prospects of quite incredible loveliness. The fleeting season, the sudden rows of trees, the twisting lanes, the steep dales and rounded summits, the half-timbered cottages and farmhouses, are a far cry from the toppled towers of Oxford Street.

Sunday 27 October – Jean left Paddington while a loudspeaker was announcing that enemy planes were at that moment directly overhead. So at least the reason for getting away was reinforced. The two of them arrived two hours late, thoroughly exhausted. I shan't easily forget the cameo of Jean dropping her case on the platform of Droitwich's darkened station while Victoria clung to her shoulder. I felt my heart lurch for they looked like refugees. Now Jean has recovered some of her stability and is studying to make herself agreeable to a stranger in the stranger's home, a task she doesn't take kindly to. Our home is to be let furnished so that my lovely leeks, carrots, parsnips, and artichokes will be enjoyed by strangers.

After a 'thundering row' with their landlady, who treated them as unpaid help, they moved to another house in the countryside, recommended by the local vicar, with whom they had become friends.

Friday 15 November – Witnessed the bombing of Coventry, which must be forty or fifty miles cross-country. On my way to the Vicarage I saw all the flares, sky-twinklings of shell-bursts, and bomb-flashes of the old days. But the wind brought no sound of the bombardment. Now people say that, like the Great Fire, the bombing was ultimately not a bad thing because Coventry was a planless, dirty, ugly city, whatever its history. Two hundred killed, eight hundred injured. I don't suppose any of the hundreds now rendered homeless thought it a planless, dirty, ugly city. This living in other people's houses has really impressed on me the tragedy of those rendered absolutely homeless and without the usual belongings.

CLARA MILBURN

In July, after weeks of waiting, Clara and Jack heard that Alan was a prisoner of war and apparently well. 'My darling dear, you are alive!' she ends her entry on 16 July. A week later the War Office gave Alan's address as Stalag XXA, Germany, and Clara immediately wrote 'a stilted little letter on a single sheet of notepaper, which is all one may do at a time'. By the beginning of October there was still no news or reply from Alan.

Sunday 6 October – I wrote the 21st letter to Alan today, and just for a few moments this evening black depression flooded over me. This separation, for such a cause, and the prospect of a long war and consequent long separation, and not knowing where he is and what is happening to him, simply engulfed me. And the stifling, choking feeling of not being able to do anything. Oh dear, it was dreadful! But 'Lift up your hearts' was said at church today and we replied: 'We lift them up unto the Lord.'

And then one's spirits just had to rise in the garden and one thought of the queer things one was thankful for personally – such varied things as the five tall cypresses on the lawn, so handsome; the bronze green of the yew hedge in the fading light, the colour of colours; a new thumbnail just grown to perfection after nearly a year; the feel of newly-cut hair and the blessing of a permanent wave; one's good bed; the rain and the sun; autumn colouring; good garden tools and a wickerwork barrow; the way Twink's ears fall and his easy action; and a thousand other things day by day. And then for one's good friends and most of all for the nearest and dearest – and home.

There was more news of Alan weeks later – he had been wounded in the leg. 'We long to know still more,' Clara wrote on 13 November.

Friday 15 November – We had a terrible night – not so much for ourselves personally as for the people of Coventry.

When we went out the searchlights were probing the clear sky, the stars looked very near, the air was so clear and the moonlight was brilliant. I have never seen such a glorious night. Wave after wave of aircraft came over and heavy gunfire followed. Scarcely once was there a lull the whole night. I should have said they came over sometimes at one per minute.

Once or twice we came up the dugout steps and looked out at the lovely moon and sky, saw the flash of the shells as they burst high over the oak tree and the sudden glare as the big gun held forth away to the east. Always there was the sound of enemy aircraft, and as the near guns fired down we went and closed the lids above us. We read at first, then tried to sleep, but I had the only chair down there and Jack sat on the bench, which was very uncomfortable. He went up once and came back with a cushion for my head, which improved matters for me.

The planes ceased going over for a few minutes now and then towards 4 a.m. and at 4.20 we came up tired out. I lay down on the living-room sofa, still clad in my fur coat, for it was very cold and the frost was white on the grass and the roofs as we came in. We slept a bit and about 5.30, after ten hours, the sound of planes ceased and the guns fell silent, so at 5.45 we stumbled upstairs and tumbled into bed.

Poor, poor Coventry! The attack is described on the wireless as 'a vicious attack against an open town comparable to one of the worst raids on London, and the damage very considerable'. The casualties are in the neighbourhood of a thousand, and the beautiful fourteenth century cathedral is destroyed. I feel numb with the pain of it all.

After blackout a woman called to ask if I could give a few nights' rest and shelter to a Coventry couple who were worn and tired, so I said 'Yes' at once, but she did not want the room tonight. Later, finding Mrs Gorton had nine people in her house, I offered to have two of them tonight, and before we could tidy the room she had brought them along. Their one idea was bed, and after a little chat we left them to go to bed and we had our dinner. Afterwards I went over to the Institute billiard-room and found many people sitting on hard chairs, babies and children rolled in rugs lying head to head on the billiard table, and a few young men playing darts – a pathetic crowd. My deckchair and rug was soon snapped up, and the husband of the woman who took it was delighted to have a pack of cards, too. Tomorrow we must see what we can do to make them a bit less uncomfortable, but it is too dark to go into the hut to look out things tonight.

Alderman Moseley, Mayor of Coventry, living in a small house in one of Coventry's lesser streets, had a distinguished visitor. His wife heard a knock and, as the bombing had upset the front door and it could not be opened, she called out: 'Come round to the back!' The visitor came round. It was the King, who is going round bombed places.

This afternoon we took laundry to Fillongley, calling at the Council Schools in which a room was being prepared for 150 people who were supposed to be trekking from Coventry. I took two deckchairs, a long cushion, rug and trays for their use, only to find that a Ministry of Health official had just arrived to say no-one would be coming today. People did not want to come to the extent they had provided for them. Evacuation of children over again! English folk cling to their homes. Those who are bombed out are the ones who have to leave. Others who are frightened (as they have every cause to be) go to friends or find their own lodgings, but those who still have their own houses seem to feel they must stay in them.

So we came home just before dark and soon Mr and Mrs Cope came along and we put them in Alan's bedroom, with the biggest and best radiator and an armchair and a deckchair, so that they could have a bedsitting-room. We had occasional sirens sounding the alert and the 'Raiders Passed' at intervals, but scarcely heard a plane and slept soundly.

Over the next fortnight, Clara provided a room for Coventry people who had lost their homes and drove others to their billets. On 25 November a letter from the War Office confirmed that Alan was in hospital with a wound in the right knee.

NAOMI MITCHISON

Writing on 7 July, Naomi begins, 'I had better get this over . . .' and her diary entry records both the birth of 'a lovely little girl' and her death the next day of a heart defect. 'And all the little things hurt, hurt, hurt, and there is nothing to be done . . . she was part of me, and wanted, all these months, and warm, and one said what a nuisance, but lovingly, and now the whole thing is ended: the love has no object.'

She envied Dick his work, wanted to be free of Carradale and 'go to the south and get into an air-raid'. But there was a wedding in September – her son Denny and Ruth, a fellow medical student – a new village hall to equip and celebrate, and, gradually, an idea for another book.

The war often seemed distant, but was coming closer.

Thursday 3 October – Letters include one from Mr Wilson at Bumpus [bookshop] in London, saying only this morning has the time bomb which has pestered us for twelve days been removed by the Engineers. I think 'pestered' is the *mot juste*! They seem to have had the shop rather badly smashed up. I wonder if River Court will survive; it sounds pretty shaky. Poor old house. I don't think I'm really properly imagining that all this is happening in London; it seems so ridiculous. Memory is solider than fact.

Thursday 10 October – **Visiting a friend in Paisley** – Mrs Hodgart talked about evacuated children, her sister's four who are still with her – real little keelies* – their father has come to see them occasionally, their mother never, but sends occasional post cards; they are part of a family of nine. All their heads were dirty and it was a month before they smelt like other children – 'the smell of the fish and chips wearing out'. Now they are sweet and clean, devoted to her sister and not wanting to go back. Then about spies; she is rather suspicious herself, said she was thankful to get rid of her refugee who had been cooking. Mrs H also talked of a German woman, wife of a doctor – she knew she was a Nazi, she had shown her a family tree with a swastika on it. She sounded Prussian to me, but I said I thought she ought to be treated in a friendly way; it would do no harm and might do a lot of good, and the woman might be terribly unhappy.

I was very sleepy, though; before going to bed Mrs H showed me their charming little air raid shelter, just in case, all tucked into an old porch and built up, with books and cushions.

Saturday 26 October – **In conversation after a talk to teachers in Argyll** – They were all too shy to talk afterwards, especially the women, but I had a little talk with Clarke, who is intelligent. He has a friend who has worked a lot on Intelligence Tests: a teacher, but a CO†: has been given exemption from military service on condition that he ceases teaching and does forestry. Things like that make one feel we don't deserve to win the war! Not that Clarke seemed to see its full implications; he said in an undertone that this chap was a Quaker, as much as to say he had B.O. The chairman of the Glasgow tribunal is Bruce who was Editor of the *Glasgow Herald* a long time ago, and was a tick then.

We had a very good tea made by the cookery department

---

* Scottish word for tough city children, especially in Glasgow.
† Conscientious Objector.

and drove back in one of the loveliest evenings I've ever seen, the West Loch glassy grey-green and Jura and Gigha transparent mauve looking like Tir nan Og.

Thursday 7 November – Bella* said Campbeltown had been bombed; we all thought it was a rumour, of course, and Archie Paterson told Mrs MacMillan she was a silly bugger for saying she's heard planes over Carradale. But by this evening it appears that it is true, that the Royal Hotel is smashed up, and that quite a lot of people were killed including Hunter, the West of Scotland Agricultural Expert, who was coming over to advise me about liming the fields. Damn silly. They were obviously going for ships in the harbour. Mr MacKillop ran out to look for his son, but found the place was being machine gunned and had to run back.

Monday 11 November – Ian MacLaren was over about the damp patch, says it is the slaters, not himself; he is in the fire brigade and helped to put out the bomb fire; he hadn't liked the raid at all, said it gave him an awful funny feeling. Everyone in Campbeltown was nervous – also here; Mrs Mitchell says they watched last night's plane circling over our house! I have since heard it being said here that Lord Haw Haw says that Carradale is to be bombed. I should suppose that someone deliberately invented this to see who would believe him.

HERMIONE RANFURLY

Wives who had illegally followed their husbands to Egypt were ordered to leave Cairo on 23 August. Hermione's trip to GHQ Jerusalem, with letters explaining the competent nature of secretaries like herself, was in vain. The commanding officer, Brigadier

* Naomi's cook.

Brunskill, with a black patch over one eye, refused to exempt Hermione, and she sailed on the *Empress of Britain* for Cape Town. There she parted from Toby, who had decided to return to her children in England.

Indefatigable, she was back in Cairo on 26 October after borrowing money to get a flight, deflecting the suspicion of a general who was a fellow passenger and, with the help of the pilot, getting past customs and immigration. Her friends Pam and Pat Hore-Ruthven agreed to hide her 'until you are found or forgiven'. Dan, who by now was working for General Neame in Palestine in the office next to Brunskill, was contacted and asked to write to Pam care of the Continental Hotel.

Saturday 26 October – How lucky I am – compared to Toby, still on that great, gloomy ship . . . I can hardly believe I was on the *Empress* just fourteen days ago.

Tuesday 29 October – I arrived at breakfast just as Pam was leaving for her office. She turned at the front door and said, 'Thank God you are here.' Then she left. I turned to Pat who was walking up and down the room and rifling his hair with his fingers, and asked why Pam had said that. 'The *Empress* . . .' he began, and handed me the newspaper.

EGYPTIAN MAIL

Tuesday 29 October 1940

EMPRESS OF BRITAIN SUNK
VERY FEW CASUALTIES

. . . some 598 survivors out of a total of 643 aboard . . .
The liner was attacked 700 miles off the coast of Ireland . . .

Thursday 31 October – Yesterday Pat met General George Clark who told him he believed I was working happily in South Africa.

I spent the day wondering about Toby and searching through the Cairo telephone book – making a list of firms who might give me a job.

Today Pam returned from GHQ to lunch in the flat. She was loaded with news: 'Dan is coming with his General to Cairo tomorrow for two nights; the news of your return is out at GHQ and there is much gossip – some think it very funny but the authorities concerned are furious and suspect you must have used someone else's passport as such care had been taken that you should not return. They are determined to "make an example" of you and throw you out again. Apparently all Naval, Military and Air Force units have been told not to give you a job.' None of this seems to matter because tomorrow I will see Dan.

I telephoned my good friend Freddie Hoffman at the Continental Hotel and asked him to book a double room and bath for Dan and me, and warned him I have no money at present and will have to pay in instalments. 'Don't you worry,' he said. 'I'll book you in as Mr and Mrs Globe Trotter.'

Sunday 3 November – Two days ago Dan arrived at the Ruthvens' flat. It was wonderfully exciting. Pat got us a gharry and put up the hood and a rather tired little horse clip-clopped us to the tradesmen's entrance of the Continental Hotel. Freddie Hoffman was waiting for us in the small garden and led us up the backstairs to a marvellous set of rooms. He stayed to have a drink with us and suggested we have all meals in the suite. 'The talk in our bar,' he laughed, 'is all about how on earth Hermione ever got back, and so quickly. Rumour has it that she travelled some of the way with the Provost Marshal.'

Dan and I forgot the war until the next morning when Dan told me, gently, that Toby was killed on the *Empress of*

Britain. It is not known exactly what happened. Some say she was in the main lounge reading a book when a bomb went right through the sun-deck and hit her – but rumour is that she was so terribly wounded on the upper deck that no one could move her and she had to be left to go down with the ship or burn in the fire. Dan insists she would not have been conscious. Dandy Wallace is going home to Scotland to their two little children. It is a frightful, shattering story. Next to my own family I loved Toby more than anyone else.

On 4 November Hermione got a secretarial job with the Special Operations Executive (SOE), Cairo office, under Hugh Dalton, minister responsible for economic warfare. When she asked if it was a spy organization, he replied, 'You'll soon find out.' On 15 November Dan received a letter from Brunskill ordering him to ensure that Hermione left or he would be sent to the North West Frontier of India and they would be docking his pay for her passage to Cape Town.

Sunday 1 December – My job is interesting but secret. Most of the employees work 'in the field' and all of them use numbers instead of names. We keep an arsenal of weapons and ammunition and in our safe are stacks of gold bars. This morning one of our people came in to collect his mail. I asked him if he'd had a good trip. He laid both his hands on my desk. The ends of his fingers and thumbs were mutilated. He'd been tortured but had escaped.

Wednesday 11 December – Great surprise and excitement here – we have advanced in the Desert.

Wherever I've been in Cairo there is a new optimism, perhaps because we've taken the initiative and a lot of prisoners – Italians – perhaps 130,000 or more.

Sadly, wounded or 'on leave' soldiers bring us news of

more and more friends who are missing or dead. Now, in my lunch hour, I go to one or other of the hospitals to take down letters for soldiers who are too ill to write home themselves.

Tuesday 17 December – I sat next to the [British] Ambassador (Sir Miles). He told me GHQ had asked if my passport could be removed. Sir Miles explained to me that to remove a British citizen's passport they must first be proved undesirable. 'As you do not appear to be a white slave trafficker or involved with drugs, I cannot remove your passport,' he said cheerfully. He went on to say that the evacuation controversy was now right out of proportion: this because there exists a very real shortage of English secretaries in the Middle East.

Monday 30 December – News kept coming in of ghastly incendiary air raids on London. We are all distressed and anxious. It will take ages before we hear if our families and friends are all right.

Dan was given a few days' leave for Christmas and we stayed at the Continental Hotel. He brought good news: General Wavell has written to General Neame to ask if he has any objection to me remaining in Cairo and General Neame has replied personally to say he has no objection. So Dan and I did not remain in hiding.

We have been out dancing and visiting friends – celebrating two victories: the one in the Desert and our own. At Shepherds Hotel we saw Brigadier 'One-Eye' Brunskill dancing with a fat woman – he was wearing a green paper hat.

THE BLITZ

The devastation of the bombing placed a heavy burden on Civil Defence teams. Firemen, air raid wardens, ambulance workers, doctors, nurses and rescue teams of able-bodied men to dig people out of their ruined homes were all called upon to help. William Sansom, a short-story writer and novelist, was a fireman during the London Blitz and published his experiences in 1947 with the full co-operation of the Home Office.*

WILLIAM SANSOM

Tuesday 17 September – **At Marble Arch** – One bomb – and only a small one – pierced the roadway above the underground subway and there exploded. The subway had been built in great strength, girders and concrete massed the roof to take the weight of heavy traffic passing round the Arch above. Apparently only the nose-cap penetrated – it made a minute hole and must have pierced between two closely-knit girders. It was the unlucky chance. The subway was filled with shelterers – some squatting and sleeping, others who had come down for a moment off the streets. So that in effect the small explosive burst in amongst the people like a heavy grenade, flew along the tunnel ripping the white tiles off as it burst and sucked its way through. When warders and stretcher and rescue parties arrived, they were faced with a terrible scene. The dead had been killed by blast – there was hardly a scratch on them, though in every case their

* William Sansom, *Westminster at War*, Faber and Faber, 1947.

clothes had been ripped off. But apart from the bursting of the bomb the sharp tile[s] had had a lacerating effect, flying swiftly and causing more casualties than there might otherwise have been. This happened only ten days after the beginning of Westminster's Blitz.

It was a bewildering, dreadful time.

BARBARA NIXON

When the theatres closed, Barbara Nixon, a young London-based actress and writer, volunteered as an air raid warden – a post generally held by men – in her local borough of Finsbury. In her second week, as she bicycled along a shabby street, she was preparing herself for her first sight of casualties.*

Tuesday 17 September – Suddenly, before I heard a sound, the shabby, ill-lit, five-storey building ahead of me swelled out like a child's balloon, or like a Walt Disney house having hiccups. I looked at it in astonishment, that bricks and mortar could stretch like rubber. At the point when it must burst, the glass fell out. It did not hurtle, it simply cracked and dropped out, allowing the straining building to deflate and return to normal. Almost instantaneously there was a crash and a double explosion in the street to my right. As the blast of air reached me I left my saddle and sailed through the air, heading for the area railings. The tin hat on my shoulder took the impact, and as I stood up I was mildly surprised to find that I was not hurt in the least. The corner buildings had diverted the full force of the blast.

At four in the afternoon there would certainly be casualties. I dared not run. I had to go warily, as if I were crossing a

---

* Barbara Nixon, *Raiders Overhead – a Diary of the London Blitz*, Scolar Press/ Gulliver Publishing, 1980, originally published in 1943.

minefield with only a rough sketch of the position of the mines – only the danger-spots were in myself. I was not let down lightly. In the middle of the street lay the remains of a baby. It had been blown clean through the window, and had burst on striking the roadway. To my intense relief, pitiful and horrible as it was, I was not nauseated, and found a torn piece of curtain in which to wrap it.

The CD [Civil Defence] services arrived quickly. There was a large number of 'white hats', but as far as one could see no one person took charge, and there were no blue incident flags. I offered my services, and was thanked but given nothing to do, so busied myself finding blankets to cover the five or six mutilated bodies in the street. A small boy, aged about 13, had one leg torn off and was still conscious, though he gave no sign of any pain. In the garage a man was pinned under a capsized Thorneycroft lorry, and most of the side wall and roof were piled on top of that. The Heavy Rescue Squad brought ropes, and heaved and tugged at the immense lorry. They got the man out, unconscious, but alive.

An article in the magazine *Local Government Service* highlighted the plight of survivors, giving an exhausting – and exhaustive – list of things to do the morning after for a mother whose husband was at sea and who had three children, one of whom had died in a raid. Each of the tasks would have necessitated a trek across the bombed-out city to a different address.

- apply for new ration books, since you have to eat
- find a communal feeding station to feed the children today
- your local rest centre having been destroyed, find a new one where the children can be left
- locate the body of your dead child
- enquire about a death certificate
- go to the war deaths department because you can't afford a private burial

- find extra clothes for the children
- at the Assistance Board make a claim for lost clothing, furniture etc.
- the cash advance they offer is limited so apply to the mayor's fund
- apply for free travel vouchers for the homeless
- apply for new identity cards
- get new gas masks
- apply for a billet in the country
- as recommended, get inoculated against typhoid

The capital wasn't the only place that autumn and winter where 'leaves [were] swept up with glass in them'.* By the end of the year more than a hundred other English towns and cities had been bombed on one or more occasions – Liverpool, Birmingham and Coventry the most heavily. In Scotland, Aberdeen and Edinburgh were targets, and in Wales, Cardiff and Swansea had eleven raids each.

ANEIRIN AP TALFAN DAVIES

Aneirin Ap Talfan Davies, 31, was a pharmacist and writer in Swansea. The back room of his shop in Heathfield Street was a gathering place for writers, poets and preachers.

January 1941 – Night falls. I head home. Halfway there the siren wails – a long painful whine, rising and falling as if some great beast is writhing in pain – the sound of all mankind's woes. Will the blitz come tonight? I've been asking the question every night since Coventry, Bristol and Cardiff – knowing it will come, but hoping against hope . . . I quicken

---

* Elizabeth Bowen, 'London 1940', in *Collected Impressions*, Longmans Green, 1950

my pace. The moon slides out from behind the clouds. On the hill I turn and look across the town and the sea and the darkened docks, before heading on up, cursing the steepness. There is an ominous hum in the air, like a swarm of bees. My heart races, and it's not just the hill: Mari will be worried ... Owen is sure to wake ... he's not three yet, but he is beginning to be aware of things. Ever since he saw the damage to his father's shop after last September's raid, I think bombs are real to him.

I reach the house. Owen is still awake. His mother has moved him from the small bed in the front room to one in the corner of the kitchen – we've been sleeping downstairs for months. Mari speaks first. 'Blitz?' We decide to move to the middle room, it will be safer there. For just a moment we sit near the fire, deciding what's best. The noise of aircraft grows. At the very same instant we both realise that the blitz is under way. There is no refuge, only a cold, brick shelter outside. We would rather stay put ... besides, Owen has a heavy cold.

The first bombs start to fall, and our guns thunder. 'Quick, under the table, Mari.' I go outside to check whether fire-bombs have fallen. Some way away. Back in the house I knock on the wall and ask our neighbours if we can shelter in their cellar. 'Of course.' We wait for the next wave to come over – I've read somewhere that there is no danger when they're right overhead – and make a mad dash out through the yard to our neighbour's back door. The husband hurries us in – no wasted words. We get Mari and Owen into the cellar before returning to watch for the incendiaries.

From the top floor my neighbour and I survey the town – our home on the hill, war's belvedere. An unforgettable sight. It is all as light as day, but not the light of the sun; instead an artificial, blue, unearthly glow as balls of light drift lightly down from the planes, followed by bomb after bomb. Together with our guns they make a satanic chorus as fire erupts everywhere. We hear the bells of fire engines as they rush through the streets. Soon their hoses are hissing like serpents, while in the air above there is still that insistent menacing hum. The incendiaries continue to explode until the town below is a cauldron of fire. Somewhere down there is my chemist's shop, but I'm strangely unworried. I've already decided in my mind that it's gone, and I fancy there's a big fire quite close by. I don't have time to dwell on it.

Down the stairs to the backyard to see if anything has landed there. Nothing. Back to the house and just as I reach the passage, in the dark, and uncertain in a strange house, I hear the whistle of a bomb descending. My neighbour yells. 'In here. Quick.' But I don't know where 'in here' is, and all I'm aware of is an unearthly noise and the front door hurtling towards me. My chest and lungs are squeezed as if by a giant's hug, just as I'm grabbed by the collar and bundled behind a nearby wall. A shower of glass and stone sweeps by.

Within seconds the pressure on my chest eases and I make towards the clouds of dust billowing from the cellar. I'm thinking that's it, they're done for, until I hear a small voice, 'Dada, dada'. Into the cellar. Everyone is safe. A miracle. Back up the stairs and into – chaos. Every stick of furniture shredded, every window shattered, every door flat on the floor.

Other neighbours rush in, terror on their faces. They had been in their own cellars – some choking, others crying. It's the same story. 'We've lost everything.' I try to comfort them. 'It will look better in the morning.' 'Where's the dog? Oh, my dog, my poor dog.' 'Thank God you're alive, Mrs——.' 'She's fainted.' 'Brandy.' And so on for hours. Comfort, comfort my people!

At last I go back into our own home. Oh God. Ap Talfan's room is dark. No ceiling, no fire. Don't cry! Every window is in pieces. Room after room. All shattered. What about the piano? – a gift from Mari's parents. I search. It, too, is in pieces. I look for my books and find them more or less undamaged. Back next door, Mari questions me like a barrister. I break the worst gently. There are no tears. What for? 'Things will look better in the morning.'

People and stories drift into the shop. It's a miracle it's still standing. I walk through the town. Fires still smouldering, but everyone – everyone? – is going to work as usual, though fatigued and red-eyed.*

* Aneirin ap Talfan, *Dyddiau'r Ceiliog Rhedyn*, translated by Geraint Talfan Davies, Foyles Welsh Co. Ltd, London 1941–2.

4. GERMANY INVADES RUSSIA

SUMMER 1941

Between the beginning of September 1940 and the end of July 1941, 50,000 high-explosive (HE) bombs rained down on London. HE bombs were always followed by incendiaries; the former made kindling out of the structures they hit and the latter caused devastating conflagrations.

In 1939 the government had forecast 3,000 dead and 12,000 wounded for each night of bombing, though the highest casualty figures were 1,436 dead and 1,792 wounded in the whole of May 1941. Nonetheless, little thought had been given to the services needed to deal with such a calamity. During the first six weeks of the Blitz 250,000 people were made homeless but only 7,000 rehoused. The lucky ones found shelter with relations but this often led to overcrowding – ten to a room in some cases or families crammed into makeshift tents in scrubby yards. Some families from the East End of London made their way to Chislehurst Caves in Kent, where a troglodyte community of 15,000 came into being.

In London the Underground stations became a home from home. Sanitation problems were addressed, bunk beds installed, evening classes organized, trains ran a 'refreshment service' and George Formby even gave a subterranean concert. Outside London a new phenomenon emerged. Each night 'Trekkers', as they were known, left the cities for the suburbs, the surrounding country or smaller towns and villages. In Portsmouth when raids were heavy they could number 90,000, but even on quiet nights there could be 30,000. In the aftermath of a raid, food and shelter were the priorities, and a natural order emerged – local authorities offered rest centres, voluntary services supplied personnel and the Ministry of Food provided food and equipment.

At the same time appeals were made for women to join the workforce, the cheese ration dropped to an ounce per week, and clothes cost 175 per cent more than they had before the war began. Imports from Europe had completely dried up and replacement cargoes of food and raw materials had to travel across the Atlantic. Hostile submarines, surface warships, aircraft and mines lay in wait for every cargo ship. Between June 1940 and February 1941 1,377 ships, carrying over five million tons of goods, were lost.

On the Home Front, people had been digging for victory since the beginning of the war. They had also collected moss for the Red Cross to use in bandaging wounds and fruit for jam, for which the government paid – two shillings for fourteen pounds of rosehips, for example. County committees had been set up to organize the gathering of dried herbs, many of which had traditionally been supplied by Germany. Nettles – used to make dye for camouflage nets – foxgloves, belladonna, male fern, conkers, burdock, broom tops, raspberry leaves, valerian root, comfrey, wormwood, yarrow, dandelion, hawthorn, lime flowers and elder, all used in the manufacture of medicines, were targeted for the war effort.

After Roosevelt's re-election to the presidency, the US Navy made fifty destroyers available to the British and Canadians, and in return America was granted the use of bases in the Caribbean and Newfoundland. In March 1941 Congress approved the Lend-Lease Act, releasing supplies to Britain on long-term credit.

Preventing the capture of the Suez Canal by the Germans was an urgent priority; as were eliminating Italy's North

African possessions, maintaining naval supremacy, anticipating any German threat to Turkey, Iraq or Iran with consequent pressure on oil reserves for the British empire and the security of India, and ridding the Red Sea area of hostile bases to ensure east African security. Egypt was vital in all these objectives and empire forces were to play major roles in achieving them.

In March 1941 in the Middle East General Wavell had reluctantly released men to help repel the German thrust into Greece. They arrived too late and were ejected from Crete, and Wavell's thinned-out army found itself being rolled back along the African coast to Egypt by the superior equipment and strategy of the brilliant General Rommel. At Tobruk in Libya, British and Australian troops had been under siege since April. On 21 May, the day after the invasion of Crete began, the German battleship *Bismarck* and the heavy cruiser *Prinz Eugen* were spotted heading out into the Atlantic. In engaging with *Bismarck*, the battleship *Hood* had blown up and the *Prince of Wales* had withdrawn.

The War Cabinet agreed to delay news of the Cretan catastrophe. Churchill's statement to the House glossed over the dire situation and emphasized that other Royal Navy warships were closing in on the *Bismarck*. As he sat down a secretary rushed into the gallery waving a sheet of paper. Churchill begged Mr Speaker's indulgence and announced the sinking of the *Bismarck*. The House cheered. Almost 2,000 German sailors died.

As May gave way to June, all the indications were that Hitler was gathering a massive force to launch an invasion of Russia, and on 21 June Operation Barbarossa began. Germany's military planners estimated that it would take between eleven and fourteen weeks, including a replenishment phase of three weeks, before Russian resistance was quelled. British Intelligence put it at a mere eight weeks.

At the end of July Churchill received an unexpected

invitation to join Roosevelt at Placentia Bay, Newfoundland. It was the first of fourteen clandestine journeys the prime minister made throughout the war. The trip, in the battleship *Prince of Wales*, resulted in the Atlantic Charter, a list of noble principles that later became the basis for the United Nations charter. At the time many within the British government hoped for a more immediate and practical outcome, but Churchill seemed content, believing that America was one step nearer to becoming a fully fledged ally.

THE DIARISTS

ANNE GARNETT

Anne started her war diary in 1939, intending it as a record of the conflict from the start. Unfortunately entries for 1939–40, kept in pocket diaries, have been lost.

After Plymouth was badly bombed in early May 1941 she enrolled as a driver in the Queen's Messenger Convoy, distributing fresh water and hot food. On 22 May she was made responsible for finding billets for 200 children evacuated from Bristol and a family that had been buried alive for two hours by a direct bomb hit in London.

Despite mornings at the Red Cross spent sewing, making jam and encouraging people to give blood, afternoons at the WVS (Women's Voluntary Service) clinic and three nights a week on duty at the mobile army canteen in Taunton, she still felt that she was not seen as useful and wrote of others who told her 'everyone who counts is in uniform these days'.

The household included a live-in maid called Gertie and a nursemaid, Mary, soon to be called up.

Sunday 1 June 1941 – The most perfect day – early mist clearing to glorious sunshine. Frank [her husband] had a Home Guard church parade and we all went to see them stepping out with band playing. Rather pathetic I thought – some so elderly and growing thin on top!

Frank resented the vicar preaching about the Holy Ghost and not referring to the Home Guard!!

After frightful news that clothes are to be rationed and we are evacuating Crete, I went out and paid a round of calls, collecting tennis players for tomorrow.

Tuesday 17 June – Very hot still and I found the clinic rather a trial, weighing 26 babies amid a horrid smell of urine and sweat. Usual piddling on floor and over my bare legs!

Cooled off in the garden after tea doing peaceful sewing – garden lovely now with all the lupins and irises out. Wot a nice home we've got.

Wednesday 18 June – Although it was the most perfect summer morning – dew, cuckoo calling and roses opening in the garden, against all instinct I went to the Red Cross and sat in the stuffy room sewing up gloves I'd knitted.

Saturday 21 June – While Sarah rode, Toots and I were led to the river by Mrs Ford, and shown where I could bathe. Toots splashed about and I soon felt so hot I got off my clothes and into the stream. Borne rapidly down in nude state, a few cows looked mildly surprised!

Did the church flowers rather pleasantly, lupins etc. This weather really is a treat and no Germans to disturb us. Peace, perfect peace, with everyone cutting their hay, Northam scythed ours this morning, we must make it for the goats.

Sunday 22 June – Took the children to school chapel, all the RASC [Royal Army Service Corps] soldiers were there.

Coming out E. asked me if I'd heard the news – Germany
had invaded Russia!! They don't arf take on these Huns. Of
course, we talked of nothing else all day, it seems incredible.
Poor Finns, Lets [Lithuanians], Esthonians etc!

Wednesday 25 June – The usual fowlery and goatery in the
evening. No wonder we get such peaceful nights with the
Russians keeping the Huns busy.
    The Sanford [pub] was closed all day today – NO BEER!!!

Sunday 29 June – A lazy day sunning ourselves – too misty in
the morning to bathe, but grilling later. Great Home Guard
manoeuvres – Frank and Bobby crawling through bracken
disguised as fawns to take the monument!* Saw Mary off by
the 5.5, then the whole family went to Bob to be inoculated
against typhoid as there's a lot about. A very sore arm by
evening, did the fowls and goats with the Griffins and two
other gardeners, then sauntered round the garden.
    Roses, hay, dew falling and a young moon!

Tuesday 19 August – A sunny morning again and we took the
kids including K., Toots' evacuee friend, out to look for mush-
rooms.
    Very few mothers at the clinic, storms of rain preventing
them perhaps, but many have gone back to London – this
long lull in raids proving too tempting. The Russian war goes
steadily on – the Huns seem to be more successful now
they're trying to break through on the Black Sea front.

Monday 25 August – Sad news this morning that David A.
is missing. His poor young wife with her wee son – only 3
weeks old. It was only David's third flight over Germany and
he didn't come back.

---

*   The Wellington Monument on the Blackdown Hills could be seen from the
    garden.

GEORGE BEARDMORE

At the beginning of February the Beardmores' landlady found an excuse to get rid of her lodgers. Jean, wanting to have her own space again, moved with Victoria to her parents' weekend cottage in Newton Longville, about seventy miles away, and George joined them every other weekend. George was more and more frustrated by the 'complete and utter boredom' of his BBC office job, feeling that his contribution to the war effort was feeble in comparison to that of his brother-in-law Jack in the RAF. His digs were cold and unfriendly. It was a dispiriting time.

Tuesday 3 June – Food scarce. I miss the vegetables most. Clothes are rationed from 1 June, not that rationing will worry Jean and me because the allowance is generous. Funny how the ordinary things of life are missed: when Jean lived here we took the bus into Worcester and there bought a small eiderdown for Victoria's cot, but because shops are now prohibited from using wrapping-paper or supplying bags we had to carry the eiderdown back home wrapped simply in string. No tobacco in the shops and cigarettes are a commodity for which one barters. No bitter at the New Inn tonight, I'm told. Queues at the sausage-shops but when you've got 'em the sausages are mostly breadcrumbs. For Victoria's second birthday Jean had raked together a feast of cake, chocolate, eggs, and custard, while in the morning we had ample bacon. I wonder what economies and fiddling Jean had made to accomplish it. As for razor-blades, one simply has to marry a shopkeeper's daughter before one can get hold of a new one.

Tuesday 24 June – Lumps like chestnuts in my throat when I left my small family safely home at Newton Longville. I told Jean that I didn't think I could bear much more of my present job but that Fletcher and the departmental head, not to mention Ernest Bevin,* wouldn't let me go. She suggested that I didn't force the issue but waited for the right opportunity. She may be right because it's odd how, when you want something badly enough, chance puts it in your way.

Now the startling news of Germany's invasion of Russia. The general verdict is that the more Russians that kill the more Germans, and vice versa, the better. This happened last Sunday morning. Jean came out of the cottage to tell me as I was walking down the garden path, having just emptied the Elsan,† and I said: 'Thank God, the pressure's off us.' Privately all I could think of was the precedent set by Napoleon, and look what a disaster that was! So far we have learned only that Brest Litovsk has fallen, that (great merciful God!) Hitler has promised Poland her independence in return for help, and that Russia has destroyed 300 tanks. We await any news – that Stalin has fled to Britain like Rudolf Hess, that the panzer divisions are in Nijni Novgorod,‡ that Hitler has shot himself. The situation news-wise is that the papers and broadcasters can tell us pretty well what they like, since it doesn't concern the security of this country, but that they can't get hold of any news to tell.

I can't convey without writing an essay on the subject how calmly people are taking the news, since the collapse of empires is now an old story.

---

* A circular from Ernest Bevin, minister of labour, had instructed government workers above a certain grade to remain in their posts. This included BBC employees.
† Chemical toilet.
‡ Nizhny Novgorod, Russian city east of Moscow.

CLARA MILBURN

A 'long-looked-for letter from Alan' from prison camp arrived in early January, and from then on a letter arrived every month, including a Christmas card on 8 February. His wound had healed, he was in 'high spirits' and grateful for the parcels Clara sent, including presents from friends and his colleagues at work.

But at home spirits were not high. Clara and Jack saw Coventry's ruined cathedral for the first time in January. There was another very heavy raid on the city in April, in which 'my old schoolfellow and dear friend Ethel and her sister Janet were killed'. In London Clara's nephew Colin, who had been a great support in gaining information about Alan, was seriously injured and his wife killed in the bombing.

Sunday 1 June – It was not until supper was over that I gardened – and only because I felt I must – and put in the rest of the snaps after raking out the rest of the tulips in the dining-room bed. I kill all the wireworms, calling them first Hitler, then Göring, Goebbels, Ribbentrop and Himmler. One by one they are destroyed, having eaten the life out of some living thing, and so they pay the penalty.

Sunday 22 June – This time last year we were dreadfully worried and unhappy about Alan and, though one can't be really heart-happy till he is safe home again, at least he is as well and contented as one can expect in the circumstances. No early church for me this Sunday and very nearly cut out the 11 a.m. service, but managed to make the effort and greatly enjoyed it. The church was beautifully cool and airy.

The big news today is that Germany, after having her forces massed along the Russian frontier for weeks, began hostilities, with all her usual claptrap and protestations. So now Russia will get a bit of what she gave Finland – and perhaps a lot more. Mr Churchill broadcast tonight and said we must stand by Russia. I suppose we must, as she is now against the enemy of mankind. But I wish we need not when I think of her ways, which are not our ways. America is sending the goods, though it is time she came in properly. It is difficult to know what is keeping them 'shivering on the brink' fearing 'to launch away'.

Friday 18 July – In Leamington this morning we had a good deal to do and shopping takes a long time. People take their ration books to the shops and they have to have the coupons cancelled as well as being served with bits of this and that.

Red currants are 2s 6d a lb, cherries 4s 6d, dessert gooseberries 3s 6d (and Mr Malins said to a customer: 'They're not worth it! Wouldn't pay it,' as he emptied them from the basket to a punnet). Potatoes are very scarce, and when I asked if I could have two pounds, Mrs Malins said: 'Have three'. So I did. Life is certainly queer now, with coupons for clothes . . . and very ordinary commodities like potatoes kept in the shops for regular customers only.

Russia seems to be keeping Germany from rushing along into her territory, though Germany is penetrating very slowly and there must be dreadful slaughter going on.

Thursday 14 August – A letter from Alan today, dated 14 July. He speaks of the heatwave at that time, of sunbathing, of a tiny pool and of a sports meeting: 'In spite of living inside barbed wire, you will gather that we are keeping pretty fit.' They took an eight-mile walk one day, which he greatly enjoyed.

By 2.15 p.m. today I was off to Coventry for a Mothers' Union meeting and, after a few inquiries, reached St Francis' Church hut, beside the pitiful little bombed church. It is a tiny hut, built up from the Scouts' Hut with £30 sent from Lincolnshire by sympathizers when Coventry was bombed.

The meeting was finished at 4 p.m. and I came away, looking very sadly at the little homes with their blank windows, damaged roofs and fences, and here and there a pathetic huddle of bricks where once had been a home. Poor, poor Coventry! It is all so much worse since the April raid.

Something impelled me to go up Grosvenor Road, where my dear Ethel Loveitt met her death in April. I saw the ruined house and thought I would call and see Maud Loveitt. But as I drew near the house I saw her talking at her gate to someone whom I did not know. As she did not notice me passing by, I drove on.

Great news on the wireless at 3 p.m. of a pact signed by President Roosevelt and Churchill somewhere on the high seas. It is called the 'Atlantic Charter'.

VERA BRITTAIN

George survived the sinking of the *Western Prince* on 14 December thanks to two acts of good fortune: the U-boat captain waited until all the lifeboats were clear before firing the final torpedoes and the captain of a merchant ship, despite orders not to run the risk of picking up survivors, came to the rescue.

Vera continued to lecture around the country, seeing ruined cities such as Coventry and Southampton. During the fearsome raid of 16 April she was in London with George. After it, she walked round Chelsea and 'was made so sad by all the smashes that I felt I never wanted to live there again'. 'What is the effect,' she asks, 'on one's mind of constantly walking about amid the utter ruins of lovely or familiar things?'

Sunday 15 June – Had queer dream in night; thought someone on staff of American *Who's Who* wrote to notify me that they were going to remove my name, as a writer whose main

characteristic was her work for peace was not worth putting
in just now. G. says I said in my sleep: 'What's the good of
living when one is so frustrated & ineffective?' But I don't
feel like that by day; I just take each thing as it comes & try
not to think too much about the complete shattering of my
life since a year ago. And two decades ago. Today is the 23rd
anniversary of Edward's death on the Asiago Plateau. He
would be 45 now. I still miss him & never more than in
these days when he would have been a source of the stability
& support which I can get from no-one in England now.

Monday 14 July – News of actual treaty of alliance signed with
Russia yesterday, but the BBC still won't play the Internation-
ale! The Russian & German claims (which say they are
almost at Kiev) as incompatible as usual – but Sunday papers
had almost optimistic articles. I think this is unwise. People
here will slack more than ever if they imagine things are
going better. Personally I don't even want to begin to hope
till there is unassailable reason for it.

Heard Churchill make one of his vindictive radio
speeches. He talked about 'inflicting on them the torments
they have inflicted on us', and gloated over the sufferings of
German civilians under our bombing – to say nothing of our
own civilians when the reprisals come back. The speech was
about on the moral level of an Old Testament Hebrew tribal
leader. Gone is the comparative decency, since Churchill
became Premier, of our distinction between the Nazi leaders
& the German people.

Saturday 26 July – Report in the *News Chronicle* of terrible raids
by ourselves on Cologne – two cinemas and a main hotel
destroyed, as well as many private houses. We can no more
hit only 'military objectives' than the Germans can. When
will both the leaders and the ordinary people of the various

nations realise just what they are doing, in destroying history's treasures in city after city? The sheer wastage now going on just beggars imagination.

Sunday 27 July – Dear Shirley's eleventh birthday* – on Sunday for the second time since she was born on a Sunday. Never did I dream when the children went to USA a year ago that I should not see her before a second birthday had gone by. As I wrote to Ruth in my long letter yesterday, the grief I feel is not only due to missing the children's lovely mental and spiritual flowering to which I subconsciously looked forward all through the period of bathing & face-washing and pram pushing. It is due even more to the sense of being cruelly deceived by the government here; of having been first encouraged to go to USA to lecture, and then, when the children had gone beyond recall, told that I could not go again owing to pacifist opinions wh. I held just the same at the beginning of the war. As it is, I parted with the children for what seems likely now to be the duration of the war without having ever decided to do so, on the assumption that I should be going to America at frequent intervals & therefore it was better for them to be there than here.

HAROLD NICOLSON

'I have no doubt that we shall win in the end ... meanwhile, I wake up with terror in the dawn', Nicolson had written in his diary for 13 April. Now he believed that the morale of the public was more vulnerable than it appeared and that the Crete defeat had created a 'trough of depression'. His work at the ministry became more wearing: other departments would not

---

* Vera posted a present of a Spanish nightdress case on 24 June.

cooperate; the BBC went its own way; it was sometimes difficult to know what Churchill wanted; Duff Cooper was away ill throughout May; and Nicolson began to feel anxious about his own position.

His anxieties proved to be justified. On 18 July Churchill wrote to Nicolson informing him that he was to be replaced at the Ministry of Information and offering a seat on the Board of Governors of the BBC. Duff Cooper, who was also dismissed, explained that the Labour Party wanted a Labour man in his job.

Sunday 22 June – A marvellous morning, with the smell of roses and hay and syringa in the air. We have breakfast outside. Vita arrives to say that the 7 o'clock news announced that Germany has invaded Russia.

Most people in England will be delighted. I am not so optimistic. It will have a bad effect on America, where many influential people do not like to see themselves as the allies of Bolshevism. It will have a bad effect on Conservative and Catholic opinion here. And if, as is likely, Hitler defeats Russia in three weeks, then the road to the oil is open, as also the road to Persia and India.

At 9 Winston broadcasts. He says that he is on the side of the Russians who defend their homes. He does not conceal that Russia may be beaten quickly, but having indicated to us the approaching collapse of India and China, and, in fact, of Europe, Asia and Africa, he somehow leaves us with the impression that we are quite certain to win this war. A masterpiece. Vita and I go out afterwards to make a little hay in the orchard. It is very hot tonight. Every flower pulsates with scent. Most people will be feeling happy tonight at the thought that we have got a new ally. I am not so sure. Not that I have the slightest objection to Russian communism. But I feel that they are so incompetent and selfish that they will be bowled over at a touch.

Wednesday 25 June – I dine alone with Rob Bernays.* He curses me for lacking in self-assertiveness. He is too polite to say so, but he thinks that I have been a softy in this job. He feels that all would be well if I had less desire to please and more desire to dominate. I confess that it has often puzzled me why a person of my ability, knowledge, experience, industry and integrity should not somehow make a certain effect. I am not exaggerating. I do not say I score more than 62 marks in any of the above qualities; but I do claim that I score 62 in each. Why the aggregate of such scoring should make so little impression on my contemporaries, I simply do not understand. I suppose it is because people say, 'Oh Harold! Well, he won't make trouble whatever happens.'

Friday 18 July – I think [the letter] might have been more politely worded. Could I afford it, I should not accept a Governorship of the BBC. But both Duff and Walter† urge me to accept. I realise that this means the end of any political ambitions which I may ever have cherished. I am hurt and sad and sorry. The PM's secretary telephones to say that he wants a reply at once, and could I send it by taxi. Well, I send it.

Saturday 19 July – I wake up feeling something horrible has happened, and then remember that I have been sacked from the Government.

I mind more than I thought I should mind. It is mainly, I suppose, a sense of failure. I quite see that if the Labour leaders have been pressing to have my post, there is good

---

* MP for Bristol North and friend of Harold. He died in a plane crash early in 1945. Harold became godfather to his baby son shortly afterwards.

† Sir Walter Monckton, a senior civil servant at the Ministry of Information, later a cabinet minister in Conservative governments of the 1950s.

cause why they should have it. But if I had more power and drive, I should have been offered Rab Butler's job at the Foreign Office, which I should dearly have loved. As it is, I come back to the bench below the gangway having had my chance and failed to profit by it. Ever since I have been in the House I have been looked upon as a might-be. Now I shall be a might-have-been. Always up till now I have been buoyed up by the hope of writing some good book or achieving a position of influence in politics. I now know that I shall never write a book better than I have written already, and that my political career is at an end. I shall merely get balder and fatter and more deaf as the years go by. This is an irritating thing. Success should come late in life in order to compensate for the loss of youth; I had youth and success together, and now I have old age and failure. Apart from all this, I mind leaving the Ministry where I did good work and had friends.

Monday 28 July – There is a rude article about me in *Truth* saying that I have 'the mincing manner of a French salon', that I lack virility and should retire from public life and bury myself in books. All rather true, I suppose. But I happen to enjoy public life. I could never be merely an observer.

NAOMI MITCHISON

In the new year Naomi went south to see family and friends, including her mother in Oxford and her brother Jack Haldane in Cambridge. It was not a period of heavy bombing and Naomi did not see the worst of the destruction in London, but she experienced the sirens and the sight of people camping out on the Underground platforms. A visit to their house, River Court, rarely used now as Dick stayed with their friends the Coles, brought back memories of life before the war, including the birth there of her three youngest. 'And now there are no more flowers or babies, and the ship in the nursery gathering dust.'

Back at Carradale, there was bad news of raids on Glasgow. A local couple had gone in search of their son: the house where he had been staying had been hit but his body not found. Naomi went to support them, as did her friends Denny MacIntosh (a local fisherman, known as Denny M) and his wife and two other men. The demolition squad had given up, but the fishermen went on digging despite the danger of collapsing walls, and found the body. In this particular death and the horrifying scenes in Glasgow, Naomi felt what she had not witnessed in London.

But, as the summer went on, there was much to enjoy: out in the boat fishing illegally at night with Denny M and the others, the news from Russia, the children back home for the holidays, working on the farm in the heat.

Sunday 22 June – Came in for the 1 o'ck news. Rosemary* and I were listening casually, but as we heard, I yelled for Murdoch to come too and they all came. As it went on I began to sob and shake with hysterics. I began to realise how I had been expecting another appeasement or worse. Now at last we are on the same side; this ache I have had all the war because of the Soviet Union, is now healed. Though goodness knows it doesn't make war any better or nobler a thing. Only something has been added.

Wednesday 27 August – We thought it would be fun to dance; for some reason all the young decided it would be even more fun to dress up, so they got out all the Slovak and other things and dressed up. By and bye [*sic*] Av went over and collected Lachie and the two Alecs; we danced to the gramophone for a couple of hours, country dances and odd

---

* Her secretary.

waltzes and things, a good eightsome. A nice flower jar was broken, which is a pity as we have very few left – the Woolworth ones survive! We gave them beer, and it was almost the end of the small cask. I have written for another, but – ? The alternative is tea, and that means sugar. And rather more washing up.

Saturday 30 August – I felt very happy; it was lovely to be getting it [the corn] in at last, to see the stocks up all over the field. It looked lovely too, the pale gold. I felt consciously and immediately happy; I had been working, I would be working again, but my muscles were standing it; I could see the new muscle in my bare arms and legs (only the muscle of my strained right thumb was sore, from pushing in the ties). I was wearing only a shirt and shorts and sandals, and a cotton square over my head. And there was no fear of rain. Denny M had brought me a bit of chocolate; Angus and Lachie looked at us gaily, coming back to work for me on a Saturday afternoon, not minding; while they were harnessing Jo, Denny M kissed me quickly on the edge of the harvest field.

ALAN BROOKE

Brooke thought Russia would resist for only a few months but that would probably give him until the following year to transform the Home Army before a German invasion. There had already been improvements, but there were still major concerns: lack of cooperation between the services, the need to increase not only tank production but also the supply of spare parts, the weakness of some commanders, the slowness of decision-making, the machinations of politicians, especially Beaverbrook.

Brooke's fascination with birds took a new turn as he built a hide at home and began filming in colour. These 'happy hours' helped him put 'the war and all its troubles right out of my mind' and 'return to work a new man'.

Tuesday 27 May – You came and had lunch and converted the day into one to be remembered amongst others. After lunch went to see S of S* to discuss questions connected with air support of Home Forces. Finally attended one of the PM's Tank Parliaments where we discussed air co-operation, and also anti-tank weapons. PM in great form and on the whole a very successful meeting. It is surprising how he maintains a light hearted exterior in spite of the vast burden he is bearing. He is quite the most wonderful man I have ever met, and is a source of never ending interest studying and getting to realize that occasionally such human beings make their appearance on this earth. Human beings who stand out head and shoulders above all others.

Wednesday 11 June – **Firth of Forth, Scotland** – Started early and finished inspecting 52nd Div by lunch time ... After lunch navy conveyed us to the [Bass] Rock, preceded by a minesweeper and followed by a relief ship! Glorious sunny afternoon and calm sea. Had a most interesting time on the Rock photographing gannets. Quite one of the most wonderful sights I have ever seen. Do hope photos will be good. Finally left aerodrome near North Berwick at 7 pm and flew back to Hendon in 1¾ hours!

Wednesday 9 July – Left 8 am. Office work till 12 noon when I went to the PM's Room, House of Commons, to attend meeting of the War Cabinet. The subject to be discussed was my proposed London exercise to deal with a parachute attack. I had to make a statement as to the reason why I considered it

---

* Secretary of State for War David Margesson, who was replaced by P. J. Grigg in February 1942.

advisable to hold the exercise and why we could not hold it as a theoretical exercise. All went well till Beaverbrook started pouring vitriol onto the idea. Purely owing to the fact that he has recently taken over the Ministry of Supply and cannot contemplate having his preliminary efforts interfered with. Attlee backed him owing to his fears of the effects of such an exercise on the public. The more I see of politicians the less I think of them! They are seldom influenced directly by the true aspects of a problem and are usually guided by some ulterior political reason! They are always terrified of public opinion as long as the enemy is sufficiently far, but when closely threatened by the enemy inclined to lose their heads, and then blame all their previous errors on the heads of the military whose advice they have failed to follow. The more I see of democracy the more I doubt our wisdom of attaching such importance to it! I cannot see how our present system of democracy can produce real qualified leaders of a nation.

Tuesday 29 July – Left Ferney Close [after a week's leave] this morning at 8 am and motored back to London with a distinct 'going back to school' feeling. Rather a sinking heart at the thought of shouldering again the burden of responsibility and all the worries and doubts which endeavour to swamp one's mind and are not always easy to keep down. Those horrible question marks which seem to be everywhere at times! Have I really taken the proper dispositions for the defence of this country? Am I sufficiently insured in the South East? Can I reinforce this corner without taking undue risks in the North? Am I under appreciating the air threat? Ought I to further denude the beaches to cover the aerodromes? If I do am I opening the door to sea invasion? Will the air support be as efficient as the Air Ministry would like us to believe? How long will the Navy take to concentrate its forces in home waters? Shall we be able to hold the thrust of Armoured Divisions in Kent during this period?

These are all questions where a wrong answer may mean the end of life as we have known it in this country and the end of the British Empire!

HERMIONE RANFURLY

On 8 April Dan was reported missing, suspected ambushed, along with Generals Neame and O'Connor. A month later the Red Cross reported Dan a prisoner in Sulmona Camp in Italy. Whitaker, who was manning the switchboard at SOE, was so overwhelmed by the good news 'that he got wrong numbers for everyone all morning'.

As early as February Hermione had nobbled Anthony Eden, on a visit to the British embassy, to inform him of her concerns about security at SOE. Nothing happened and in early June she spoke to the chief of staff, General Sir Arthur Smith, who asked her to make up a dossier of evidence for the minister of state, soon to arrive in Cairo. This entailed smuggling documents out in her bra each night, copying them in longhand and returning them first thing each morning. It helped to know that the general planned to recommend her for the post of assistant private secretary to the high commissioner in Jerusalem, Sir Harold MacMichael, once the 'horrible job' was done.

Sunday 22 June – Germany has attacked Russia. The general opinion here is that Russia will be beaten in a few months – that she is ill equipped and without military leaders. Bonner Fellers* is the only person I have met who thinks the Russians will survive – he has been to Russia fairly recently and says the Germans have bitten off more than they can chew.

I received a letter today which cheered me very much. It was from an RASC Captain McClure in Alexandria:

---

* Military Attaché to the US Embassy.

I was listening to Radio Vatican yesterday . . . The announcer
was calling out a list of prisoners of war . . . I heard him send
one message as follows: 'Lord Ranfurly sends his love to his wife
Countess Ranfurly, the Continental Hotel, Cairo.' All messages
were repeated twice and it was only after hearing the Continental
Hotel, Cairo, mentioned I took notice. The majority of messages
sent kind regards or wished to be remembered. Yours was the
only one in which love was sent. I am taking the liberty to write
to you in case you did not receive the above message. I have
honour to remain, Madam, Your Ladyship's obedient servant
J. K. McClure (Captain RASC)

Thursday 3 July – Today I went to say goodbye to the Wavells[*]
who are going to India. General Archie's departure is a real
blow to all ranks and particularly to my generation. He is
one of the very few senior soldiers who back young methods
of war and enterprises like the Long Range Desert Group.[†]
Tough luck on David Stirling that he must operate without
such a leader. How they would have enjoyed each other. I
found Lady Wavell and Nannie packing in their petticoats.
I felt as if my own family were leaving.

Thursday 10 July – Today I received a letter signed by the
Deputy Adjutant General saying that he understood I had left
my job and he wished to remind me of my promise to leave
the country if such circumstances arose. I replied that my
change of job had been arranged in the full knowledge and
consent of the Commander-in-Chief and I was sorry he had
not been informed.

---

[*] After the recent failure to relieve Tobruk, Churchill had decided to swap
Wavell with Auchinleck, commander in India.

[†] David Stirling's fledgling SAS. Hermione knew all four Stirling boys: David,
Peter, Hugh and Bill. Hugh was killed in April 1941 at El Alamein. Peter was
third secretary at the British embassy in Cairo.

Tuesday 15 July – **In the train** – When I crossed the canal at
Kantara and heard the frogs croaking I felt, suddenly, desolate. Palestine will be different this time: Dan is in prison
in Italy; Toby is dead; the Sherwood Rangers are besieged in
Tobruk; and Whitaker is left behind in Cairo.

As the train puffed its way north I felt increasingly afraid
lest, from panic over my job in Cairo, I'd made a huge mistake.

Wednesday 16 July – **Jerusalem** – After tea Sir Harold told me
the terms of my appointment. He emphasised that leave is a
privilege and not a right. I am to work under his Private
Secretary, Donald MacGillivry. My hours are 8.30 a.m. to
7.30 p.m., with a lunch break, seven days a week.

For comfort and beauty few places can equal this – but I
am wondering, all over again, if, when Dan is a prisoner and
all our friends are in the Desert or besieged in Tobruk, or
being bombed in England, I should be so sheltered. My only
hope is to work extremely hard.

Tuesday 22 July – General Jumbo Wilson, who commands this
area, came to see Sir Harold this evening. His ADC told me
that the General had received a letter from Cairo GHQ,
asking that I be sent back immediately and quoting the old
evacuation order. The General replied that as my husband
had been in enemy hands for some months he considered the
initial reason for my evacuation extinct and furthermore I'd
been sent to Palestine with the consent of General Wavell.
He concluded, 'This lady has outmanoeuvred every General
in the Middle East and I do not myself intend to enter the
arena.'

Saturday 16 August – I miss knowing first-hand what is happening in the Desert – what the 'grown ups' (GHQ) and the
Desert Rats are saying (always so different). It is a very dark

hour for us whichever way one looks. I'm going to send all the news cuttings on the Atlantic Charter to Dan. If the Nazi censors hold them up it will still do them good to read them.

Despite sending a note to Dan every day, and the authorized single parcel every three months, Hermione had still not heard from him.

THE DESERT WAR

The Desert War presented unique problems: there was no front line and Axis and British formations criss-crossed the terrain in search of each other. To make themselves less vulnerable to air attack, the British moved in widely dispersed lines, travelling under cover of darkness to pitch camp (or leaguer) some distance from their last position. This posed additional problems to the supply columns who had to locate the camps each night.

Identifying friend or foe was difficult – both sides used captured vehicles and equipment and both first appeared as a dust cloud on the horizon, while frequent sandstorms and long distances made radio communication unreliable. The frequency of sandstorms was put down to the increased movement of vehicles across the desert floor. A. Morrison was a 21-year-old lorry driver from Liverpool. He'd volunteered for Palestine early in the war having 'heard many romantic stories of the mystic east' and was now a Tommy with the RASC attached to the 7th Armoured Division (the Desert Rats). After their vehicle took a direct hit from an enemy fighter plane, Morrison and his co-driver hitched a ride in a fifteen-hundredweight truck but this became separated from the rest of the column as night fell.

A. MORRISON[*]

We set off after the column, in the direction we thought it was going, as fast as we could, over great ruts and bumps, stopping occasionally, switching off and listening, until finally we heard the column, caught it up and took our position again, thankfully eating dust as we thought how lucky we were!

After a short interval we all stopped again, as the moon began to rise. To our delight we saw that the men in front were putting down their blankets to sleep. We followed their example and lay down beside the truck. Shortly afterwards I felt wide awake – why, I don't know; but as I lay watching the tip of the moon just breaking over the desert, a chap came walking up with a large jug in his hand. 'Coffee,' he muttered. I grabbed a mug from under the driving seat just above my head, blew the dust out of it and held it up with a grunt. He filled the mug and walked off, the others obviously still asleep. As I sat drinking my coffee, I felt my scalp prickling as I examined the shape of the tank a few yards in front of me in the growing light; for on closer inspection I could see the large black cross on the turret. I realised I was drinking the enemy's coffee!

I quietly woke the others and quickly explained the situation to them. At first they thought I was joking, but they soon realised the truth. We knew we had to move quickly, as no doubt the Germans would soon post a guard. Quickly and calmly the lads crawled on the back of our truck, I got behind the wheel, turning it to a full left lock as R. got in beside me; I switched on the ignition, put it in gear, clutch in, pulled the starter and prayed it would start at first go,

---

[*]   A. Morrison, private papers: unpublished ms, 'On the Road To – Anywhere!', Imperial War Museum 75751. First name not noted.

which it did. I don't think I've ever travelled so fast in the desert before or since!

The Allies had captured the workable port of Tobruk from the Italians on 22 January 1941. While Tobruk remained under Allied control, the Axis would have difficulty reaching the all-important Suez Canal. On 10 April an Italian–German force under Rommel surrounded the thirty-five-mile perimeter, which was manned by 14,000 Australian and 10,000 British troops. The siege was to continue for 242 days.

A. O. McGINLAY
Major, 7th Royal Tank Regiment*

We wanted to prove to the Aussies that it was quite safe to lie low in a ditch or trench and let a tank drive straight over them. To this end, as each Brigade came into reserve, which they regularly did – the other three brigades manning the perimeter – we had them dig slit trenches, lie in them, and ran over them. Apart from the odd mouthful of sand, they were unhurt.

This training paid off, and when Gerry broke in about the end of May, the infantry just laid low whilst the Mark IV Gerry tanks rolled over them, then came up, wiping out the Gerry infantry following them. This left the Gerry tanks completely cut off from their support, and both the Royal Artillery, firing over open sights at short range, and our tanks, 1st RTR [Royal Tank Regiment] and our squadron of 7th RTR, had a field day, knocking all of them out. Gerry took a long time before he attacked again.

* Major A. O. McGinlay, private papers, Imperial War Museum 93111;
  Robert Lyman, *The Longest Siege: Tobruk – The Battle That Saved North Africa*,
  Macmillan, 2009.

Water was rationed to one and a half pints per man per day with an additional cup of tea supplied with the evening meal. Small sponges that could soak up water for washing and then be squeezed out again so that the water could be re-used became invaluable as the men sought to wash, shave and clean their teeth in half a mug of water. A daily shave was necessary to avoid skin rashes.

VERNON NORTHWOOD
Captain, Australian 2/28th Battalion *

First thing in the morning everyone stood to and expected – anything. Perhaps nothing happened; perhaps some shelling, some mortar ... Then about midday a heat haze would settle over Tobruk. Everything became distorted – a camel became a twenty-storey building. That was when you could move around safely, wander over to the platoons and have a talk to them. We encouraged the men to take their boots off and walk about barefoot in the sand – that's the only way we kept our feet clean. We took our shirts off and the sun baked the perspiration into salt, and we rubbed it off. You were always rubbing salt and dust off your body.

The men slept and invariably ate in their coffin-sized dugouts. Rats and fleas were a constant problem. Pyrethrum powder, the only insecticide effective against the fleas, did not reach the army until October. Soldiers were also pursued at all times by swarms of flies desperate for moisture. Many resorted to carrying their mosquito nets around with them in order to eat inside.

*   Captain Vernon Northwood, Oral History Reel 16, Imperial War Museum 22161; Robert Lyman, *The Longest Siege: Tobruk – the Battle that Saved North Africa*, Macmillan, 2009.

ALAN MOOREHEAD
War correspondent, London *Daily Express**

The food of the front-line men had to be cooked near the town and taken up to the trenches in the starlight. The men who had lain all day in the sun facing the enemy would crawl through the trenches to the dug-outs where the bully stew and brackish tea was served out. And they would relax there for an hour or two at night to smoke, talk and read. Before the morning came they would walk back to their posts. By any standard they were very fine troops. They were the Rats of Tobruk.

All these men – some 25,000 of them – were maintained solely by naval supply. The siege ended on 7 December 1941 with the defenders breaking out to link up with the advancing 8th Army. A total of 5,989 Allied soldiers had lost their lives, many of them to be buried in the sand, and a further 539 members of the Royal and Royal Australian Navies had died at sea in the 'Suicide Run' between Alexandria and Tobruk.

* Alan Moorehead, *African Trilogy*, Hamish Hamilton, 1944.

5. THE WORLD AT WAR

WINTER 1941–2

When Germany invaded Russia in June 1941, Hitler had hoped to capitalize on the fact that Stalin's purges of the 1930s had left the Red Army in disarray, stripped of its experienced officer corps. The German battle plan was straightforward. Nineteen panzer divisions with more than 3,600 tanks would strike like lightning into the heart of the country and then turn to envelop the enemy from the rear while the German infantry poured in through the initial incision and closed the cordon from the front. Surrender was bound to follow.

What Stalin knew, and Hitler did not, was the strength of his reserves and the logistical capabilities of the Soviet Union. Millions of men could be moved west and hundreds of factories moved east. Hitler knew only how to play a short game; Stalin knew he could afford to play long. The further into Russia Hitler's armies progressed the longer their supply lines grew. Particularly irksome was the fact that the Russian railway gauge differed from the German, so new tracks had to be laid. As autumn and then winter set in and the temperature dropped dramatically, the German decision not to equip their soldiers with winter clothing proved disastrous.

Britain's continuing concerns were the Atlantic and North Africa. From the end of November 1941 the two sides milled about in the desert, described by one German general as 'a tactician's paradise and a quartermaster's hell'. Eventually it was the supply problem – by ship across the contested Mediterranean for the Axis force, or all the way round Africa via the Cape for the Allies – that decided the immediate outcome. The siege of Tobruk was lifted, and by February 1942 Rommel, running out of fuel and ammunition, was forced to withdraw and regroup.

When Japan signed the Tripartite Pact in September 1940, joining the Axis of Germany and Italy, Holland and France were under German control and Britain was seemingly next in line. Japanese occupation of French Indo-China went unopposed by Vichy France, and Japan's continuing war with China, begun in 1931, had only resulted in trade embargoes on oil and steel. However, by the autumn of 1941, with Britain undefeated and Germany locked in combat with Russia, the embargoes were beginning to bite. Roosevelt had moved the US Pacific Fleet to Hawaii and ordered a military build-up in the Philippines. The United States now had a strong naval and air presence in the Pacific, and any Japanese attempt to advance into the Dutch East Indies or the British colonies would be blocked.

Over ninety minutes on Sunday 7 December 1941, Japanese planes devastated the US Pacific Fleet in Pearl Harbor. Within twenty-four hours of the strike, Japan had launched attacks against Malaya, Hong Kong, Guam, the Philippines, Wake Island and Midway Island. Four days later Hitler and Mussolini declared war on the USA. The whole world was now at war.

In the Atlantic German submarines seemed unstoppable, sinking HMS *Ark Royal* in November and in January, the first month of Operation Drumbeat, thirty-five Allied ships. On 11 February the German battle cruisers *Scharnhorst* and *Gneisenau* left the French naval base at Brest and headed up the English Channel. Failures in British radar and communications and the downing of six Swordfish biplanes meant that both reached Germany, albeit slightly damaged.

The humiliation felt in Britain was deepened by events in the Far East, where the Japanese were determined to stake claims in as many arenas as possible before the Americans could recover from Pearl Harbor. From Malaya they advanced quickly south towards Singapore. On 15 February, suddenly and devastatingly, Singapore surrendered to a Japanese force less than half the size of the island's garrison. One hundred and thirty thousand Allied troops were captured. As with events in Norway early in 1940, the public had been led to believe one thing and was shocked when the opposite prevailed. Churchill was alone at Chequers when the news came through. 'It was his darkest hour,' wrote Lord Beaverbrook.*

THE DIARISTS

HERMIONE RANFURLY

A letter from Dan, dated 11 April 1941, had finally arrived on 10 September, confirming that en route for Tobruk his party had been ambushed at night by German commandos. No one had been hurt. He asked for news of Whitaker and said that he was 'desperately worried' about Hermione. She had written back immediately to reassure him of the joys of deciphering coded messages in her dressing gown at all hours, but had heard nothing since. The waiting was appalling: they were always waiting

---

* Quoted in J. R. M. Gwyer, *History of the Second World War*, United Kingdom Military Series, *Grand Strategy*, Volume III, Part 1, HMSO, 1964.

for something – for letters, for the outcome of battles, 'for news from everywhere; for the war to end'.

Saturday 6 December 1941 – **Jerusalem** – A big tank battle is raging in the Desert near Sidi Rezegh. I think the Sherwood Rangers may be involved. Perhaps, after all, I am lucky that Dan is a prisoner and not in the midst of this turmoil.

I am afraid we are not yet as well armed as the Germans – their Mark 3 and 4 guns are excellent and they have the awful 88mm gun.

Monday 8 December – Old Nick burst into the billiard room this morning – his face pink with excitement. 'You've been across the Pacific,' he said. 'Just where is Pearl Harbor – it's not marked in my Atlas?'

'Go away,' I said. 'I am struggling with a cipher signal.'

'To hell with that,' he said, 'the Japs have bombed Pearl Harbor, destroyed a lot of American ships and the USA are coming into the war.' We danced round and round the billiard table.

Wednesday 10 December – Wonderful news: we've advanced in the Desert and raised the siege of Tobruk. For us in the Middle East this is wildly exciting. Through the dark days of 1941 the defenders of that shattered town have been an inspiration to us all, except perhaps for dear Lady MacMichael who announced at lunch she could not find Tobruk on her map of Russia.

Thursday 18 December – Japanese troops have landed on Hong Kong. North, south, east and west of us war goes on and spreads. Nothing seems to improve – except our geography.

Thursday 25 December – A letter has come from Dan dated 10 May, written two days after he arrived at Sulmona POW camp in southern Italy. He wrote they had a terrible journey back across North Africa to Tripoli. Nearly all the prisoners had dysentery.

Monday 29 December – The MacMichaels have gone on holiday to Syria and I have been granted two weeks' leave. I am tired and glad of a rest. When I get back I think I should ask for a half day off each week.

She spent the new year visiting old friends in Cairo.

Thursday 1 January – **Cairo** – Last night soldiers on leave in Cairo saw the New Year in with a vengeance. They behaved disgracefully but were so funny and happy no one seemed to mind. Whitaker and I hired a gharry and drove round and saw chariot races in Kasr el Nil, bank notes fluttering on the pavements, and military police convulsed with laughter, hopelessly trying to restore order.

Friday 2 January – I visited Bonner Fellers in his office and looked at his fascinating maps and photographs while he finished dictating in his colourful, downright way. He drove me to lunch in his 'hearse' as he calls it – a camouflaged van which has a bunk in the back, which he uses when he goes up to the Desert.

And he told me 'I am getting unpopular here. Not so much with your people as with the US Embassy in Cairo and in Washington; they think I am a defeatist but that's not going to stop me saying what I think about the military situation, which is my job to do. The trouble is your top brass are overconfident which they've no right to be: your gear is still inferior to the enemy's, and you are less well led – too many senior officers sitting on their arses in GHQ. If I get levered out I shall join MacArthur – he's the best soldier we have.'

As I was leaving he said, 'Remember one thing: we've got a helluva lot to learn – your country and mine. I reckon if we don't stop worrying about our different customs and snobberies then Russia will take the lead in tomorrow's world. You people are so busy with tradition and mine so stuck on making money that I guess it will serve us right if they do.' A grin and he was gone.

As I was leaving Shepherds Hotel, a tall, gaunt, scruffy figure climbed out of a taxi and asked me to pay the fare. It was David Stirling – just back from the Desert. Considering the length of his beard he must have been there for a long time.

'How many men have you got now, and what's the score?' I asked.

'Four officers and fourteen men, and around ninety enemy planes destroyed on the ground,' he said and added he now only had one idea in his head – a bath. Before I had time to congratulate him on his Honour (the DSO – Distinguished Service Order) he hurried away saying, 'Meet me here for dinner.' I did.

Sunday 4 January – I dined with Peter Stirling at his flat. David was there. [He] hates talking about his nocturnal raids so I felt honoured to hear a detailed account. Mo, with the dignity of an English butler, served dinner and handed round captured Italian wine, murmuring, 'Mussolini, Sir?'

ALAN BROOKE

The previous autumn Brooke had been to his friend Dill's wedding. 'I do hope he will be happy; if anybody deserves it, he does.' But now there were rumours that Churchill wanted to replace Dill as chief of the Imperial General Staff (CIGS). Brooke knew that Churchill did not share his admiration for Dill, and he also believed that Beaverbrook was undermining Dill's position. Brooke and Dill were good enough friends to discuss the situation honestly and openly. Dill was clear that if he had to go Brooke should be his successor.

Sunday 16 November – **At Chequers** – After dinner PM took me off to his study and told me that as Dill had had a very hard time and was a tired man he wanted to relieve him. He then went on to say that he wanted me to take over from Dill, and asked me whether I was prepared to do so.

It took me some time to reply as I was torn by many feelings. I hated the thought of old Dill going and our very close association coming to an end. I hated the thought of what this would mean for him. The thought of the magnitude of the job and the work entailed took the wind out of my sails. The fact that the extra work and ties would necessarily mean seeing far less of you tore at my heart strings. And finally a feeling of sadness at having to give up Home Forces after having worked them up to their present pitch.

The PM misunderstood my silence and said 'Do you not think you will be able to work with me? We have so far got on well together.' I had to assure him that those were not my thoughts, though I am well aware that my path will not be strewn with rose petals! But I have the greatest respect for him and real affection for him, so that I hope I may be able to stand the storms of abuse which I may well have to bear frequently. He then went on to explain the importance he attached to the appointment and the fact that the Chiefs of Staff Committee must be the body to direct military events over the whole world. He also stated that his relations with me must for now approximate those of a Prime Minister to one of his ministers. Nothing could have been kinder than he was, and finally when we went to bed at 2 am he came with me to my bedroom to get away from the others, took my hand and looking into my eyes with an exceptionally kind look said 'I wish you the very best of luck.'

On 1 December Brooke took up his post as CIGS. He quickly concluded that there needed to be an overall strategy that consistently focused on a planned priority and that this should determine the deployment of men and weapons.

Wednesday 3 December – I am positive that our policy for the conduct of the war should be to direct both our military and political efforts towards the early conquest of North Africa. From there we shall be able to reopen the Mediterranean and to stage offensive operations against Italy.

Thursday 4 December – At the War Cabinet – Debate became interminable. Anthony Eden like a peevish child grumbling because he was being sent off to see Uncle Stalin without suitable gifts, while Granny Churchill was comforting him and explaining to him all the pretty speeches he might make instead. Finally Eden succeeded in swinging Churchill round to a gift of some 300 tanks and 300 aircraft. During most of the debate the conduct of the war seemed to have been pushed into the background, self interests seemed to pre-dominate.

After dinner Chiefs of Staff met at 10 pm with the Prime Minister presiding, and Attlee and Anthony Eden present. During the dinner interval the PM had swung right round again, tanks and aircraft had been put aside, the gift was now to consist of 10 squadrons of aircraft to be made available immediately after the Libyan offensive was finished. Portal* agreed, but said offer was too definite. This produced the most awful outburst of temper, we were told that we did nothing but obstruct his intentions, we had no ideas of our

*   Chief of Air Staff.

own, and whenever he produced ideas we produced nothing but objections, etc. etc.! Attlee pacified him once, but he broke out again, then Anthony Eden soothed him temporarily, but to no avail. Finally he looked at his papers for some 5 minutes, then slammed them together, closed the meeting and walked out of the room! It was pathetic and entirely unnecessary. We were only trying to save him from making definite promises which he might find hard to keep later on. It is all the result of overworking himself and keeping too late hours. Such a pity. God knows where we would be without him, but God knows where we shall go with him!

On 12 December Churchill left for the USA. Brooke argued in favour of Dill accompanying him and staying as the country's representative, liaising with General Marshall*. Brooke later wrote, 'Thank heaven I succeeded in convincing Winston as few men did more in furthering our cause of final victory than Dill.' On Christmas Day, Brooke officially became CIGS and spent most of it in a meeting with the chiefs of staff. The next six weeks were also spent in many similar meetings, which he frequently found both dull and inefficient. With the war going badly in North Africa and the Far East, he could not have taken up his new post at a more difficult time.

Wednesday 11 February – The news of Singapore goes from bad to worse and now poor Archie Wavell has injured his back! PM sent for me this evening to discuss with him last wire from Wavell about Singapore from where he had just returned. It was a very gloomy wire and a depressing wire as regards the fighting efficiency of the troops on Singapore Island. It is hard to see why a better defence is not being put up, but I presume there must be some good reason. I can't see the place holding out more than a day or so now. The

---

*   Eisenhower's Chief of Staff.

losses on the island will be vast, not only in men but in material.

I have during the last 10 years had an unpleasant feeling that the British Empire was decaying and that we were on a slippery decline!! I wonder if I was right? I certainly never expected that we should fall to pieces as fast as we are and to see Hong Kong and Singapore go in less than 3 months plus failure in the Western Desert is far from reassuring! We have had a wonderful power of recuperation in the past. I wonder whether we shall again bring off a comeback?

CHARLES RITCHIE

Ritchie continued to move in aristocratic circles, weekending in England's great houses. In February he had met the Irish novelist Elizabeth Bowen at the christening of Billy Buchan's* child. They struck up a close friendship. Bowen was unhappily married to an alcoholic academic, Alan Cameron. In September he recorded that Elizabeth had said, 'Take it from one of the best living novelists that people's personalities are not interesting, except when you are in love with them.'

Sunday 7 December – The attack on Pearl Harbor has caused very human sardonic satisfaction to everyone I have happened to see today.

For years I have seen movies of United States reconnaissance planes circling away from the US base at Pearl Harbor to spy out the Pacific for just such an attempt as this. What were they doing when those five aircraft carriers sneaked up close enough to disgorge those planes? We listened to Roosevelt's address to Congress on the wireless in Mr Massey's big office at Canada House under the great glass chandelier – the

---

* William, brother of John, now Lord Tweedsmuir.

room where he told us of the declaration of war on Germany.
Roosevelt was moving and had dropped his mannerisms. He
sounded profoundly shocked and bitterly angry. His speech
was just right.

I have not heard one word of sympathy for the United
States here but when the number of US battleships sunk
began to come in an Admiralty official said, 'This is getting
past a joke.'

We Canadians feel that once the Americans have got over
the initial shock they will get on the band-wagon and will get
into the war one hundred percent and be producing tanks,
planes, etc., by the million when the Japs are finished. The
English have no real faith in the United States. Now it is our
business to begin boosting the Americans here.

Tuesday 20 January – Elizabeth and I dined at Claridge's. She
was in an easy and cheerful mood. She said, 'I would like to
put you in a novel,' looking at me through half-closed eyes
in a suddenly detached way like a painter looking at a model.
'You probably would not recognize yourself.' 'I am sure I
wouldn't,' I lied.

A redhaired young man came up to me and said, 'I have
met you somewhere before.'

In the end I remembered it was when I was staying with
the Fullertons. He played Chopin in the drawing-room. Since
then he has been shot down in an airplane, lost a lung, and
gets six pounds and six shillings disability allowance. I think
he must have landed on his head. He has a wild look in his
eye.

Friday 23 January – I feel this country cannot – in the end –
escape the European civil war. My friends seem to me to be
waiting offstage to take up their parts.

There are friends of mine mostly now employed in
Military Intelligence who might qualify for a post-war secret

police. My role is indicated – the diplomat who hangs on until the last moment, feeling it his duty to defend his country's actions right or wrong, reluctant to give up his career.

Tuesday 27 January – Heard the Prime Minister defend the Government's conduct of the war in the House. It was the greatest speech I have ever heard. For an hour and a half he developed the central theme of the grand strategy of the war and at recurrent intervals sounded the note of his own desire for a vote of confidence from the House. It was an orchestral performance. To read it would be to lose half of it – the implications in his slightest side-glance were significant.

One small thing that struck me before the Prime Minister got up to speak was the reception given to a question asked by a Labour MP as to why certain people were still allowed to have three or four domestic servants in their employ. The question was greeted with ironical laughter from Conservative MPs, the implication of the laughter being that there were no such persons. The Cabinet Minister who answered the question pooh-poohed it and said that he could not accept that such a situation existed, yet they must have known as well as I do (better since most of them no doubt still have got three or four domestic servants of their own) that in any country house you choose to go into there are still domestic servants in threes and fours. A small thing but typical.

George Ignatieff* is shocked that behind closed doors in the War Office the MI [Military Intelligence] boys express the hope that the Russians will be defeated and that *three days* later the German army itself will collapse. It is, and has been

---

* Then a member of staff at Canada House, subsequently Canadian ambassador to the UN and NATO. His elder brother was in the Russian and Scandinavian section of British Military Intelligence.

all along, the ideal British solution. The Russians know this as well as we do.

Tuesday 10 February – Dined at the Conservative Club. Gossip about Stalin – they say he wishes Cripps* would not come and bore him by talking communism to him. Stalin hates bores but takes a great interest in the Windsor–Simpson story. He cannot understand why Mrs Simpson was not liquidated.

HAROLD NICOLSON

Criticism of Churchill grew, including within the Conservative Party. For Nicolson, however, Churchill remained 'the embodi-ment of the nation's will', and he was 'disgusted' by the small-mindedness of his critics. Although Churchill won the vote of confidence on 29 January (in which Harold witnessed 'the wind of opposition dropping sentence by sentence' as Churchill spoke), doubts about his leadership did not disappear.

Thursday 12 February – What has saddened me is not merely the bad news from Singapore and Libya, but a conversation with Violet.† She had been to see Winston yesterday, and for the first time in their long friendship she had found him depressed. Underneath it all was a dreadful fear, she felt, that our soldiers are not as good fighters as their fathers were. 'In 1915,' said Winston, 'our men fought on even when they had only one shell left and were under a fierce barrage. Now they cannot resist dive-bombers. We have so many men in

---

*   Stafford Cripps, a former Labour cabinet minister, had been expelled from
    the party in 1939 for advocating an alliance with the Communist Party. He
    had been British ambassador to Moscow since 1940.
†   Lady Violet Bonham-Carter, a fellow BBC governor.

Singapore, so many men – they should have done better.'
It is the same, of course, in Libya. Our men cannot stand up
to punishment. And yet they are the same men as man the
merchant ships and who won the Battle of Britain. There is
something deeply wrong with the whole morale of our Army.

Sunday 15 February – In the evening Winston Churchill speaks
[on the radio]. He tells us that Singapore has fallen. He is
grim and not gay. Unfortunately he appeals for national unity
and not criticism, in a manner which recalls Neville Chamberlain. Moreover, although he is not rhetorical, he cannot
speak in perfectly simple terms and cannot avoid the cadences
of a phrase. I do not think his speech will have done good,
and I feel deeply depressed and anxious.

Tuesday 17 February – Winston made his statement [in the
House] this afternoon. It started all right, but when people
asked questions, he became irritable and rather reckless.
He spoke about 'anger and panic' which infuriated people
and will, I fear, be broadcast throughout the world by our
enemies. The pity of it is that he had a good case, and if only
he had kept his head and produced his promises in the right
order, all would have gone well. He was not at his best.

Friday 27 February – I do a talk on Winston for the Empire
programme.* I cannot bear the thought that this heroic figure
should now be sniped at by tiny little men. I fell asleep for
one moment last night and dreamt of pain and anxiety, and
then suddenly I felt Vita's hands upon my shoulders. 'Is it
you?' I asked. 'No,' the wraith answered, 'I am Defeat.' I
woke unhappily and remained awake.

---

* This became the BBC World Service in 1965.

CLARA MILBURN

The news from Alan was always cheerful: he sent a snapshot
showing himself looking 'fit and determined'. Though he was safe,
Clara was all too aware of the slaughter at home, across Europe
and now in the Far East. She tried to keep up her spirits, listening
optimistically to the news each morning at 8 a.m. but finding she
was 'plagued with a gentle melancholy' that came with the day's
end.

Monday 26 January – Aeroplanes were busy around here last
night from dusk till 2 a.m. at least, but after that I got to
sleep. Daily work filled this morning and at 12.30 p.m. I took
Twink in the fields. It was not a pleasant morning. The wind
was bitterly cold and I went out in Alan's leather helmet,
worn first by him as a little boy, with his green sledge
'Rocket' in the field at Stoneleigh (and what a dangerous
place for such a winter pastime – a steep slope with the deep
river at the bottom; it makes me shudder to think of it). Since
then it has been worn by a succession of girl-friends going
out with him in his open car. The old fur coat with the collar
up, gauntlet gloves and gumboots kept out the worst of the
wind, but even then I wept.

Twink made his first 'kill' today and didn't enjoy it. He
rooted a little mouse out of its nest in a tuft of grass and then
feebly bit it, distastefully giving it one nip and later another.
Poor little thing! I finally had to help in its dispatch.

Russia is still marching forward through the snow and
Germans are being killed in thousands.

Sunday 15 February – The fall of Singapore has been announced
and this – on top of the outcry in *The Times* yesterday and
the *Sunday Times* today on the matter of the German warships

slipping comparatively easily through the Channel – has made a black week. Everybody feels thoroughly down, but it is no use staying down.

Mr Churchill is criticized for keeping too much power in his own hands. Everyone feels what a marvellous leader he is, but many wonder whether he ought to do quite so much personally and feel he should depute some of his jobs to others. He spoke at 9 p.m. tonight, reviewed the situation calmly, remarked on the vote of confidence recently, and reminded us that a free Press, such as this country has, can be abused. He gave no promises for the future, only spoke of things as they were after Dunkirk and then last year. He felt there was something better now than then. We were then alone, and now have Russia, America and China with us – all powerful countries of unlimited resources. He spoke firmly, not minimizing our difficulties, prophesying more setbacks in the near future, but a hope of the tables being turned eventually. The papers have been very churned up, but Churchill was calm and sane in his words. He is undoubtedly the leader and a Prime Minister to be proud of.

VERA BRITTAIN

In October Vera and George moved to a flat in Richmond, an area they both loved. She was trying to make headway with her new book about pacifism, *Humiliation with Honour*, and was therefore reluctant to take on extra work. However, she was persuaded to join the PPU's new campaign for famine relief in Europe.

Cut off from the children, losing friends because of her views, threatened by the possibility of her Peace Letter being suppressed, at odds with some of the male leadership in the PPU and above all often alone in the flat as George's work took him out of town, this was a difficult time.

Sunday 4 January – Worked all day on 'H w H' after tidying up the flat. In afternoon walked over to Richmond cemetery – which was much nearer than I expected – to see Father's grave. It was quite tidy, but the inscription is getting rather moss-grown & the sun-dial wants cleaning. Must see to it.

Tuesday 6 January – Much upset by arrival of letter from Ruth [Colby], dated 16 August, enclosing clothes list for autumn for the children, and all too reminiscent silhouette drawings of their feet. Letter didn't even leave St Paul till 3 Dec. Wrote CORB asking to fix some method by which this censorship by delay could be avoided where children concerned. Could have howled with grief and exasperation.

Saturday 24 January – Jap. landings in New Guinea. Great agitation in Australia; demands for reinforcement and attack. How much of the British Empire will be left in six months?

Spoke at the London Group PPU food relief meeting at the Aeolian Hall. Felt as though I were climbing a steep hill. Thought the audience must be indifferent or hostile, yet at the end they proved to be solidly behind us and unanimously backed the sending of a telegram to the Govt.!

The excellent bulletin 'Famine' was on sale at the door & in the streets. After the meeting, Muriel Lester* spoke to me for a moment saying how glad she was that an effort was being made to rouse public opinion at last about the starving Belgians and Greeks.

Sunday 25 January – Walked with G. along towing path of river in both directions, but too cold for pleasure; bitter wind. G. showed me the lock across the river between Richmond and Kew bridges, & I suddenly realised to my great relief that

---

* Long-time Christian pacifist and activist, who, like Vera, was no longer free to travel abroad.

Father couldn't have drowned himself in Richmond since his body was found at Isleworth on the other side of this lock, in August when the river is low. I always wondered how he persuaded a taxi to take him the long drive to Richmond in the middle of the night, and I think now he must have gone to Hammersmith Bridge, where he used to go & look over. I feel so thankful to know that our theory held for 6½ years is wrong, and that this shadow is lifted for me from lovely Richmond.

Monday 9 February – Grimness of position at Singapore gradually becoming clear through the usual fog of censored news. Rationing of soap announced; buzz of talk among the women at the Ashburton indicated that it was more important to them than Singapore.

Tuesday 10 February – Singapore situation worsening. Work very difficult; 1940 tension back again. Criminal folly of those who started this war which we could have avoided becoming more and more self-evident. In this mood of waiting I cannot write at all.

Thursday 12 February – Work impossible today; news too grim. Singapore going, if not gone. Tension the same in my mind (though not apparently in that of most people here) as at the fall of France.

Kipling unknowingly prophesied this hour of our history when he wrote 'Recessional'. Everywhere voices asking more and more loudly: 'Will Australia go? Will New Zealand? Will Burma? Will India?' This evening G. returned from lunch* to say that within 6 weeks there will be a showdown, now preparing, in the H. of Commons, wh. will shake down the Government & perhaps Churchill himself.

---

* With Conservative MP Albert Braithwaite.

The anguish of Singapore, its soldiers and civilians (who were deceived about the situation by our censorship until it was too late for them to escape), has been with me all day like a palpable presence. It is an overwhelming and sobering experience to have been born at the end of the prosperous Victorian era, and live to witness, while still only middle-aged, the collapse of that civilisation – thanks to two great Wars & the interests which brought them about.

ANNE GARNETT

The autumn had seen Frank promoted to Home Guard Intelligence. Anne remained on the driving list for the Queen's Messenger Convoy delivering to bombed-out areas of Exeter and Plymouth and the mobile unit for Taunton. The WVS had been asked to prepare for at least 300 evacuees 'from possible blitzes being dumped on us at a moment's notice'. Members of the Polish Air Force had become regular drinkers at the pubs, their dogfights with the Luftwaffe clearly adding to their sex appeal. At the end of January Anne visited friends and family in London.

Monday 12 January – **With the mobile unit in Taunton** – From 1.30 a.m. we had a continuous rush and I moved in a daze of soldiers and Vikings [armoured vehicles]. One sailor thought I must be on duty every night, as he's seen me whenever he came! At 7 I got a cat-nap for 15 minutes, perched on a hard chair. A soldier said he thought they could sleep in odd positions but had never seen anyone asleep like that before!

A bitter night freezing hard and snowing up and down the line.

Home at last to fall asleep at the family breakfast table with my head in the butter-dish!

Wednesday 28 January – Only four in carriage – nice boy just discharged from army, has been in hospital ever since Dunkirk. Poor thin, pale face which broke into smiles at getting to London once again. London to me seemed strangely empty and silent ... I walked round a bit, hurrying past hideous ruins and yawning pits with averted face, they didn't seem decent somehow! It's rather like someone you know with beautiful teeth, and when you meet them they open their mouth and it's full of black gaps and ugly stumps.

Friday 30 January – Shuddered at the remains of John Lewis'. Those gorgeous fabrics, sodden among heaps of rubble and twisted girders – Ugh! The ruined bits of London make me feel quite sick.

Thursday 5 February – **Back home** – Snow-storms and a piercing wind. Did the usual jobs and then to WVS room. An unfortunate woman came in to show me a chilly note from the Army pay corps 'As your husband is absent without leave we regret we are unable to forward your allowance.' Col. Langford is trying to get help for her – I could only suggest a stiff letter to husband.

Mended socks solidly all evening, listening to wireless. A high-minded airman spoke about the noble deeds of heroes in the RAF. A pity we can't produce some of these lofty ideals and morals for peace-time instead of for carnage! These very heroes will probably be bloated stockbrokers or touting vacuum cleaners in a few years.

Sunday 8 February – After putting children to bed, getting supper etc. departed to Sanford where I met B., and having drunk whisky and ginger-ales we went into Taunton, calling at Bradford for Mrs L. on the way. Then began the familiar grind – endless throng of soldiers to be served, the heat and steam and smell of burnt toast and wet dirty tea-cloths and tobacco smoke. How one's feet ache and smart after a few hours there! Ten and a half hours is too long a shift we all feel. We had a rest of about an hour and a half when we got terribly sleepy, but from 3.40 onwards were busy till 7.30.

Came home terribly tired but fairly bright – my efforts at liveliness not appreciated by Frank at the breakfast table!

Monday 23 February – There is very little news in the paper now, save gloomy articles on the fall of Singapore and the bad way things are in out East. Today we hear the Japs have crossed the Bilin river in Burma and it looks as if Rangoon is doomed. It's all evacuated and made ready to be blown up.

O O Oh . . .

GEORGE BEARDMORE

The BBC sent a circular to staff asking about their qualifications. George sent a list of his published titles, but it led to nothing except the recommendation that he stay in his current post. 'Well, that settles it. I must leave this drudgery whatever the urgency, put the whole lot behind me and try to forget it.' He and Jean, still 70 miles apart, missed each other and missed London too.

Sunday 21 December – For the last four days I have been suffering from the foulest cough, bronchitis, and asthma I ever remember. When specks of blood began to appear I struggled to the medic's at Bromsgrove and he made me feel a lot better at once by saying that the lungs were unharmed. Being poorly in an official billet is just too difficult.

Wednesday 31 December – Took a week of my annual holiday to visit Harrow with Jean and the infant. (She, by the way, has got as far as getting her words wrong e.g. 'Sing Song Eightpence', 'Tell story little of nothing', and 'Tell story New Lamps of Old'.) Lunched at the Strand Brasserie, still amazed at how little London, or that quarter of it, has changed despite the bombings.

Thursday 29 January – Three weeks ago my pharynx seized up and brought on chest trouble and sleeplessness. I felt as though I would cry if spoken to, which is no condition in which to pursue a living. Eventually I had to ask for three days sick-leave, which was grudgingly allowed. Came to Newton by bike along ice-covered rutted roads.

Eventually, when recovered enough, I was sent by the local medic to University College London because he suspected that the heart might be a bit out of position due to much coughing. Glad to find myself interested in other people again. Four different wretches with the genuine stuff of life in them also waiting for verdicts.

Sunday 1 February – The X-ray revealed that all organs are sound. The lethargy is purely nervous, due to working eight hours a day or more in an army-hut at the far end of a frozen field, without benefit of family, change, or worthwhile conversation. The medic suggested that I change my job. So there it is, that's how it's going to happen.

Saturday 14 February – Still at the cottage, still without much energy, still surrounded by snow and ice. The doctor continues to give me weeks off because I look tired and still have poor nights because of nose and chest. Have ascertained at the local Labour Exchange that I am not bound forever to the Corporation, that I am still on a weekly notice basis, and that if I become unemployed I shan't instantly be pushed into a munitions factory.

Sunday 15 March – A week of bronchitis, waking up gasping in the small hours and relieved only by ephedrin and amytol, taking the hill [to his digs] in five stages and lying on my bed afterwards to recover – and all the time going to the office and nine hours of ledgers.

Came back about 26 February resolved to stay there no longer. Put up to it by Fletcher, the head called me in, in the first place I daresay to tick me off for my absences but in the end giving me leave to go. I don't know – men like him are no doubt shaping the world we live in but he doesn't know much about people – he alleged for instance that as a writer I must think engineers an inferior breed, and did I not think radio engineering was an art. O God. The whole conversation made unreal by the squeaky voice left me by the pharynx. So that's it, then – when I remember walking round Newton Longville one frosty night praying and praying to be taken out of the present impossible situation, I can't help but believe that God intervened to help me. I must, however, stay on until the end of April.

NAOMI MITCHISON

As America entered the war, Naomi continued to try to make Carradale a haven. She felt a growing closeness with the local people, especially the fishermen, and when family and friends came to stay for a traditional Christmas and new year, the locals were included in the celebrations. In February she went south to Cambridge to visit Murdoch, her eldest. He had been offered a Carnegie scholarship but had refused it 'partly because he feels he oughtn't to be out of the country or to shirk joining up. I think he's quite right yet Dick and I were both sorely tempted to say what a good idea it was.' While in Cambridge she met many young people in her son's rooms, 'mostly going, both boys and girls, to war jobs this summer'. 'It was all so hellishly like last time.'

She found everyone 'on edge with the news' of the war, and faith slipping in Churchill – there was a rumour he would resign. The bitter winter continued as she returned to Scotland.

Wednesday 21 January – It's not because I want to own them or to get anything out of them or to exploit them or their families in any way; I just simply like them; I like their shapes, I like their eyes, their smiles, the way they have of speaking or laughing; I want, as it were, not just a slip, not a tease, but the whole thing. Yet I know that if I were to take it, it would be misinterpreted, probably by them, certainly by anyone connected with them. I don't suppose they would go as far as to think out the implications of their condemnation, they wouldn't say to themselves, we condemn her because she is taking something that belongs to someone else; they would just condemn me plain, say I was a whore and leave it at that. And because I am doing work here, trying to give people other ideas of human relationships, starting with the simplest form of it, my own relations, first towards my family, then towards my friends, I mustn't jeopardise that. If they do condemn me in one thing they will condemn me in everything. And I couldn't blame them considering their historical conditioning and this god-awful church that thinks of sex as sin.

It's much more important that I should be able to change people's minds about one another in this other way, to try to show them non-possessive, generous human relations in other ways. If I can do that, the other thing will follow in time, a hundred years say.

Well let's hope nobody reads this who won't try to understand it.

Wednesday 4 March – The Glasgow train, late and, as usual, dirty and over-crowded and stinking with cigarette smoke. No non-smoking carriages, of course, at least not thirds, and even so, people always smoke in them now if they feel like it. I suppose it's a necessary drug to most people.

Most of the passengers were soldiers, some reading 2d 'books' of a semi pornographic kind, again. One party with a nice, cheerful ATS girl with them. She seemed at first to be being rather uncomfortably much ragged by them, but I think it was really quite friendly, and they all liked it. The 1st class ladies waiting room at Dumfries largely pencilled with semi-obscene drawings and rhymes, with much use of the words fuck and tool. I wondered if they had been done by males or females.

Got to Glasgow in a mild blizzard. No taxis. Put luggage in a cloak room and ultimately got a car to take me to Anna's;* difficult to see the right stop but everyone very helpful. Anna's room beautifully warm, the snow dripped off my hair. We talked about friends and relations, her school work – she is now with the seniors, teaching maths. Very short of staff, and large classes, hampered also by having missed time earlier on. I gave her my bacon which she was delighted with, used my own butter. She says soap is difficult for anyone living alone; she used to wash out her stockings every day, so did most of the girls. Meant one could do with fewer. She's had gastric flu and only half a pint of milk in two days.

Thursday 5 March – By myself to the Cosmo; a lovely, and rather moving, early Russian film, *Shchors*, so much better than the present ones! Also *March of Time*, a good *Silly Sym-*

---

* Anna Simpson, a teacher who had been been evacuated to Carradale in 1939 and with whom Naomi had become friendly. She was now living in Glasgow.

phony,* *Tale of Two Cities*, and *Song of the Clyde*, a really lovely documentary, only marred by an English commentator; a lot of photos of Glasgow, everyone talked and laughed and pointed things out – the attraction of the familiar! I started clapping afterwards, and lots joined in.

Back – very slippery – to Anna's, ate toast and tea, and talked again. She's been working hard at the station canteen. During the holidays drives taxis and lorries for the family business – the remaining brother will probably be called up. We talk little of the news but feel rather gloomy. I have one of my more unpleasant defeatist dreams in which more and more countries come in against us.

THE FALL OF SINGAPORE

Between 1923 and 1939 the British government had poured resources into making Singapore impregnable. Churchill called it the 'Gibraltar of the East', and the island was a vital military base against Japan's increasingly aggressive expansionism. But no one anticipated that a threat to Singapore would materialize at the same time as a major war in Europe; nor that an attack would come from the land rather than the sea. The Japanese army's thrust down the Malay Peninsula was swift and brutal and Singapore fell with shocking speed.

* *March of Time* was a newsreel, and *Silly Symphony* a Disney animation. *Tale of Two Cities* starred Ronald Colman.

THOMAS KITCHING*

Tom Kitching was chief surveyor of Singapore and had spent twenty-five years in the Malayan Survey Department. On his last home leave in the spring of 1940, with his wife Nora and young son Brian, Tom had been given the option of remaining in England or returning to their spacious bungalow at 24 Mount Rosie Road. Tom and Nora had not only chosen to return to Singapore but had taken their 17-year-old daughter Joan, who had just finished at boarding school, back with them. Their eldest, Colin, was at Oxford, where he remained, though he had plans to join the navy.

The attack on Pearl Harbor on 7 December altered life beyond recognition. Nora and Joan were working long hours at the hospital while Tom dealt with increasing numbers of refugees. But it wasn't until 31 December that Tom and Nora took the painful decision to send 9-year-old Brian to the safety of a family in South Africa. By mid-January 1942 Tom, who was in charge of the Fullerton Building, which housed his offices, had instigated the digging of a well to secure a water supply in the event that supplies were interrupted by bombing.

Sunday 18 January – The Japs have crossed the River Muar at Muar. However, we now have some Hurricanes and they are much better than the Buffalo. The Naval Base was bombed this morning and petrol tanks were fired.

Our cook says the police are pinching all the bikes. We ring the police and this is true – the military have requisitioned 5,000 and they just seize any in good condition, unless the rider can produce evidence he is in essential service e.g. ARP. So our cunning cook deflates his tyres.

---

* Brian Kitching (ed.), *Life and Death in Changi: The War and Internment Diary of Thomas Kitching – The diary of Tom Kitching who died in Japanese hands in Singapore in 1944*, William Culross & Son Ltd, 1998.

Wednesday 21 January – What a day!

We were about to leave when the alert went and continued with a very brief intermission until 11.30 am. Bombs fell very near the Fullerton Building – one in mud, 50 yards from Anderson Bridge, and the remarkable thing is that the mud came right over the roof – say 150 feet high – and bespattered walls; bomb-splinters made holes in the walls.

Nora and Joan were at the hospital from 2 to 9 pm. There was a lot of work to do – there were many casualties coming in – ghastly.

The Japs dropped 128 bombs today.

Thursday 22 January – There was roof spotting for me – there were two alerts. In the second, I spotted about 27 Japs coming straight at us and I sounded the klaxon. They got the airport to some extent and dropped some near us.

Tuesday 27 January – Joan [friend] is very insistent that I should remove Joan [daughter] – and Nora too, if possible. I don't know what to say. They are both doing very useful work in the hospital. No – when I think and think, I cannot see the fairness of doing yet another bolt when you are trained for the very emergency which has arisen.

Thursday 29 January – The power station was hit and there was no electricity. The police have been disbanded and the military taken over.

I book Nora and Joan in a troopship to the UK.

Friday 30 January – Nora won't go. She refuses. Cancel her passage.

At 1.30 p.m. we arrive at the docks [taking Joan]. A direct hit on something has started a large fire; our normal route to the ship (the *Empress of Japan* – ha! ha!) is out of action. We have to cross 200 yards of sea in a tender; this is an appalling scrum of men, women, children and luggage – and no porters.

Joan is very brave about it; she doesn't really want to go.

There is an alert about 10 p.m. I see nothing. I slept having had only two hours sleep last night. The afternoon weather was grand for Joan's ship getting away – rain!

Sunday 1 February – The Battle of Singapore begins. There is a lovely sunset through light rain. I take several photos on spec.

I got Nora's passport made valid for a journey anywhere outside British Malaya. Then I ruthlessly sorted out books etc. and got everything in the way of personal records into one suitcase, which I hope to get away, if it comes to it.

I had dinner early, then had a marvellously quiet night with a full moon.

Thursday 5 February – There is an alert at 5 a.m., but nothing near us. The war has some curious effects. In the morning now, I look at the sky; if it is brazen, I think, 'Ha! We'll be able easily to spot the little yellow devils this morning!' If cloudy, 'Hmm – going to be difficult today.'

M came in with a very urgent message from the Military Police Bureau: all European able-bodied men are to help immediately in the demolition at the Naval Base – to ensure denial of materials to the enemy. Does this mean we expect the enemy to gain a foothold on the Naval Base?

Friday 6 February – The Royal Singapore Golf Club is occupied by hundreds of Bali cattle. The RAF has nearly all gone; the Navy occupies the Club House, but I still get a demand for a $8.80 subscription. Why?

Saturday 7 February – When I get home I find a new menace has arisen – artillery fire from the mainland. Conolly says the shells went whistling over the house. He had four officers in and they finished his beer!

Monday 9 February – I held a meeting in my office about the destruction of maps, machinery etc. if necessary. Jap landings between South Kranji and Pasu Laba on the west coast in the dark hours of last night are confirmed. I have tea with Lieutenant Paterson from Fort Canning. He says there is a chance we can hold the Island. I hope he is right – I don't see it; we haven't the air support.

Wednesday 11 February – The Japs seem to be approaching from the North West.

There are troops everywhere in town; it seems peculiar there should be so many apparently doing nix.

All transmitters of the Malaya Broadcasting Corporation were destroyed this morning. Now our only means of communication with the outside world is a secret military transmitter, which connects the GHQ, London. The Government is still buying cars!

Thursday 12 February – My Chinese chief clerk asks, 'Cannot I get away?' He thinks I ought to; for the first time, he fears the worst. 'The Singapore Free Press' is a sheet 11 by 8 inches. It says the enemy has been held at all points! And it contains an announcement by the Government – all spirits in anybody's possession are to be destroyed by noon tomorrow!

Yesterday, also, the Japs invited us by polite letter to a parley – it was no use carrying this on any longer. We are to send a car with a special flag along Bukit Timah Rd. We refuse.

I had a final stengah [whisky and soda with crushed ice] in the Swimming Club. They have 200 cases of whisky, to be destroyed at noon tomorrow – stupidity.

Friday 13 February – Nora rang at midday; she has received her order to go. So I went to the hospital at 1 pm and took her to the docks at 3.15 pm. What a mob! I tried to get my suitcase with the records away, too; Nora took it. I hung about in case of any hitch, then there was one hell of a raid and a rain of bombs fell very near her ship. I managed to get let into the docks – very difficult! I found to my horror there was a walk of about a mile. Poor Nora. Had I known, I'd never have inflicted the case on her. I walked to the quayside, passing blazing cars and lorries all the way and a corpse and several wounded. I arrived. Nora is away on her tender and her ship, I am told, is one of the China river steamers. I stood on top of a saloon car – goodbye to the last survey wife! There are crowds of men waiting to go, so I look round to see if Nora's luggage is away – and find my suitcase! So I brought it back – alas!

Saturday 14 February – We must watch the water now – there must be corpses in McRitchie Reservoir. The big bar-room at the Swimming Club is being converted into a hospital.

At 3 pm I hear the Japs have broken through and we are counter-attacking. There is no water – have the Japs got McRitchie Reservoir?

At 9 pm I made coffee for six on my stove and they pronounced it very good, which will tickle Nora if I ever see her again.

Sunday 15 February – Our troops are all over the place, loafing, lounging – a dreadful sight.

If the Japs have the water – and I think they have – the City must be finished. Why didn't I go on Nora's boat?

Unknown to Tom, Nora's boat, the naval auxiliary *Kuala*, had taken a direct hit a short distance out of the harbour. The bomb had dropped through the engine room sinking the boat. Survivors were machine-gunned in the water, and rescue craft were also bombed.

Monday 16 February – An officer, don't know his name, rings from my office to Fort Canning: All was over at 8.30 last night. I don't know the terms, he says it's 'unconditional surrender'. The present orders are to 'stay put'.

A Chinese came in, expressed sorrow and asked for a souvenir! I gave him a napkin ring.

Tom and other civilians were ordered to go to the Singapore Cricket Club for 10.30 the next day.

Tuesday 17 February – There are hundreds of people, but not as many as I expected. We had a long, hot wait and were grouped in nationalities – British, New Zealand, South African, Australians etc. why I don't know. The Japs will observe international law as regards internees.

We are to go near the Sea View Hotel and wait. We are to walk. We are to take our own food. This is bad. Most of us have none.

We sleep; it is very hard, very hot and the mosquitoes never stop biting – and we are hungry! There is nothing to eat all day. And then lukewarm water is not thirst quenching. My final reflection is that Brian would like pancakes today; so would I! It is Shrove Tuesday.

Tom died on 14 April 1944 in Changi Prison from cancer of the oesophagus. His diary, on tiny scraps of paper, was smuggled out by a fellow inmate.

6. SETBACKS AND SAVAGERY

SUMMER 1942

The war on the Eastern Front ground on with massive attrition on both sides. Despite steady advances German casualties averaged 60,000 per month; Russian losses were even greater. While Hitler planned a huge summer offensive, Stalin agitated constantly for the Allies to establish a second front in Europe to draw German divisions away from the east.

Reports from the Atlantic were, of necessity, scarce. Convoys were increasingly important but advertising their existence carried obvious risks. Even when merchant ships reached their destinations with relatively few losses, announcing this would enable the Germans to calculate departure dates. For those with relatives at sea this lack of hard information created huge anxiety.

In the Pacific, although the United States continued to accelerate mobilization and arms production, Japanese troops occupied more and more islands. Eventually, General Mac-Arthur was ordered by Roosevelt to abandon his defence of the Philippines and relocate to Australia. He did so reluctantly, promising to return.

On the night of 30 May 1942 the new head of RAF Bomber Command, Air Chief Marshal Sir Arthur Harris, mounted the first thousand-bomber raid on Germany, targeting Cologne to prove his theory that a sustained campaign of mass bombing would help win the war by terrifying the German population into surrender. From his point of view the raid on Cologne was an unqualified success. Bomber Command's strategy was judged effective and more planes were ordered. Twenty years later, when official historians sought to publish their account of the air offensive on Germany, they were requested to deny that a policy of area bombing had ever been adopted.

On 26 May the war in the Western Desert took an unexpected turn. Rommel launched a new offensive: using Italian divisions as diversions, the Afrika Korps swept south-east and then north to Tobruk. The British were caught off guard and on 21 June the port finally fell into German hands. The news reached Churchill in Washington. 'Defeat is one thing; disgrace is another' was his chastened reaction. President Roosevelt immediately promised tanks, guns and planes and Churchill flew back to Britain to face a Commons motion of confidence on the conduct of the war. He won the vote easily, but with the war now almost three years old, what he really needed was a military success. What happened next, however, although not quite a victory, was a welcome relief.

The British had withdrawn to a forty-mile-long front stretching from a small railway halt in the north at El Alamein to the Qattara Depression in the south. For the first time in North Africa the line was anchored at each end and could not be turned. Rommel was confident he could break through to Cairo, but everywhere he tried he met fierce rebuffs from British, New Zealand, Australian or South African units. He and his troops were physically exhausted, ammunition and fuel were all running low, and his supply lines were stretched to breaking. Rommel had overreached himself.

In July an American delegation arrived in London seeking to persuade the British that a cross-Channel operation involving US troops was still possible in 1942. In the event an Allied invasion of French North Africa was agreed upon. Churchill wanted to tell Stalin personally about this development, and decided to visit Moscow, travelling via Cairo. Accompanied by Alan Brooke he embarked on a tour of 8th Army units. As a result General Auchinleck was replaced by General Alexander and General Ritchie by Lieutenant General Montgomery, a leader with the operational panache to match that of Rommel.

There were now 200,000 Canadian troops in Britain. On 19 August 5,000 of them were involved in an exercise that proved to everyone that this was not the year to launch a cross-Channel invasion. Almost 3,500 were killed, captured or wounded in a failed raid on Dieppe. It would take two more years to turn the lessons of this failure into a recipe for success.

THE DIARISTS

HAROLD NICOLSON

In addition to his work as an MP and BBC governor, Harold was working on the second volume of his family history. He took his turn at fire-watching in the Houses of Parliament and was one of the MPs who took up the invitation to contribute to the war effort by working in a munitions factory. He was still a supporter of Churchill, remembering 'what Winston did in 1939 and 1940', but he was well aware of the slump in the prime minister's popularity. In April he wrote in his diary, 'How foul is public life and popular ingratitude.'

Thursday 11 June – BBC Board. We discuss whether the clergy should use the microphone to preach forgiveness of our enemies. I say I prefer that to the clergy who seek to pretend that the bombing of Cologne was a Christian act. I wish the clergy would keep their mouths shut about the war. It is none of their business.

Monday 22 June – Another lovely day, and I bathe before breakfast. I have not slept well, as I kept on waking up with the word 'Tobruk' echoing in my ears, and rolling from side to side with gigantic apprehensions. I do most of Chapter IV, but I am a little discouraged by the book.

I weed the lime-border, and after dinner, under a sickle moon (which hangs over Tobruk), Viti and I slash weeds by the lake. Great thistles fall to our slashing.

The *Chicago Sun* rings up to ask me whether I think the fall of Tobruk will lead to a major political crisis. I think it may, but I do not say so. If there were any alternative to Winston, he might be severely shaken by this event.

Wednesday 24 June – I go to Vincent Square and do munitions work. I am put in overalls, set to a bench and stand for three hours filing a thing into another thing.

Wednesday 1 July – To the House for the first day of the debate on the Vote of Censure. Wardlaw-Milne* is an impos-ing man with a calm manner which gives the impression of solidity. He is in fact rather an ass, and the position he has acquired as one of the leaders of the back-benches has caused his head to swell badly. He begins well enough but then suddenly suggests that the Duke of Gloucester[†] should be made Commander-in-Chief. A wave of panic-embarrassment passes over the House. For a full minute the buzz goes round, 'But the man must be an ass.' Milne pulls himself

---

* The Conservative MP who tabled the motion of no confidence.
† Brother of the King.

together and recaptures the attention of the House, but his idiotic suggestion has shaken the validity of his position and his influence is shattered.

Roger Keyes seconds. He is a very dull speaker, and most people troop out to lunch.

Thursday 2 July – The second day of the Vote of Censure Debate. Winston sits there with a look of sullen foreboding, his face from time to time flickering into a smile. He rises stockily, his hands in his trouser pockets. He makes a long statement which really amounts to the fact that we had more men and more tanks and more guns than Rommel, and that he cannot understand why we were so badly beaten. He gives no indication of how the battle of Egypt is likely to go. In the end, after one hour and thirty minutes, he is quite fresh and gay. He gets his vote of confidence by 472 to 25, plus a great ovation afterwards. But the impression left is one of dissatisfaction and anxiety, and I do not think it will end there. The only thing he could do is to bring back Wavell as CIGS. I feel deeply sorry for him. Every weapon he uses smashes in his hands.

Wednesday 8 July – I go to my munitions factory. I am worse than ever. I file a thing too short and another thing too long. My belt jumps off the other thing five times. I have discovered a trick by which I can adjust my belt and avoid the incessant kindly reproach of my instructor. But I go away at 9 covered in oil and frustration.

Thursday 30 July – Dine with Sibyl.* Go away early and firewatch. There are two alerts during the night, and I dress and patrol with my little torch. In and out of the Prince's Chamber and the Royal Gallery I go, and into the dark House

---

* Lady Colefax, an old friend.

of Lords. I am tired and sit on the Woolsack with my tin hat on and my torch giving the sole illumination while the guns thunder outside.

HERMIONE RANFURLY

A letter from Dan dated 3 October and sent from Campo Concentramento, PC No. 12, PM 3200, had arrived in January: 'imagine an old castle restored in the worst Victorian style, grey and featureless with enormous battlements and a tower in one corner ... General Neame does needlework most of the time; General Gambier-Parry plays poker extraordinarily badly and we all win his money ...' In a second letter, written in the spring and taking only five weeks to arrive, Dan wrote, 'It made us laugh that you sent General Carton [de Wiart] a parcel because he gets twice as many parcels as anyone else. I am endlessly amused by him. He is a really nice person – superbly outspoken. He reads a lot and so will enjoy your books.'

Monday 22 June – **Jerusalem** – The Germans have taken Tobruk. No news has shocked us more since Dunkirk. The retreat must be worse than last time. Tragic that Churchill could not understand Wavell and moved him. Now our leadership is not so inspired. At present, we have superb troops but no great leader.

Friday 26 June – Wounded are pouring into Palestine because the hospitals in Egypt are overflowing. Each day between one and five I go down to a hospital in Jerusalem to help washing soldiers, making beds and emptying things. Today I washed four heads which were full of sand. I am learning a lot about pain and courage and getting used to smells and sights. The soldiers make fun of everything, and, even in the long ward where the serious cases are, no one ever grumbles.

I cannot describe the courage of these men. Only when they ask me to help them to write home do I glimpse their real misery: some of them are so afraid their families will not want them back now they are changed. They call me 'Sugar'.

Tuesday 30 June – We can no longer hide our anxiety. Down in the Desert the battle, now only about four hundred miles away, has reached a terrible intensity. Reuter reports: 'The noise and heat are terrific – it cannot go on much longer . . .'

Last night I dined with Pat Hore-Ruthven. He left for the Desert this morning. We sat under a full moon, which must be very unpopular in the Desert. Pat was pleased and excited to be going to do some fighting and my heart felt like a gallstone as he chattered about the battle and joked about saying 'shalom', the Jewish greeting, in Germany if he were taken prisoner. He gave me messages to send to Pam and his mother, and spoke of his little son Grey.

It is always the same. These young men come on leave or courses to Cairo or Palestine, or for a while they are on the staff. They take you out to dinner and talk of their families and what they are going to do after the war; they laugh and wisecrack and spend all their money in the short time they can be sure they are alive. Then they go down to the Desert leaving their letters, photographs and presents to be posted home. So often they never come back. When people write from England saying, 'You must be having a whale of a time in the Middle East,' I have not the heart to reply that so many parties are farewell parties in the truest sense of the word.

Saturday 4 July – The Germans are only seventy-five miles from Alexandria. Rommel has made himself very vulnerable; his supply line is stretched taut like elastic; if only we could cut it.

I have told my family to keep sending good news of me

to Dan even if things get worse. Poor Dan, it must be hell
reading Italian newspapers.

Sunday 12 July – Robin Stuart French* has arrived recently
from England. He came on the *Queen Mary* via the Cape in
twenty-eight days which is probably a record. There were
ten thousand troops on board. In spite of the cramped
accommodation, the terrific heat and their unattractive destination, Robin says none of the soldiers grumbled. Cairo,
which is now so near the front line, is still fairly serene.
The British Embassy and GHQ have been burning official
documents.

While we were talking several people joined us and soon
an argument began as to whether we can hold the Germans
in Egypt and what will happen if we don't. There was talk of
evacuation which I still find rather a sore subject. 'Lord Byron
said women and cows should never run,' I said.

A little man who was standing nearby turned round – he
had a red, rather belligerent face: 'And what use would you
be?' he asked.

Robin came to my rescue: 'She would fight with the rest
of us,' he said. 'Can you shoot?' the stranger asked me.

I shook my head – I was beginning to feel foolish.

Red Face glared: 'Well,' he said, 'I like that bit about Lord
Byron. I'll teach you to shoot. Be at the police station on the
Jaffa Road at six tomorrow.' He stumped off before I could
ask his name.

Monday 13 July – This evening I went straight from the hospital
to the police station on the Jaffa Road. Red Face was waiting
for me in a bare Arab room. I asked his name. 'Call me Abercrombie,' he said, 'it's as good as any other. Now, sit down,'
he continued, 'I shall tell you all I know. I was taught in

---

* Work colleague from early Cairo days and officer in the 11th Hussars.

America by "G" men and I am a bloody fine shot. Make the gun part of your arm. You must get so accustomed to it that when you point at anything you damn well hit it. What do you do when you eat? You put your fork in your mouth, not in your cheek. See? When you wipe your nose, you find it first shot.'

Monday 20 July – Today I had my last lesson with 'Abercrombie'. I shot with his Smith and Wesson, a Browning, a Mauser pistol and a tommy gun at dummies, playing-cards and oranges on trees. At last he said, 'You'll do. If the Germans break through at Alamein I reckon you'll make your contribution, you and Lord Byron.'

CHARLES RITCHIE

Ritchie was working on the application of the Atlantic Charter, 'the treatment of Germany after the war, etc.'. Daily, he vacillated between desiring to see the 'Old England of Tradition' pulled down and fearing the consequences if this really were to become 'the century of the common man'. Similar contradictions governed his love life. Although he was besotted with Elizabeth Bowen – 'this attachment is nothing transient but will bind me as long as I live' – he kept an eye out for other lovers, combing hair over the bald spot beginning on the back of his head as if he were 'adjusting a wig which the wind might blow out of place'.

Friday 5 June – Some slightly drunk and defiantly cheerful American soldiers were piling into a taxi tonight in Berkeley Square shouting and in general throwing their weight about. Surprised looks on the faces of two elderly English gentlemen of military bearing who were waiting to cross the square – an 'old-fashioned look' – contempt concealed beneath policy.

Monday 10 August – Although there are no indications that we are winning the war, I feel that the Germans are committing suicide, that even if they won they would be incapable of profiting by their victory. They have not got what it takes to organize Europe and rule it as the British ruled India. The rebound from their tensed up national effort must be towards materialism, individualism. The dream of the masses everywhere is comfort – the American standard of living. It will be the same for the Germans. Once out of the iron circle of fear, hate, slaughter, and revenge they will turn passionately to materialism.

Dined at the St. James's Club among the remnants of the Diplomatic Corps. Outside the narrow windows a November-like gale tossed the trees in Green Park. From the walls the blank frames stared eyeless forth. The Club sent its pictures into retirement in the days of the Blitz. They have moved their funniest marble nymph from the foot of the stairs to the lavatory.

Tuesday 11 August – The waiter in these flats is trying to get me to give him one of my suits. He talks to me as though the revolution had already come. If it ever does, God defend me from the city hotel servants, and all the hangers-on of the rich, spoiled and eaten up with envy, full of dirty tricks and cruelty to each other. Gorky in one of his books suggests that the revolution should protect itself by bumping off such people.

Reading Rebecca West's book about Yugoslavia.* What the Croats felt about the Serbs is (I hope in a minor degree) what the French-Canadians feel about us. What the top-dogs cannot imagine or understand is the degree of resentment which the under-dogs feel. Because we know ourselves as Anglo-Canadians to be fairly mild and good-natured we feel

---

* *Black Lamb and Grey Falcon*, which had just been published.

injured that we can be so hardly thought of, but it is not only cruelty that people resent, it is unconsciousness, lack of insight, the bland shrug of incomprehension. The British are paying for this attitude now all over the world.

ALAN BROOKE

When Brooke met his American counterpart George Marshall in April, he discovered that Marshall frequently did not see Roosevelt for a month or more, whereas 'I was fortunate if I did not see Winston for 6 hours.' The prime minister and his chief of staff saw even more of each other over the summer as they travelled to Washington (where the 'staggering blow' of Tobruk reached them), Cairo, Tehran and Moscow. Both were critical of Auchinleck's performance in North Africa. Brooke tried to protect him from Churchill's impatience, which he felt could easily undermine the command and worsen the situation. It was crucial to Brooke's long-term strategy of delaying a second front in France that North Africa should first be cleared of Germans so that the Allies could advance into Italy.

Travelling separately, Brooke and Churchill arrived in Cairo to assess the situation on 3 August. They were joined by Jan Smuts, the prime minister of South Africa, a man Brooke greatly admired.

Wednesday 8 July – At 12.30 Cabinet meeting at 10 Downing Street at which PM ran down M[iddle] E[ast] army in shocking way and criticized Auchinleck for not showing a more offensive spirit. I had an uphill task defending him and pointing out the difficulties of his present position. Also the fact that any rash move on his part at present would very quickly lose us Egypt. However PM was in one of his unpleasant moods going back over old ground and asking where the 750,000 men in the ME were, what were they doing, and why were they not fighting. After being thoroughly unpleasant during the Cabinet meeting, with that astounding charm of his he came up to me afterwards and said to me 'I am sorry Brookie if I had to be unpleasant about Auchinleck and the Middle East!' Then you came to lunch, and I forgot about all my worries.

Thursday 6 August – One of the most difficult days of my life, with momentous decisions to take as far as my own future and that of the war was concerned.

Whilst I was dressing and practically naked, the PM suddenly burst into my room. Very elated and informed me that his thoughts were taking shape and that he would soon commit himself to paper! I rather shuddered and wondered what he was up to! Ten minutes later he burst into my room again and invited me to breakfast with him. However, as I was in the middle of my breakfast by then he asked me to come as soon as I had finished. When I went round he made me sit on the sofa whilst he walked up and down. First of all he said he had decided to split the ME Command in two. A Near East taking up to the canal, and a Middle East taking Syria, Palestine, Persia and Iraq. I argued with him that the Canal was an impossible boundary as both Palestine and Syria are based administratively on Egypt. He partially agreed, and then went on to say that he intended to remove the Auk to the Persia–Iraq Command as he had lost confidence in him. And he wanted me to take over the Near East Command with Montgomery as my 8th Army Commander! This made my heart race very fast!! He said he did not require an answer at once, and that I could think it over if I wanted. However I told him without waiting that I was quite certain that it would be a wrong move. I knew nothing about desert warfare, and could never have time to grip hold of the show to my satisfaction before the necessity to attack became imperative.

Another point which I did not mention was that after

working with the PM for close on 9 months I do feel at last that I can exercise a limited amount of control on some of his activities and that at last he is beginning to take my advice. I feel therefore that, tempting as the offer is, by accepting it I should definitely be taking a course which would on the whole help the war the least. Finally I could not bear the thought that Auchinleck might think that I had come out here on purpose to work myself into his shoes! PM was not pleased with this reply but accepted it well.

After lunch Smuts asked if he could see me for a bit, and we retired to a quiet room. He then started on the same story as the PM in the morning. Telling me what importance he attached to my taking it, and what a wonderful future it would have for me if I succeeded in defeating Rommel. I repeated exactly what I had said to PM. Thanked him for his kindness and told him that he did not really know me well enough to be so assured I should make a success of it. However, he replied that he knew I had taken a leading part in saving the BEF in France. At last I got him to agree that Alexander was a better selection than me. I have been giving it a great deal of thought all day and am quite convinced that my decision was a right one, and that I can do more by remaining as CIGS.

Saturday 8 August – Auchinleck refuses new appointment and prefers retirement. He is I am sure wrong – the Iraq–Persian front is the one place where he might restore his reputation as active operations are more than probable. However, I am not certain that we are not better off without him.

Back to Embassy again to receive a long lecture from PM, with all his pet theories as to how essential it is for Alex to command both ME and 8th Army. I again had to give him a long lecture on the system of the chain of command in the Army! I fear that it did not sink much deeper than it has before!

On 13 August Brooke arrived in Moscow. The next two days were heavy going (not least because of the overly generous supply of food and vodka), and Brooke was sceptical that much good had been done, although as he wrote much later, it created 'the beginnings of a strange understanding between Winston and Stalin'.

Friday 14 August – By the end of dinner Stalin was quite lively, walking around the table to click glasses with various people he was proposing the health of. He is an outstanding man, that there is no doubt about, but not an attractive one. He has got an unpleasantly cold, crafty, dead face and whenever I look at him I can imagine him sending off people to their doom without ever turning a hair. On the other hand there is no doubt that he has a quick brain and a real grasp of the essentials of war.

Tuesday 18 August – **Back in Cairo** – Determined at last to have a good night's sleep. I slept soundly from midnight to 8.30 am. Whilst dressing the PM breezed in in his dressing gown and told me he had been thinking over the urgency of the attack against Rommel. He then started producing all the arguments that I have so frequently battled against for speeding up the date. I had to point out it was exactly 2 days!! ago that Alex had taken over and Monty arrived, and that there was a mess to put right, etc etc. I know that from now on I shall have a difficult time curbing his impatience.

Back to the Embassy to see Auchinleck after he had said goodbye to PM at 12 noon. Did not look forward to this interview, but he was in a much more pleasant mood and the interview went off well. We parted on friendly terms.

Churchill, Brooke and Alexander drive to 8th Army HQ four hours away in the desert.

Wednesday 19 August – There Monty gave us an excellent appreciation of the situation and what he proposed to do if Rommel attacked before he was ready and also his plans in the event of his starting the offensive. He is in tremendous form, delighted at being sent out here, and gave me a wonderful feeling of relief at having got him out here. We dined at their Mess and I slept in an ambulance converted into a caravan for Alex. Very comfortable, lovely night with the sound of the waves only a few yards away. On way to bed PM took me down to the beach, where he was transformed into a small boy wishing to dip his fingers into the sea! In the process he became very wet indeed!!

VERA BRITTAIN

Vera continued work on her book and, during the spring, spoke in support of famine relief, as well as giving other talks about her pacifist beliefs. These were given new urgency by the intensive bombing of German cities and the reprisal attacks on Bath and other historic towns. As the summer progressed, she became increasingly involved in the PPU's Food Relief Campaign, which pressed for the lifting of the blockade of supplies to occupied Europe, and their campaign to stop the RAF's bombing of Germany's civilian population.

Sunday 31 May – Got out *Humiliation with Honour* and spent wretched day over it. As I was arranging notes for Ch. 3, realised that the thing was dead, read like a tract, must be rewritten in accordance with some new technique that would make it live. Suddenly got inspiration of doing it as a series of letters to John [her son] – based on Ruth's information of his criticising and questioning my pacifist ideas while Shirley loyally champions them. Began drafting first short letter but felt tired, depressed & bad-tempered after wrestling with it all day.

Tuesday 2 June – News of huge raid on Cologne yesterday followed by news of another similar one last night on Essen & district. Churchill spoke in the House tonight – vulgarly jubilant as usual over the suffering caused to Germany. Why can't he at least be as dignified & regretful as Abraham Lincoln was over the South? At lunch-time people said to be leaving London area again for fear raids return.

Spent day re-writing Chap. 2. Beautiful warm day, magnificent evening, but felt too bitterly ashamed of our raids to feel anything but its incongruity. Ipswich raided last night.

Thursday 11 June – Letters from Shirley, one to me alone, one for G. and me jointly. Mine contained an excellent impressionistic sketch of a thunderstorm. She begs for a dog when she comes home. I had a letter from Ruth also, mainly to enclose a sketch for an oil painting which John had done called 'Arsenal of Democracy', some rough drawings of a girl he met at Stillwater [summer school], a word-impression of early morning in Chelsea, & a really brilliant study of his life at the Community Centre at Stillwater called 'The Hypocrites' (tho' Ruth says he enjoyed it all!). She herself comments on his brilliance, extravagance & egotism. He certainly isn't an easy boy to handle – never was in a way, yet always I have felt in tune with him, never irritated.

Vera discovered that it was possible to book the children a passage home from the USA, and that they might arrive before September. 'But G. was very damping when he came home, having as usual apprehensions about the general situation and wanting J. and S. to stay longer.' They agreed a compromise and 'booked them definitely for next May'.

Saturday 25 July – At Food Relief mass demonstration in Trafalgar Square – Donald Soper* wound up, proposing resolution. Carried nearly unanimously; only 3 voted against. Large crowd was very orderly; little heckling; police had nothing to do & looked v. good-tempered. Managed first speech all right but it was a bigger effort than Hyde Park (no microphone), & I was almost voiceless by the time I had to make a second speech on another side of the plinth. One is v. high above the audience & the buses are very near.

Vera sent the manuscript of *Humiliation with Honour* to her publisher Andrew Dakers.

Tuesday 4 August – Funny to finish such a book on the 28th anniversary of the First Great War.

Felt thankful & relieved to have finished this exacting little book.

Friday 7 August – Fire-watching 3 a.m.–6 a.m. Only got odd snatches of sleep before it as I was wakened first by a searchlight streaming into the room & later by distant guns. But no Alert went and I spent the watch writing to John & Shirley.

Got up to find several letters, among them one from Andrew Dakers, which said of 'H. w. H.': 'I started reading it after going through my mail this morning & everything had to wait until I had finished it. It is a shining thing in a dark world; better & lovelier than I had dared to expect. Your restraint gives it power . . . The book moved me deeply, & is the best statement of pacifism for non-pacifists that I have come across.' This at any rate is cheering.

Thursday 13 August – Alert at 3 a.m. Some gunfire; saw first searchlights & then guns firing across the river somewhere in

---

* A Methodist minister and leading pacifist.

the Ealing direction. Later papers reported 7 killed by a bomb somewhere in the London area. All clear about 3.30.

Caught up on correspondence during morning. G. went off after lunch. Felt much depressed at having to spend the night so often alone in this flat, be wakened by the Alerts & lie thinking about the children. But G. regards this as just tiresome & unreasonable on my part. But it is so long since I heard from them. Sometimes I can't believe that this endless period without them is not a dreadful nightmare, from which I <u>must</u> soon wake up.

From Winifred's death onwards they were all of my life that matters. If I could only see & talk to my darlings just for half an hour. How long – oh, how long?

Vera dedicated *Humiliation with Honour* to 'the victims of power'. She longed for her own children, and she longed for the much greater suffering of others to end too, including the starving:

Their numbers are so great, their family lives so tragic, and their sorrows so fathomless, that we who have implored our Government to show pity on them by lifting the blockade sufficiently to permit the passage of some limited supplies, can picture their catastrophe only if we 'break it up small' and see it in terms of some beloved child on the verge of starvation. What should I do if for months I had watched you and S. getting thinner, paler, darker under the eyes, more quietly apathetic, until at last I knew that I had only enough for one more meal left in the cupboard? That is how I try to look at it.

Today our conscience is stirred by the crimes of the Nazis, but not by the European sufferers from our own blockade. We do not rid ourselves of responsibility by saying that their plight is due solely to Germany. In the case of Greece and Belgium it cannot be, since before the War both these countries imported over 40 per cent of their food. If we could save the victims of famine, yet deliberately refrain from doing so, we are morally as responsible for their deaths as any Nazi conqueror.*

The book was published in October 1942, and the first edition of 6,000 had sold out by the end of the month. John did not read it. 'No doubt she realised,' he wrote in his autobiography, 'that the lessons of the book were quite beyond my experience.'

NAOMI MITCHISON

Most of Naomi's time was taken up by the farm, including the hands-on work of ploughing, sowing and fertilizing. Dick was home at Easter and for other occasional breaks from his busy legal practice and the manpower survey. In May she heard from Ruth, her daughter-in-law, that she was pregnant – news that she received with both pleasure and envy but also as 'one in the eye for Hitler'. Her second son, Murdoch, at Cambridge studying medicine, was expecting to be called up, and was thinking of joining the army.

Friday 29 May – Walked round with Dick in the afternoon. Felt ill and depressed, all the more so as I have to fill in three govt forms, one for petrol, one for ditto for the motor mower, one about the farm. No letters I want. Wish Murdoch weren't going into the army. Dick says it will be over next year; I say it will never be over. We've all got into the habit of it; that's the way total war is. And equally I feel ashamed not to be more in it, not to have been in London during the proper blitz. Wish they'd go for Edinburgh next

---

* Vera Brittain, *Humiliation with Honour*, reprinted in *One Voice*, Continuum, 2005.

week while I'm there. Though I would be awfully frightened.
Feel as if nothing I did was any good.

In Edinburgh, her home town, Naomi stayed with a cousin and
enjoyed the 'civilised' life. She then travelled north to stay with an
uncle and visited the chapel in Gleneagles where there was a
memorial stone to her parents – 'there would be just room for
me under my father'. She also arranged to borrow a tractor from
her uncle's farm.

Tuesday 2 June – **Edinburgh** – Had a wire from Murdoch
yesterday: Possibility of general war research job alternative
to army – intelligence required rather than scientific knowledge – civilian at home military abroad further details Sunday
what do you think. It seemed to be a good idea, and I also
rang up Dick; it might lead to something afterwards, is
anyhow likely to be much more interesting than plain army.
But of course one's thinking all the time about their safety.
Not that one can guarantee that. Either way. I think there
will be some definite military development, whether a second
front or something of the kind, within a few weeks, days
perhaps. If only this Libyan news was better. I think it's
pretty bad really.

Wednesday 8 July – Murdoch [home from Cambridge] and I
went over and got some paraffin to start the tractor; I wanted
to try her out with wrack.* The girls went down to the beach
to collect it. Lachie and Murdoch and I with some trouble
got the tractor started. I didn't want to take it on to the
beach but the others all thought it was firm enough, and
none of them could really manage the wheel-barrows up
from the sand. I took her down and at first it worked, then,

---

* Seaweed, used as fertilizer.

with a full load on the trailer, she stuck a few feet from the edge of the old track, and dug herself in. It was wretched, I do hate getting into a mess with a thing, we unhooked the trailer, but it made no difference. Finally and raging, I got all the men and we dug her out, and got her up, leaving the seaweed in a dump. I felt all the time that everyone would say this came of a woman driving, and I said to Angus and Lachie that they were not to say so, and indeed, I don't think they really think it, they are really pretty sympathetic; it was the hell of a job as the gears are very stiff, and one gets bumped on the rough ground. I was awfully tired in the evening, when a few turned up to dance.

Friday 31 July – A lovely day, with a mild breeze. We picked fruit in the morning, put up the rest of the hay in the afternoon; there is now just the stuff round the house. People just turning up for fruit all the time and all with some kind of special plea, children or invalids or something. Meanwhile I try and get on with the early local orders.

Murdoch back, and with a satisfactory interview, will probably go into Tank operational research. Probably getting a fortnight first. He has had his hair rather firmly cut, so as to give a better idea to the Board!

Sunday 2 August – I was very tired going to bed, had an awful dream that the Germans had invaded south England, were taking one town after another, Bath, Oxford, and the BBC making soothing noises, and now they were within a few miles of London (where I was in the dream) and I felt despairingly that we <u>must</u> stand, it mustn't be Paris over again, but if we did we'd all be killed.

ANNE GARNETT

As first Yeovil then Bath burned, Anne wrote, 'Hitler says these are reprisals. It would save a sight of bother if we stayed at home and bombed our own towns!' When Exeter was flattened on 6 May, she drove the WVS canteen to deliver beds, blankets, lavatories and food. The High Street was 'just a goat's track between shattered walls and heaps of debris, choking white dust under the hot sun'.

Anne had single-handedly taken on the Ministry of Health to prevent two families of evacuees, who had fallen outside the billeting scheme, from being returned to London. The result was a reputation for being 'aggressive' and a 'trouble-maker'. Nonetheless she would not ignore the needs of the men, women and children passing through the WVS office: the little Polish girl with a label 'This child has no family' or the sailor (one of seven out of seventy-five to survive the sinking of his ship) wanting a lift to collect his wife and new baby from hospital, to name just two.

Wednesday 3 June – I write this feeling sore and mentally lacerated in spite of the lovely June evening. This morning as I sat in WVS office, Howard Fox* came in and proceeded to give me a terrific rowing over my letter to the M. of Health! He wouldn't listen to what I had to say, but held forth about 'meddlesome interference' and was extremely unpleasant and rude. Then Loïs [fellow WVS worker] came in and he took a milder tone, and apologised before he left 'if he'd said too much'. I was furious, but forced myself to be polite and accept his apology, but he has left me very sore and angry! Does he think he is in Germany? I rushed on to do the lunchtime feeding of baby ducks etc. and Red Cross collecting and

---

* One of the owners of a worsted factory, Wellington's biggest source of employment.

home very late to pour it all out to Frank, who was speech-less with wrath, and having a slight attack of hypoglycaemia, rolled his eyes in a truly alarming manner!!

Wonderful warm June evening but I'm too sore to enjoy it. News of the 'Battle of the Gaps' in Libya pretty good – we sent another 600 planes over Essen last night, and left it in ruins.

Saturday 27 June – **On holiday in Bude, Cornwall** – The children rushed to the beach and Toots returned saying the 'ride' had come up so high as to almost drown her!

Late this evening watched convoy slowly struggling up Channel: barrage balloons abob above it, and the throb of its guardian planes. Counted 36 ships.

Monday 29 June – We went into the town after breakfast to try and find a bathing-cap for me and some surf-boards: no caps anywhere but a kind draper told me of a lady who had one – too small for her – for sale. So I unearthed her at her house, tried on and bought the cap with much gratitude. To what a pass has the loss of Malaya* brought us?

We managed to get one surf-board at the Council Offices and it depressed me beyond words to see all the files marked evacuation and the dreary tea-kettle on the gas-ring, all exactly the same as at the Council Offices at home.

We had tea on the beach, cowering behind rocks from the fog and then a lively bathe with surf-boards, two bor-rowed ones for the children which were a bit too big for them. Sarah quite got the knack of it and had some lovely rides right up the beach.

News tonight rather depressing, the Germans claim the fall of Marsa Matruh† and the BBC man announced suavely

---

* And its rubber plantations.
† Approximately 500 kilometres north-west of Cairo.

that there really isn't any suitable line of defence until you get to the Nile Delta. Sebastopol still holds out – amazing.

Monday 6 July – **Back home** – Oh the washing and the chores! It comes hard after doing nothing but enjoy myself for a week! As I shopped my fellow WVS greeted me on all sides with 'So glad you're back to carry on with the nettles,' and the clerk at the bank complained that no one had been to fetch his father-in-law's nettles and the old man was hopping mad. After tea went forth to grasp the nettle – disgusted to find that the dry ones have not yet been sent off, they told me for lack of sacks, but I found 4 sacks full of mouldy nettles at the foot of Molly's ladder. I had to empty them on her rubbish heap. Feel this deeply!

The following month an 'all-black' battalion of American troops arrived. 'All-black' meant African-American soldiers but white officers.

Saturday 8 August – On going to milk early yesterday I met a large Negro* standing forlornly in the road, directing traffic, and a party of black pioneers have arrived to dig a hole outside the Donovans. The camp is to be on the fields behind the Griffins – lovely meadow land producing tons of hay. I take this hard after an Agricultural broadcast yesterday urging us to use every inch of soil for food. With the heathery hill-tops so near it seems criminal.

Wednesday 12 August – Wellington a seething mass of darkies nowadays, followed by trails of children who can't leave them alone. Three hundred have now arrived and there's a

---

* The terms used here for African-Americans which are now considered offensive were in common usage and do not in themselves prove racial prejudice on the part of the user.

forest of tents in the field behind the Griffins – lovely for them as they're woken at 5 AM by terrific chatteration, laughter and blowing of whistles!

Babs and I went down to collect for St Dunstans at the local cinema. There was a short film about the blind, then the lights went on and in we went with our tins and the awful collector's smile pinned on our faces. £17 odd has been got in this way in 3 days. Niggers of course gave lavishly: their opinion of England 'a place where there's hardly any food and no money'.

In October Gertie caused a bit of a stir by inviting one of the soldiers to the house. He arrived with a bottle of beer and offered Anne some. Anne tried to dissuade Gertie from going out with him by saying, 'Nasty Incidents happen in the blackout,' then adding, 'Fathomed from G's face that any such incidents happened weeks ago.'

GEORGE BEARDMORE

George returned to London in April, but without a job. He sold his motorbike. He managed to find alternative accommodation for the tenants occupying his house in Harrow and spent the last weekend in May with Jean packing for their return home.

He secured some work with *Picture Post*, and went with their photographer Bert Hardy to report on Chinese seamen in Liverpool and then roadsweepers in Kent and a monastery near Hereford.

Sunday 7 June – Yesterday Jean and I and the infant visited 45 for the first time since it had been vacated and found its condition not so bad as we feared, but more shabby than we liked. We were working until 11 p.m. lugging the heavy furniture downstairs and sorting it out, from where it had been stored in the back bedroom; carpets beaten, table assembled, light pendants hung, and so on. I couldn't wait to get out into the garden so, as the growing season is now well advanced, I planted thirty runner beans, erected the poles for same, and dug over and fertilised the ground ready for planting tomatoes.

Jean said that it was her happiest day for years and, with recollection of those insufferable billets, I bet it was. She confessed that quite recently she had woken up with the cold horrors, imagining herself back at Mrs B.'s and shut in her rooms for the afternoon. Although by going into the country we were spared the latter end of the bombing and perhaps the nervous troubles her parents are suffering, we made a mutual promise not to leave our home again in any circumstances, unless forced out or bombed out. By God, no.

In the evening, although weary, she asked me what I should do for a living, whether I thought I could live by my pen, what hope there was of being able to put penury behind us. Didn't come to any firm conclusion (one seldom does, I notice) but it must have been three or four in the morning when we found ourselves wide awake, this problem still on our minds. I said words to the effect that, Look, penury or not, I have been given my freedom when old friends . . . are in uniform and separated from their wives and homes. Therefore it's up to me to find something worthwhile to do for the country rather than interview roadsweepers in Kent. For some reason I didn't confide to her my old haunting memory of the homeless in the Underground. Also a recollection came back of my seeing in Willesden mothers with their children milling round the entrance to a church, near which two clerks were seated on stools at trestle-tables interviewing them. Included in the picture were two small boys, one limping about on a crutch and the other bandaged round the head. Homeless, I was told – the bombed-out whom the Council is sorting out and trying to find shelter for; as for the church, it had been loaned to the Council and was being used as a Rest Centre. A sort of weary helplessness came over me as I lay there at Jean's side, wondering why the hell I couldn't be in there with them and help out?

Eventually we went downstairs and made tea. At four-thirty it was already light and I walked round my garden, mug in hand, thinking about nothing much. At least it was my own garden I was walking in.

In July George had the good news that his 'broadcasting book' had been sold on the strength of the four chapters he had so far written. It was a novel drawing upon his research into the history of radio. He also had an idea for a thriller set in a monastery (sparked off by his *Picture Post* assignment) but that would have to wait. There was less good news of Jean's parents, both of them in George's view 'invisible casualties' of the strain of the bombing.

Sunday 19 July – Jean's mother suffers from an extraordinary lassitude in addition to a greenish-brown tinge of skin. The medics suspect an infection (or possibly TB) of the endocrine glands. She is bent like an old, old woman. And when I remember what she was before the bombings! I hope Hitler's pleased.

CLARA MILBURN

Work in the garden intensified during the growing season, and was not made easier by news of Tobruk and other setbacks. Clara was appalled by reports of Nazi savagery, especially the reprisals in Czechoslovakia following the assassination of Heydrich, and welcomed the bombing raids on German cities. To Clara they were as necessary as her attacks on the pests in her garden.

Tuesday 21 July – A busy morning at home for me and Jack, setting out a trench on the small orchard patch to sow, well and hopefully, a last row of peas. Good luck to 'em! I bought my weekly groceries when I biked to the grocer's this afternoon and they came to 2s. 7½d.!!! Many things were not obtainable, and so one just had the weekly ration of butter, lard, margarine, cheese, bacon and sugar – 2s. 7½d. And on top of 2s. 7 ½d. I have ordered a present for Jack at 47s. 6d., but I'm not sure whether I can get it. That was the last price at which this particular commodity was offered, but now I do not know what price it will be! One might say 'What a thing to buy now.' Well, on the principle of buying a packet of white lint and bandages and then finding a use for them almost at once, I am hoping to buy a —— well, I think I'll leave a space.

Tuesday 28 July – This afternoon I sadly decided to take up all my beautiful bed of onions, badly attacked by the onion-fly grub. It was no use to leave them to be eaten off one by one, Hitler fashion, and I shall not grow them again. They were a back-aching job to plant out, and I have spent many hours on their culture – all for nothing. Most disappointing. In fact – and I might as well record it – I am at the moment fed-up with the garden. Every year we slave in it, take years off our life with overwork, and by July it is dried up through lack of rain.

This year it promised well, with good rains in the spring, and the pear tree border was nice and full, but now the plants are withering in the drought. Pests of all kinds are rife, but not only in this garden. I suppose one will get over it, but I wish there was a little less to do sometimes.

Fierce fighting goes on at Rostov* which the Germans claim to have taken. The slaughter is terrible.

---

*   A city north-east of Moscow.

On 3 August Clara gave Jack a Union Jack for his birthday – to be flown when the war was won.

Wednesday 12 August – An American professor visiting England is amazed at the health of the people after three years of war, and says the children are splendid. The health of the nation is better than before the war, says our Ministry of Health. There is no malnutrition. We shall probably have to tighten our belts a bit more this winter, but it is wonderful what has been done in the way of food-growing.

What the Germans are doing in the occupied countries, with the persecution, is frightful. Oh, the wickedness they perpetrate in exterminating people everywhere.

Wednesday 2 September – Gathered many pounds of apples from our Early Victorias in the orchard. I have already given many pounds away and sold many more for the Red Cross. We have had a fine lot this year.

The Russians have had a bad time lately and today we hear that Stalingrad, the city of which they are so proud, is in grave danger. The Germans also advance into the Caucasus. They seem to have endless tanks, aeroplanes and men, and yet they lose so many in the hard fighting in Russia that their strength and military might must surely be sapped. They are like a loathsome disease spreading and spreading over Europe.

GETTING NOWHERE FAST

AFRICA

The North African desert was the perfect arena for tank battles, although Rommel, for all his tactical brilliance, could do nothing without supplies. Without ammunition a machine gun is just a heavy lump of metal. Without fuel a tank is an even heavier one. With Hitler favouring the Russian Front over North Africa both in terms of strategy and of resources, Rommel found his progress repeatedly stymied and was forced to withdraw to resupply. This relieved the pressure on the Allies. However, the loss of Tobruk was a catastrophe for the British.

The diary of J. L. Dixon, an ordinary soldier with the British army inside Tobruk, reveals the frustration of ordinary soldiers with a high command that was unprepared and the agony and confusion of surrender itself.

J. L. DIXON
Gunner, 4th Durham Survey Regiment, Royal Artillery*

After the order to stand to at first light the sound of heavy firing was heard coming from the eastern sector. We all sensed that this was no ordinary probe by the enemy to test our defences, the firing was too prolonged and consistent.

As we watched all hell broke loose as the 'planes playing follow the leader took turns in diving on the almost defence-less town and docks. A huge black cloud rose into the air, the

---

* J. L. Dixon, private papers, Imperial War Museum, 87341.

result of a direct hit on one of the oil tanks and spread slowly over the town turning day into night.

The battle on the eastern sector raged unabated while the rest of the perimeter remained silent. There were no troop movements or reinforcements being drawn into the battle area, so we presumed that the enemy were either being contained or in the process of being repulsed.

About 10 a.m., a deathly silence descended upon Tobruk, the firing ceased and we began to wonder if our defences had held. Climbing out of the slit trenches, we gathered in small groups awaiting the outcome of the battle from battle HQ. None of our officers had the slightest idea of what was happening, they were just as much in the dark as we were.

The first signs of activity occurred when we saw one of our vehicles approaching carrying several high ranking officers. But what surprised us most was seeing a huge white flag being held aloft.

As the vehicle reached our positions, an officer jumped off and made his way to our command post, where our officers awaited with bated breath for the news. They stood talking earnestly for a while then the messenger returned to the waiting truck. Fall in was called and when we were all assembled, our ashen faced captain let it be known that Tobruk had surrendered. He had been instructed to inform us that the surrender terms included the handing over of all weapons and equipment plus all food stocks. We just couldn't believe our ears; it seemed unbelievable that such terms could be accepted by our general staff. But we were assured they were and had to be carried out to the letter, immediately.

The first reaction after the news had sunk in was a feeling of repulsion for the whole of the high command in the Middle East. It seemed we would get nowhere fast until the whole system of selecting our field commanders was changed and someone with fire in his belly introduced into the desert war. Our fate had been decided by someone totally out of touch with reality.

The least that we could do to make amends for the disgrace that we all felt was to see that nothing of value fell into the hands of our enemy. Setting to with gusto we destroyed everything in sight. Trucks, guns, small arms of every description, all available food supplies were sent up in flames. Even personal effects went the same way.

When the Germans were finally sighted, coming from the direction of the town, everyone stood up. Led by a column of Panzers, with foot soldiers following behind, they approached our positions. There they [the panzers] halted while the infantry continued until they stood before us. We were not unduly worried at meeting our enemy face to face, in fact it was an exciting experience. The ordinary soldier was quite friendly but their officers were cast in a different mould. With shouts of 'Raus' and 'Schweinhund' the officers ordered us to be searched for concealed arms while they berated our officers for allowing the destruction of the equipment.

After being searched for hidden weapons and in some cases watches and other valuables, we were told to assemble on the roadway and await further instructions. The strained atmosphere of just a short time before had now eased and in no time at all we were deep in conversation with our enemies. Cigarettes were exchanged and 'Jerry' cans of water were passed round. The Germans [regular soldiers] were very friendly and offered us their commiserations on being captured and tried to lessen our fears for the future behind barbed wire. While their officers still showed resentment over the wilful destruction of our equipment, the rank and file of the German army agreed with us that it was a soldier's duty to prevent anything of value from falling into the hands of the enemy.

INDIA

Having conquered Malaya and Burma, the Japanese were intent on India – after Britain the empire's greatest source of military manpower, manufactured goods and raw materials, and close to the oil fields of the Middle East. Japan aimed to take control assisted by a popular revolt against British rule. Since the Indian independence movement had been gathering strength following Gandhi's return to India just after the First World War, some sort of rebellion was by no means impossible.

Near Bombay 35-year-old Rations Corporal Clive Branson, who had seen active service in the Spanish Civil War as a member of the British Communist Party, was exasperated by the failure of his superiors to deal with this double threat. Forbidden to keep a diary, he expressed his frustrations in censored letters to his wife.

CLIVE BRANSON*

Thursday 11 June – **Gulunche, near Poona, India** – I had an amusing interview with an officer today. The conversation went as follows (much abbreviated):

He: Well, Branson, I want to thank you for your work on the rations, blah, blah, blah. No doubt the new Lt. Quartermaster will have you in mind if he wants a job done, etc.

Me: I don't want a job like that again, etc. I want to get some training. I want very badly to be a soldier.

It shook him all right, and perhaps it will result in my being put in charge of a fatigue party whose job it is to line-up the blades of grass as they come up out of the earth since the rain began.

These last few days I have been suffering from an 'upset tummy' which has not improved my temper when dealing with those bloody idiots in the regular army who want to indulge in the abuse of the Indians. They treat the Indians in a way which not only makes one tremble for the future but which makes one ashamed of being one of them. Really some of the most ignorant men here are to be pitied. They joined the regular army to get away from family trouble in blighty. They never write home; they try to suppress all feelings about blighty, they vent their own misfortunes on any hapless and helpless Indian, and they look upon army life as a scramble (all against all) for good jobs. The art of war, the character of this war, the outcome of the war outside of India just does not concern them; *they dare not let themselves be concerned* for fear of burning homesickness that smoulders beneath their simulated toughness. I have had the chance of talking to a few – My God, what *hideous* lives they lead. Eternally on the scrounge for petty gain; eternally feeling they are being swindled by the paymaster, by the canteen, the shopkeeper, etc., and therefore ready always to swindle someone else.

Two things have just happened which stagger one in their contrast. Tobruk has fallen, and we have been ordered to polish all brasses on all our equipment.

Since I wrote the above, a new programme has been put up which promises that from next week on we are going to be really busy, which is heartening. Many of us are so longing to get on to the job so as to end this bloody war as soon as possible, and any signs of real work raise our spirits no end. As a mere sideline on the subject of politics in the army – two points of view have been expressed by the CO and Squadron Leader. The CO said the old army method of the horse trough [dunking] was still the best way of teaching a man patriotism. The SL said that we were all paid certain rates for certain jobs by the Government and if we did not do our work properly we were not keeping the contract. It is extremely lucky that the bulk of the men here are, on their own, anti-fascist, and feel this to be the purpose of the fight, otherwise there would be no idealism to spur on our fighting morale.

Saturday 20 June – This morning we had the first meeting of the debating society committee which I am on. Our first debate is for next Thursday. The subject is 'Woman's place is in the Home.' I proposed this subject as it appeals to the men, they all have ideas on it, and it will lead to some pretty good discussion when they get back to their tents. Among other subjects I put up were, 'Tradition is a hindrance to Progress' and 'We should treat the Indians as equals.'

This morning we went out on a scheme on foot in units representing tanks. We covered ten or more miles over ploughed fields, etc. It was magnificent exercise and although I felt pretty tired I enjoyed it no end. That sort of thing will make real soldiers of us.

But tonight I had a terrible set-back. On parade this morning we were asked who had seen active service. I said I had. When we came back from the scheme I was informed that I was to go to an inspection by the Duke of Gloucester in a few days' time. This is apparently the purpose of asking about active service. This parade is a purely bull-shit parade. It will take several days to polish boots, brasses, etc. It will take days and nights for some eight Indian tailors to alter, clean, press, etc., etc., clothes for the white-sahibs to wear like bloody waxworks. The Indians will, of course, not be on parade, the lucky fools. I have often been asked, 'Have we got a fifth column here?' Yes, we have! for nothing could help the enemy more by undermining morale, destroying enthusiasm and making us incompetent fighters than this kind of tomfoolery.

It would be another eighteen months before Clive Branson saw any action. On 25 February 1944 he was killed fighting the Japanese on the Arakan Front.

7. HOPE OF VICTORY

WINTER 1942–3

In the summer of 1942 Hitler had two objectives on the Russian Front. The first was to push south-east to the Caucasus Mountains and the oil fields on the Caspian Sea. The second was to advance east to Stalingrad, the most important industrial and transportation centre on the Volga River. Capturing Stalingrad wasn't strategically crucial, but Hitler's pride and perhaps the city's name led him to devote more resources to it than was strictly required. The constant switching of the axis of attack between the Caucasus and Stalingrad compromised both campaigns.

By the end of August German forces led by General Paulus had reached the outskirts of Stalingrad, but they were now overextended and protected on the flanks by less committed and less well equipped Axis troops drawn from Romania, Hungary and Italy. Stalin ordered that the city must not fall to the Germans, and the Soviet high command devised a plan to bring the Red Army sweeping through from the north and the south-east in a pincer movement to cut off the Germans around Stalingrad. For the next two months the Russians and the Germans waged a bitter battle of attrition around the beleaguered city.

In North Africa Rommel had moved his tanks into position for an assault which he thought would finally open the road to Cairo and Alexandria, giving the Germans control of the Suez Canal. In early August he sent a long detailed signal to Hitler, relaying precisely his plan of attack, which was intercepted by British Intelligence. The information that Montgomery, who had taken over command of the 8th Army, cherished above all was that Rommel acknowledged the risk he was taking with his supply lines. If the RAF or Royal Navy could prevent fuel tankers reaching Benghazi, the start of Rommel's overland supply route, and Montgomery could prevent Rommel advancing, there could be only one outcome. By the end of the first week in September it was all over: Rommel had been forced to withdraw yet again.

On the night of 23 October Montgomery launched the Battle of El Alamein. Rommel returned from sick leave to discover that his second in command was dead and the fuel supply situation was worse than ever. Eleven days and nights of fierce fighting ensued, with terrible casualties. On 4 November the BBC Home Service advised listeners to avoid switching off before midnight when 'the best news for years was coming'. The Axis forces were in full retreat. During a speech at the Lord Mayor's Luncheon at the Mansion House on 10 November, Churchill said, 'Now this is not the end. It is not even the beginning of the end. But it is, perhaps, the end of the beginning.' On 22 November the Red Army's pincers closed around the German troops at Stalingrad, trapping them, and Churchill's words seemed even more apt.

At last there was good news from the front. And on 1 December the British government published the Beveridge Report, which promised good news at home too. The most significant and far-reaching report of twentieth-century British politics, it would lead to the post-war welfare state. Its timing couldn't have been better. With Montgomery's successes in North Africa quickening the national pulse, thoughts were naturally projected forwards to a demob-happy peacetime

Britain. Here was a plan for the future behind which everyone could rally.

But many would not survive to see the end of the war. At the beginning of December Jewish representatives met MPs to inform them of the increasingly horrific persecutions in Europe. Anthony Eden, the foreign secretary, addressed the House of Commons on 17 December to put the government's concern on record.

In January 1943 Roosevelt and Churchill met at Casablanca for the first of a series of meetings between the Allied leaders and chiefs of staff. Stalin declined the invitation to join them in the light of the ongoing battle for Stalingrad. He did however remind his allies that he wanted to see a second front in Europe before much longer. There was prolonged discussion about what the Allies' next steps should be. As argued by Roosevelt, it was agreed that the war would only end with the unconditional surrender of the Axis powers. It was further agreed that aid would be sent to Russia but that there would be no cross-Channel invasion of Europe that year. Instead, the Allies would invade Sicily and advance through Italy. In addition, there would be heavy strategic bombing of German industrial areas.

At the end of January the Axis troops in Stalingrad were still surrounded. Hitler, aware that no German field marshal had ever been captured, promoted General Paulus to that rank. Clearly Hitler expected Paulus to succeed or do the honourable thing and kill himself rather than be taken prisoner. Paulus, however, surrendered on 31 January, and by 2 February the Battle of Stalingrad was over.

On 28 February Nazi plans for an atomic bomb were fatally sabotaged. Nine British-financed Norwegians destroyed heavy water-electrolysis chambers in a former fertilizer plant at Telemark on Norway's highest plateau. What made this operation all the more remarkable was the fact that the Germans had initially been expecting saboteurs, but presumed they could not have survived the winter hiding out on Europe's most inhospitable terrain. According to the Wehrmacht general sent to investigate, it was 'the most splendid coup I have seen in this war'.

THE DIARISTS

HAROLD NICOLSON

On 6 November Harold had been invited to Downing Street for lunch ('sea-kale, jugged hare and cherry tart – not well done'). It was two days since the news of the victory at El Alamein had been received, and all those present shared in the triumph with Churchill. Back in August Harold had attended a meeting with Beveridge to discuss health services, old age pensions and family allowances. He came away 'more cheerful and encouraged than I have been for weeks'. He welcomed the publication of the report at the start of December.

Wednesday 2 December – The Lobbies are buzzing with comment on the Beveridge Report. The 1922 Committee* were addressed by Beveridge and gave him a cordial reception. The Tory line seems to be to welcome the Report in principle, and then to whittle it away by detailed criticism. They will say that it is all very splendid and Utopian, but we can only begin to know whether we can afford it once we have some idea what our foreign trade will be like after the war. They also suggest that in many ways it is an incentive to idleness, that some people are better off under

---

* Conservative backbench MPs' group.

the present arrangements, and that in fact it is the old Poor Law immensely magnified.

Wednesday 9 December – We have a Committee meeting at which several representative Jews tell us of the extermination of their fellows by the Nazis. They have ringed off the Warsaw ghetto and transported two-thirds of the inhabitants in cattle trucks to die in Russia. It is a horrible thing to feel that we are so saturated with horrors, that this Black Hole on a gigantic scale scarcely concerns us. They put lime and chloride in the cattle-trucks and bury the corpses next morning. They are particularly vindictive against children. I have a sense that my fellow-Members feel not so much 'What can we do to such people' as 'What can we do <u>with</u> such people after the war?'

Thursday 17 December – Eden reads out a statement about the persecution of the Jews, and to our shame and astonishment a Labour Member (having been deeply moved by a speech by Jimmy Rothschild) suggests that we should all stand up as a tribute. The Speaker says, 'Such an action must be spontaneous,' so everybody gets up including the Speaker and the reporters. It is rather moving in a way.

Harold's son Ben left for Cairo at the end of October and Nigel for Algiers three weeks later. Harold wrote to them every week until June 1945.

Letter to Ben and Nigel, Sunday 20 December – The military arrived at Sissinghurst. It consisted of the Headquarters of a tank Brigade on exercise, heralded by a young officer of the name of Rubinstein. Recalling how but three days before I had stood in tribute to the martyred Jews of Poland, I was most polite to Captain Rubinstein. His parents, it appeared, live in Leicester. He told us that his Brigadier, plus five officers plus cook plus batmen, would appear by tea-time and wanted to stay the night. We showed him the brew-house, the oast-houses, Nigel's room, Ben's room and the loft beyond. He said that it would do nicely, and departed to inform his Headquarters what a pleasant little welcome was being prepared.

It was at that moment that Mummy remembered the onions stored on the floor of the loft. They number between two and three thousand. She said that the Army always stole onions and that we must remove them at any cost before they arrived. I said that we were only having a Brigadier and his officers, and that (a) they would probably not want to steal more than three onions each, and (b) we should not miss them much if they did. She said that you could never tell with officers nowadays, so many of them were promoted from the ranks. So we got three sacks and two shovels and all afternoon till darkness came we carried the sacks across to the Priest's House and spread them on the floor of Pat's room. We had scarcely finished with the last onion when the Brigadier appeared. He was a nice well-behaved man and looked so little like an onion-stealer that Mummy at once asked him to dinner.

NAOMI MITCHISON

During the autumn Naomi became involved with the newly formed Scottish Convention, a coalition of the left following a split within the Scottish National Party. There was much discussion in Carradale about the Convention, and also about the Beveridge Report. The Mitchisons knew Beveridge and were friendly with Frank Pakenham (later Lord Longford), his personal assistant. Dick's work had contributed to the evidence base for the report, and the Mitchisons' socialism and commitment to their community gave them a deep interest in the proposals. It now seemed possible to plan for a future beyond the war.

The family gathered at Carradale for Christmas, but without Naomi's two eldest: Murdoch was unable to come, and Denny and Ruth stayed at home with their newborn baby.

Friday 25 December – Woken early by Val bringing me my stocking; we all undid stockings and raced round one another's rooms. The children had given me all sorts of things, Val had made me slippers, Lois had given me six coupons! Rosemary came back from her dance, which had been a bit of an orgy, as they had collected most of the drink in Campbeltown, but quite fun. She brought a great whack of mistletoe which we hung up. I gave the maids £2 each – twice last year – and got much kissed, we undid parcels after breakfast . . .

Lilla, Peter and Ellen came to dinner, we had a goose from the Lochgair hotel instead of the usual turkey; it was very good. The maids had a chicken; we each had a pudding, and I had kept some ginger.

Then the children began to come for their Christmas party; we lit the candles, and brought them in. There were about 18, mostly small ones, including small Anne Jackson. I had a book for each, mostly Penguins and Puffins, and a whistle or blow-out, relics of pre-war or immediately post war. Goodness knows what I'll have next year. They were all thrilled with the tree, which did look lovely. We played musical bumps and blind man's buff, but they tended to segregate rather firmly into boys and girls. We had made jellies with some rather peculiar jelly guaranteed to contain nothing, and some tinned fruit, but they didn't like it much, or the milk shake which I think is so good. We also had buns and biscuits with chocolate spread. We had the tree in the musical box from Munich turning round and tinkling.

The children left at 6.30, and after supper there was a meeting in the village hall. Even though it was Christmas Day, Dick talked about the Beveridge Report and made some proposals to put to the government about securing the future of their fishing community.

There were finally about thirty-five people there, but none of the fishermen; Johnnie's wife had said he was very keen to be there, but she didn't know if he'd be back. They can't risk losing six or seven hundred pounds!

Dick had been preparing this all day, and made a very good job of it. He spoke for an hour and a half, and I think held everyone's interest. He explained it in some detail, but it's difficult to remember figures at all. It would have been better with a blackboard. There were quite a lot of questions. Dick suggested things the fishermen should do, and old Mr Cook said they ought to take it up. Willie was in the Chair. It was all very informal, and worth doing. Some came back to the house afterwards to go on asking questions.

On the way out I drew Donald Jackson's* attention to the mistletoe – whereat he seized me, took me right off my feet and gave me no end of a kissing. I had no idea he would be so strong though of course he's a farmer's son.

Sunday 10 January – The Beveridge thing most interesting; I rang up Johnnie and asked him to get hold of some of the others and come over this evening. It's very difficult to understand, all the same.

Johnnie, Rob, Sandy and Gilbert 'Tosh turned up, Denny M still in bed with flu. We had a long discussion. They didn't know much about the Beveridge report to start with. Apparently most of the boats now are insured so part of Dick's security proposals had to be re-written. They all want

---

* Head teacher of the village school.

unemployment pay of some kind, but see the insuperable difficulty of deciding about it. Most of them make up their stamp books when they stop fishing in March; they are worried at the much larger payment involved under the Bev scheme, especially for the skipper.

Dick went back and worked on the letter till the small hours. I was pretty miserable, as I seem to have seen very little of him and there was a lot I wanted to discuss before he left.

Although both victory and political change seemed possible, the war was still inescapable. Naomi heard from her friend Margery Spring Rice that her son Stephen's submarine was long overdue, and she feared the worst.

Sunday 31 January – Awfully tired. Couldn't sleep, kept on thinking about crises, also about Margy. I don't get her and Stephen out of my mind at all. Dick talking about Carradale after the war and things that could be done. But I think there will be revolution and everything utterly different. Sometimes I want that violently, other times I only want a lovely holiday and everything done for me by pre-war maids!

She later heard that Stephen had been killed when his submarine was torpedoed.

ANNE GARNETT

After Sarah's form mistress joined up in the summer, Anne and Frank had taken the painful decision to send her to boarding school from September. To help finance this, Anne agreed to give up the WVS clinic and look for paid work. For the time being their younger daughter would stay at home.

In October Anne landed a job in a factory, Bell Bros, run by husband-and-wife team Jean and Ron, producing water-purifying equipment for the Ministry of Defence. Her job was to check trays of glass ampoules for cracks that might render them useless. She was almost as frustrated by her failure to spot 'duds' as her employers. Six weeks into the job, although she worked carefully – checking forty-four trays in a day to her co-worker George's hundred – she still missed 3 per cent. This meant all of her work had to be re-examined and stamped as checked by someone else. However, this seemed a trifling irritation when compared with the pain of her friend whose husband had been reported missing in Egypt.

Friday 6 November – Oh God, the heartache in the world. I keep seeing Dorothea's little face, pinched and white, dark circles under her eyes. She said today (to her mother) 'What shall I do when the war is over and everyone has their men coming home?' It's all so pitiful. I spent the morning with them, went down with flowers and persuaded her to come for a walk as it's a lovely day. We trudged through the mud along the old canal, leaves fluttering down: D. very silent but bravely keeping her end up. She's incredibly brave. Got some whisky and ginger-ale and oranges for her to have tonight, and took in on my way to work. Found I'd passed 23 duds yesterday, but feel too sad to care.

Monday 9 November – Fine autumn morning and I cycled to work in high glee, to have a crushing blow dealt me by George who found 30 duds in my Friday's work. Feel this is serious, and had a chat with Ron over our morning coffee. He is quite puzzled as he thought I'd be good at the job, however he still hopes I may pull through; and has my stamp ready for me in his drawer! Am longing to really master the D-things – today they were vile and full of every kind of fault, so I could only do 38 trays.

Wednesday 9 December – Down to milk in pitchy darkness, by torch-light, all very reminiscent of Bethlehem – animals

crunching hay and a warm milky smell. To a lecture at the
Police Station where our new Police Sgt. appealed to us to
help combat the spread of VD in Wellington. Terrific stir
among the local ladies (audience entirely composed of WVS)
and much chit-chat: he told us hair-raising yarns of local
girls and soldiers which were much appreciated, concluding
'If I was to tell you who had VD in Wellington you'd fall
down – you would straight!'

Sunday 13 December – Discussion as to sexual morality in bed
last night, could think of no reason why promiscuity should
be banned except for the illegitimate children and the VD
question. Remove dangers of these, and why should one
object? Yet one still does! Prejudice I suppose – result of years
of moral training. Still, people being as they are, I should
advocate contraceptives and lots of clinics, and licensed
brothels complete with medically examined girls, rather than
have the babies and VD we're now faced with. I do think
it's cruel of the USA to send us their darky troops with no
provision for their sexual needs – poor old England, what we
have to do for our allies!

Started work at 10 and did 88 boxes – George found 3
duds in my yesterday's lot. The work is mounting to the
ceiling and George and I are like mice nibbling at it! If only
Ron had given me my stamp. It's locked in his drawer, and
he in town!

Tuesday 15 December – Portioning out the money [from the
government] as fairly as I could among the many herb-
gatherers. The dried nettles are paid for at the rate of 4d per
pound and the foxgloves 1/6d. No mention of money for
horse chestnuts so I totted up all the collectors, it came to
over 1,145 pounds of conkers! Even as I worked little boys
swarmed in to know if the money had come!

Sunday 20 December – When I'd put the kids to bed I sat for a bit in the gloaming enjoying the tree all lit with little steadily burning coloured lights, it seemed to me as if it was burning and shining for all the men away overseas who are fighting for our homes and for a Christmas Peace on earth. Magic tree!

Tuesday 29 December – Had to tap re-sealed ampoules all afternoon, the glass flew all over the place and I got a bit in my eye, very nasty. Mr D [a co-worker] couldn't see it, but I got a glimpse of it and got it out in the end.

Tuesday 12 January – I got soaked pedalling back from the town in spite of mackintosh and gum boots. Not that my GBs are much good now, poor old dears, they are in tatters round the tops and all cracked at the ankle, but have done well being 11 years old. My grateful Govt. refuses to let me have new ones as I'm not a *whole* time farm worker (as if you can't get just as wet part-time!)

Friday 22 January – We're nearly in Tripoli now – wonder what Rommel has up his sleeve, some foul trick I feel sure, he'd never run like this otherwise.

Frank furious at fire watching becoming compulsory in the town which means he'll have to pay 3 people 3 shillings a night each to watch the office. Three people – but who? They'll never find enough to go round, we're all in the NFS [National Fire Service], HG [Home Guard] or something.

Thursday 28 January – On to drive the salvage lorry. What a nasty job it is – smelly tins and bones, tomato sauce and household milk all over one's hands and dirty water slopping out all over you as you stagger down the street bearing an old bath piled high with tins. Frank gave me a lecture on how silly I was to take it on, and really I was almost agreeing with him by the end of the morning.

Tuesday 2 February – Babs [Griffin] full of dark prophecies about the latest call-up of workers this evening at ARP duty. It seems that all women under 40 (without small children) can be switched off now and put into anything the Government needs them for. How people can run businesses I can't imagine – staffed either with babes-in-arms or aged crocks in bathchairs!

Wednesday 3 February – Why does it always rain on my way to work? Rather embittered the other day, after battling with a 60 m.p.h. wind all the way home, to find C in her large car: 'I felt I simply couldn't face my bike today in this wind, so I'm doing my shopping with the car.' She still gets a petrol allowance for 'essential purposes'.* Galling to those like myself, who get none!

Saturday 6 February – Bustled home at 12 to use up the rest of the 'point coupons' in our ration books, as they expire today. One of the major issues of war. 'How Best to Use One's Points.' I find American sausage-meat (in tins) one of the best buys, you get a large tin for 9 points and the meat is coated in thick white fat which does for pastry or cakes.

GEORGE BEARDMORE

George finished his 'Broadcasting book' early in December – 'a long book, my first serious one, of which I have high hopes' – and applied successfully for a job in the Housing Department of

---

* Petrol was strictly rationed and allowances given only to civilians required to use their cars for war work.

Stanmore Council, close to home. His mother-in-law came out of hospital, and he and Jean decided that she should now live with them.

Monday 16 November – Now that Jean's mother has returned from hospital she has been installed in our back room, the very same that sheltered us during the bombing. Indeed, we look upon her as though she herself were a victim of shrapnel or flying glass. Talk of 'being without her' and 'executors' brings tears to Jean's eyes, as to her father's. He is so filled with gratitude to us for taking her in and nursing her that he cannot see me doing anything but wants to better it for me. He sees me polishing my shoes and offers to go up home for some special Probert's oil. He found me putting up an extra coat-rack and presently I found his tin of Rawlplugs in my hands. He is getting draft-proofing for the front room (draught-proofing – it's 7 p.m. and I am tired) and arranging for us to have a telephone.

My chief concern of course is Jean.

Sunday 10 January – On Boxing Night at ten to seven in the evening Mamma woke from a drowse that had kept her unconscious on and off for a couple of days and asked for her milk. The Guv'nor was at hand to comfort her and stepped out of the room to boil it. When he returned he found that in turning over to ease her cramped legs she had died. I heard him call out – I was washing up at the time – and in the hall he said: 'I think she's gone.' I went inside and felt the pulse – a queer sensation to feel the wrist still warm but with no tick in it. A tear had rolled onto her nose. Jean astonished me by her resource and strength.

The office is going very happily – plenty of freedom, little worry, fresh faces, and home for dinner. The work entails finding lodgings for nurses employed at the Orthopaedic Hospital at the top of Stanmore Hill. It is said to be chiefly occupied with mending broken airmen. Worthwhile work, therefore, but surprising the resistance one meets in house-holders. I knock at the front doors of well-to-do households and am met with the widest variety of women and excuses. The most common response is: 'Oh, you're from the Council. No, thank you,' and a door shut in my face. As one might expect, it's the poorer people who have most sympathy, but there again it's the poorer people who have most children and therefore all their rooms occupied. Still, so far I have managed by guile and much smooth talk to get three nurses accommodated.

Sunday 21 February – The publisher's list with 'All Space My Playground' came this morning. Out in March.

A good many people think the war will be over this year. The Russians have recently retaken Rostov-on-Don and Khar-kov. Our own forces are in Tripoli and pushing on to Tunis. It's very naughty of them, but the office men – all old soldiers of the last war – are secretly delighted that the Americans have suffered a reverse in Tunisia. Clowes said: 'That'll teach the buggers.' The 67-year-old Churchill, just returned from Casablanca, Turkey, Cyprus, and Tripoli, is now getting over a bad cold. We have had a three-day Commons debate on the Beveridge Report (on the feasibility of a National Health Service) and it has been officially declared possible provided that the country can find the money after the war.

CLARA MILBURN

The sound of bells again (for Alamein) – first, on the wireless from Coventry and other bombed cities, and then outside from nearby Berkswell village – 'caught at my heartstrings'. Clara's best days were those when a letter arrived from Alan – his camp had been closed down, and he was now in Oflag VIIB. Prisoners still ran a 'camp university' to alleviate the boredom and he seemed well, but the letters were censored of course, and perhaps Alan was also selective about what he wanted his parents to know.

Wednesday 16 December – At last a letter and a postcard from Alan, dated 24.9.42 and 24.10.42. He talks of hockey, soccer and touch-rugger, describing the latter game and appearing quite interested in hockey. He does not mention the tying of prisoners. He had a cold after scorning those 'who spent their time sneezing', while he who was so bronzed and healthy 'spent his time in the fresh air'.

Thursday 31 December – A letter from Alan again today, dated 19.11.42, and a cheery one too. It tells of him getting up at 7 a.m., shaving 'by feel', working at his studies till 8 a.m., and again after breakfast and lunch as 'the exam' (Assoc. Member of Mech. Engs.) is in ten days' time. Joan Spencer* has had several letters, and one tells of 200 officers being manacled. But 'they are quite humanely treated and no-one need worry', he says. The manacling lasts 18 days for 12 hours a day. Of course they make fun of it, but Nevill remarks 'how extraordinary it is that a man's mind should be so like a child's mind'. The German Censor lets this through, it seems.

Thursday 21 January – There was a letter from Alan dated 28.11.42, in which he said they were having a cold, damp day, and that his exam was imminent. He feared the April parcel was lost, which is a pity as it contained the gumboots and a beautiful pullover knitted by Florence.† However he does not seem very short of clothes, which is a good thing.

---

* A friend of Clara, whose son Nevill was also a prisoner of war.
† A cousin of Jack and close to the family.

Sunday 21 February – Three years and five months since war began. Three years and six weeks since Alan went away. We go to bed, we get up, we work, we play a little. The daily round goes on. How much longer will it all go on? The light is breaking – how long till the full day?

VERA BRITTAIN

When the bells rang again for the victory at Alamein, Vera wrote, 'Their ringing should have been postponed till the end of the War,' adding that it was 'rather childish premature rejoicing'. She and George were concerned about the children, particularly John, who had moved to another school without them being consulted. They had been thinking about how to bring them home. One plan had been for them to travel on a Portuguese ship, as Portugal's neutrality would protect the vessel from U-boat attack, but they were now advised against it. The war in the Mediterranean made it too risky. Vera's anxiety about her own children made her all the more sympathetic to mothers in Europe desperate for food. Her campaigning on behalf of famine relief continued.

Wednesday 16 December – Most depressing – in fact devastating – letter at last arrived from George Brett about John. As I suspected, his change of school was due to a falling off of work at the St Paul Academy. He has obviously been wrongly handled and made recalcitrant (partly, no doubt, because Shirley seems very obviously the favourite at St Paul). George thinks John should come home in May & so do I; he appears to believe that transport will be available. Alas & alas! I have gone without the children for 2½ years, only to produce this situation. I knew all along they shouldn't have gone.

Thursday 17 December – Felt better about John today; realised that he is just being the same old John who, so far as a boy

can be of a girl, is a replica of my 15-year-old self reacting
adversely to affectionate friends who have treated him with
a little less than complete wisdom. Wrote a long letter to
George about him of wh. I asked him to send a copy to Ruth.

Saturday 19 December – G. & I sent a cable to John for his
15th birthday on Monday. I still feel bad about him, & could
kick myself for not having both children back last summer.
40 children and 12 adults have arrived in Lisbon from another
Portuguese ship, but after a very bad voyage.

Monday 28 December – Rung up on telephone while it was still
dark by a long Christmas cable from Ruth. The first part
contained Christmas & birthday messages;* the remainder
said: 'Pan-American friend advises plane earliest possible
midsummer all children's exits regarded unpatriotic now,
wish you could come instead.' Felt very depressed about
this all day. It won't be so bad if a 'plane is available
at midsummer, but more likely then we shall be told that
nothing can be done for another 3 months etc. In consequence G. kept talking about Portuguese boats.

Wednesday 6 January – Long letter from George Brett about
putting the children on a <u>British</u> boat made us decide to go
to Cook's & discuss possibilities.
      They confirmed impression about 'plane & we made
provisional arrangements to put John on a Portuguese boat.
Had tea with Mother & came home very depressed by the
grim alternative between leaving my dear boy in U.S. for
the duration, perhaps to be called up, & bringing him home
through the dangers of wartime travel. G. came home in a
vile temper & we had the usual quarrelsome argument abt.

* Vera would be 49 the next day.

whether J. should come home or not which left me completely pulverised.

Sunday 17 January – Had dinner latish & not till then did G. show me a cable received during the afternoon from the Colbys, saying John was fearing badly prospect of sea voyage, did we insist? British Consulate was objecting, & coming now would mean forfeiting re-entry permit. (Could not understand these two last statements at all.) G. & I were discussing this when a large raid started in retaliation for our raid on Berlin last night. Much noise & heavy gunfire round here but we hardly heard it as problem of deciding whether to call off plans for John & perhaps not see him for duration was so grim. Went to bed very tired by exhausting problem & was woken again at 5.0 by another raid. Terrific gunfire & huge shells bursting into smaller ones – some over this flat.

Tuesday 19 January – Agitating & exhausting day. Late morning a cable came from George Brett saying John unlikely to leave before mid-March. Wondered all day whether I wanted John to travel against his will – & finally decided that I didn't yet, however much it was George's advice.

Had violent headache by the time I got home. Decided send cables postponing John's booking; then had to go to bed.

Thursday 21 January – Arrival of Famine Relief material notifying that great effort is now to be made since the Foreign Secretary turned down the scheme for very moderate relief for Greece & Belgium recently put before him by the Archbp. of Canterbury & Card[inal] Archbp. of Westminster. The Archbp. is to address both Houses of Parlt. on this on Feb. 17th. Suddenly it came over me that I could probably reach a large, non-pacifist public of novel-readers with a personal pamphlet on this. Felt a real call to write it. Wrote Edith Pye [secretary of the Famine Relief Committee], & Andrew Dakers to ask if he would publish it; said I'd give the royalties of H. with H. to it if these would help. Then started to write the pamphlet, wh. is to be about 10,000 words. Made scheme & collected relief material together. Felt I must make this effort.

She finished it, including the typescript, at 1 a.m. the following Monday. Despite her efforts, the archbishop decided not to refer to it, unwilling to be associated with any criticism of the government. Vera's pamphlet – 'a plea to parents and others for Europe's children' – was published in February as *One of These Little Ones*, and sold 30,000 copies. She donated the profits to the campaign. The archbishop's speech on 17 February 'was a flop because everyone was listening to the debate on the Beveridge Report'.

CHARLES RITCHIE

Ritchie's brother Roley had come over with the Canadian army in 1941, serving as assistant deputy judge advocate with the 3rd Division stationed in Sussex. Although Ritchie had no real intention of joining up, his brother's selflessness disturbed him.

Friday 1 January – Last night the end of the year with a wind howling down the steep gully of flats outside my window. I feel both sad and excited as though I were seventeen. Christ! Why has it all happened?

Sunday 3 January – Elizabeth has borne with all my attempts to play-act my life, although she has so little patience with histrionic characters, without ever making me feel a fool. She has shown me up to myself – good money to some extent has driven out bad.

Monday 4 January – Now arises the question of whether or not I should join the army. Elizabeth thinks that I might make a 'useful soldier'. She says if I join the army she will join the ATS. I doubt if either of us will do either. I can see that this idea of joining the army is closing in on me unless I can prove to myself that it would be unfair to the service I am now in and just a piece of heroics. Unfortunately the work here has been so slack recently that I find it impossible to believe that I am pulling my weight in the war.

What a joke it is – a cosy bachelor pried out of his shell and being drawn principally for reasons of face-saving into the horrid prospect of army life. What a short story for someone. By suggesting that I should become a soldier I have put myself in for stakes which I know I cannot afford to play, and depend on other people to get me out of the situation. Perhaps no one will be bothered to do so, and that in itself has a sort of attraction for me. I have now a card to play against myself.

Sunday 31 January – I went to visit Roley in the hospital with jaundice at Horsham in the heart of the Canadian-occupied district. Everywhere Canadian soldiers, often with local girls. I suppose somewhere under the surface a Sussex rustic life goes on. An occupying army irons out the character of a neighbourhood – everything looked down-at-the-heel as in London. The rich settled bloom has gone, the stripped naked country-houses are all barracks or hospitals, the avenues morasses of mud from military vehicles, the fences down, the gardens neglected – the little towns submerged in khaki.

Saturday 6 February – Shaftesbury Avenue was lined with American soldiers just standing there, very quiet and well-behaved, watching the crowds or waiting to pick up a girl. The American troops are everywhere in the West End. They make a curious impression, very different from the legend of the swashbuckling, boasting Yankees abroad. I wonder what they really think about it all. They are so negative that they arouse one's curiosity. They themselves seem completely incurious. They look as though they were among strange animals. The Canadian soldiers up against the British try at once to establish human contact – they make jokes, pick quarrels, make passes, get drunk, and finally find friends.

HERMIONE RANFURLY

By the end of September 1942 the old restlessness had led to Hermione giving Sir Harold MacMichael one month's notice. Friends in Cairo, the Caseys, thought they might get her work there with General Alexander. While Hermione was visiting them in November they invited the general to lunch. Hermione refrained from discussing the subject directly. On his way out Alexander left a message for Hermione. As he was going to be in the desert for some time he did 'not want to employ a woman'. He recommended instead that she try General Jumbo Wilson in Baghdad.

Monday 7 December – **Baghdad** – Mark Chapman Walker, now Military Assistant to General Jumbo, met me at Habbanyeh. As we drove through the outskirts of a poor little town I interrupted Mark to ask its name. 'Baghdad,' he said. Soon afterwards we drew up at a small villa surrounded by a sea of mud: our Headquarters.

General Jumbo was sitting at his desk with his tin spectacles on the end of his nose; he held a fly swatter in one hand. Tall, immensely fat, with kind little twinkly eyes, he looks exactly like an elephant – an elephant standing on its hind legs.

After I had seen the General, Mark showed me a telegram which had just come from General Alexander:

Personal for Wilson from Alexander

Ranfurly left for you today. I have the honour to take your
place as the only General in the Middle East who has not
been outmanoeuvred.

Scrawled on the bottom in General Jumbo's handwriting was:
'Reply: "Better to have Ranfurly in the bag than Rommel on
the loose." ' Then I settled down to study the files.

The Embassy stands on the edge of the Tigris. This
evening a dead camel floated past the windows. Save for my
lacquered fingernails and the General's red tabs, there seems
to be no colour here.

Tuesday 15 December – At first I thought Baghdad a dreary
place but I have learned to love this town which has a mulled
beauty all of its own. Kingfishers live in the river banks;
painted boats lie beneath the latticed windows that overhang
the river; there are parrots in the grain shop near the bridge.

The streets are crowded with Indian, Iraqi, Polish and
British troops.

Friday 8 January – The American Persian Gulf Service under
General Connelly is going to take over our base headquarters
at Basra; we will continue to be responsible for the internal
security at Persia and Iraq, but the Americans will take over
the transport of aid to Russia. Bombers are being flown direct
to the Stalingrad front. They are often in action eight days
after being unloaded at Basra. Fighters, tanks and other
equipment will go by the arterial road from Khorramashar
and Badashabir to Tabriz. We have built a bridge across the
Shat-el-Arab river.

Tuesday 19 January – The siege of Stalingrad has been raised.
We are thrilled.

Sunday 24 January – When news reached us that the Eighth Army had entered Tripoli I could hardly believe it. As soon as I could escape the office I took a pony and rode out into the desert to think.

I thought of General Wavell and how tragic it was that Mr Churchill could never like or understand him – what a combination they would have been; of Auchinleck, so handsome and charming but not quite able to cope with the intricate Desert war; and of Monty whom few of us like or admire – who did not go into action until he was reinforced beyond Wavell's wildest dreams. And I thought of Rommel who, in spite of being our enemy, gained our admiration and respect – almost our affection.

I remembered all the friends I'll never see again; the shattered lives of the seriously wounded and the multitude of heroes who have made it possible for us to reach Tripoli. Most of all I thought of Dan, still incarcerated in an Italian castle – now nearer to our Forces but still so far away.

As I cantered on tears ran down my face but I did not know if they were from joy or sorrow.

In February 1943 Wilson was appointed commander-in-chief, Middle East, and he and his staff moved to Cairo.

Tuesday 16 February – **Cairo** – When at last I got to the Continental Hotel I found Whitaker waiting for me in the cool, old-fashioned bedroom which is to be my new home. His kind fat face was set and serious and he pulled a newspaper out of his pocket. 'I hate to tell you, my Lady, I have bad news . . . His Lordship's best friend and best man at your wedding is dead.' On the front page I read that Pat Hore-Ruthven had died of wounds in an Italian hospital on Christmas Eve.

After a while Whitaker, obviously miserable, announced

he had more bad news: David Stirling and his brother-in-law, Simon Ramsay, are both missing. If I must learn such ghastly things I was thankful to have Whitaker with me. We stayed up late – talking of Pat, David and Simon. When Whitaker departed to go to his digs he said, 'My Lady, you'll have to write and tell all this to His Lordship. I don't envy you writing the letter or him reading it. Please tell him we're going to win this war and that you and I will stick together until it ends – come what may. Tell him that the likes of me will never surrender.'

Wednesday 17 February – Mark brought with him one of the green parrots from the grain shop in Baghdad and gave him to me as a souvenir. The parrot is beautiful. His name is Coco. Poor little bird – he is still nervous from the journey but already he will sit on my shoulder and feed from my hand.

Cairo is cool and sunny and far emptier than when I was last here. Now it feels a long way from the war. This afternoon I went with General Jumbo to the zoo to see Said the Hippo who is an old friend of the General. The two outsize personages seemed pleased to renew their friendship.

ALAN BROOKE

Brooke began 1943 in optimistic mood and took stock in his first entry of the year.

Friday 1 January – New year started. I cannot help glancing back at Jan 1st last year when I could see nothing but calamities ahead. Horrible doubts, horrible nightmares, which grew larger and larger as the days went on till it felt as if the whole Empire was collapsing round my head. Wherever I looked I could see nothing but trouble.

And now! We start 1943 under conditions I would never have dared to hope. Russia has held; Egypt for the present is safe. There is a hope of clearing North Africa of Germans in the near future. The Mediterranean may be partially opened. Malta is safe for the present. We can now work freely against Italy, and Russia is scoring wonderful successes in Southern Russia. We are certain to have many setbacks to face, many troubles, and many shattered hopes, but for all that the horizon is infinitely brighter.

From a personal point of view life is also now a bit easier. With 13 months of this job behind me I feel just a little more confident than I did in those awful early days when I felt completely lost and out of place. I pray God that He may go on giving me the help he has given me during the last year.

On 13 January Brooke arrived in Casablanca for the Allies' conference. Over the next ten days he argued in favour of his preferred strategy over that of the Americans: an advance across the Mediterranean into Italy rather than initiate, at this stage, a second front in northern France. He found the Americans 'friendliness itself' but exasperating. He thought Eisenhower was 'deficient of experience and of limited ability', Marshall 'has got practically no strategic vision', King was 'biased entirely in favour of the Pacific' and Patton 'at a loss in any operation requiring skill and judgement'. Despite everything, agreement was reached by 20 January. Then there was a last-minute hitch, when it seemed that the majority of the British team wanted to invade Sardinia rather than Sicily from North Africa.

Friday 22 January – Such a change at the last moment was not to be contemplated. The Americans I knew would not look at Sardinia and might well accuse us of not knowing our own minds, and wish to close down operations in the Mediterranean. It was with some difficulty, and against their inclination that we had succeeded in drawing them away from a re-entry into France for a continuance in the Mediterranean. The meeting however went off far better than I had hoped, and the determination to proceed with our plans for Sicily were confirmed subject to a revision at a later date as regards resources and training. This was really the culmination of all my efforts. I wanted first to ensure that Germany should continue to be regarded as our primary enemy and that the defeat of Japan must come after that of Germany. Secondly that for the present Germany can best be attacked through the medium of Italy in the Mediterranean, and thirdly that this can best be achieved with a policy directed against Sicily. All these points have been secured, and in addition many minor ones connected with Turkey, command of operations in Tunisia* and at home, etc. It has been quite the hardest 10 days I have had from the point of view of difficulty handling the work.

After tea I went for a walk. Found five of the small owls and a marsh harrier.

From Casablanca, Brooke and the rest of Churchill's party flew to Cairo, Turkey, Cyprus and back to Cairo. They then flew to the airport outside Tripoli, passing over El Alamein and the other recent battlefields for the first time. They were met by Alexander and Montgomery in preparation for inspecting the victorious troops.

Thursday 4 February – At 9.30 am we all assembled and started off by car for Tripoli. It was most interesting seeing the place for the first time. The streets and housetops were lined with sentries, who held back the local inhabitants. When we arrived on the main square and sea front we found there the bulk of the 51st Division formed up. The last time we had seen them was near Ismailia just after their arrival in the

---

*   Alexander was to be Eisenhower's deputy.

Middle East. Then they were still pink and white, now they were bronzed warriors of many battles and of a victorious advance. I have seldom seen a finer body of men or one that looked prouder of being soldiers. We drove slowly round the line and then came back with the men cheering him [Churchill] all the way. We then took up our position on a prepared stand and the whole Division marched past with a bagpipe band playing. It was quite one of the most impressive sights I have ever seen.

As I stood alongside of Winston watching the Division march past, with the wild music of the pipes in my ears, I felt a large lump rise in my throat and a tear run down my face. I looked round at Winston and saw several tears on his face, from which I knew that he was being stirred inwardly by the self same feelings that were causing such upheaval in me. I felt no shame that tears should have betrayed my feelings, only a deep relief.

Sunday 7 February – A cold and uncomfortable night. At 9 am we were over the Scilly Isles and 10 minutes later came to Land's End. Clouds were low and the going very bumpy. By 1 pm we arrived in London where to my great joy you met me.

I had finished a journey of some 10,200 miles, which had been full of interest and had resulted in agreements with Americans and Turks far above anything I had hoped for. In the last two years I have flown just under 55,000 miles!!

I now foresee some hard work ahead to convert some of the paper work of the last 3 weeks into facts and actions.

WOMEN IN THE SERVICES

Women had served in all-female units of the services in the First World War and nearly half a million served in the British forces between 1939 and 1945 – in the WAAF (Women's Auxiliary Air Force), WRNS (Women's Royal Naval Service), FANY (First Aid Nursing Yeomanry) and the ATS (Auxiliary Territorial Service), which had been established in September 1938 to supply women volunteers to work in the army as cooks, clerks and orderlies, releasing men for the fighting zone.

In December 1941 conscription was introduced for unmarried women between 20 and 30 and the ATS was granted military status.

JANE BEGG
Junior officer, ATS*

Jane Begg from Caithness was one of the original volunteers for the North Highland ATS. She specialized in army catering and became an officer in May 1940, commanding a platoon of sixty girls on the south-east shores of Kent during the Dunkirk evacuation.

The girls are issued with a complete set of clothes, underwear and brushes whenever she joins up but these must be handed back, except for a few articles, when she is discharged. Consequently there are endless inspections of kit where every

---

* Jane Begg (Mrs J. R. Macbeth), private papers: lecture delivered February 1943 to Reay Women's Guild, Imperial War Museum, 91271.

detail is laid out so that officers can see they are clean and mended.

There is a monthly medical inspection and here the girls often have the benefit of Harley Street specialists who have volunteered for Army Service. The girls are stripped and examined from head to foot, in the presence of their officer.

Their fiancé may have been killed at Dunkirk – they went on parade that morning and reported for duty in the cook-house as though nothing had happened – even although they probably fainted over the wash-up in the process. Their homes were bombed or blasted to wreckage – their fathers, mothers, sisters or brothers killed – the ATS their only home.

Women were barred from serving in battle but soon took over many vital supporting roles – as drivers, radar operators, military police, anti-aircraft gun crew and wireless operators. They were expected to complete their training in a third of the time traditionally given to their male counterparts. As early as 1936 Air Chief Marshal Dowding had recommended women for the role of plotter – the vital link between radar operators and the officers responsible for ordering the movements of aircraft or ships.

IRENE STORER
Corporal, WAAF*

Women were initially considered far too weak physically to have anything to do with barrage balloons. Nonetheless, even in this exceptionally dangerous line of physical work, good training and good organization allowed them to succeed, as Irene Storer, from Derby, explains. In the winter of 1942 Irene was operating

* Irene Storer (Mrs I. Forsdyke), private papers, Imperial War Museum, 86371.

a barrage balloon with an all-woman crew from a cemetery in Sheffield. The team in charge of a balloon had to eat and sleep on site. It was a constant, round-the-clock responsibility: '2 hrs on 4 hrs off throughout 24 hrs, then moving on by 2 hrs each day until a day off on the seventh'. Irene much preferred the cemetery to the slag-heap site she'd worked on previously and there were 'plenty of colourful flowers to enjoy!' – although they did have to clean their teeth at a tap, 'lining up with people waiting to fill jars and vases for graves'.

The giant balloons, made of two-ply Egyptian cotton, proofed and silver-faced to deflect heat, were kept aloft with 19,000 cubic feet of hydrogen gas in an inner compartment. The crew had to be able to haul in the balloon speedily if bad weather threatened or their own aircraft were in the area. It was a dangerous business and Irene complained that HQ rarely gave them storm warnings.

The whole purpose of the balloons was to hold up cables. It was the cables which were lethal to aircraft. Viewed from the ground the balloons seemed miles apart, but from the air a balloon barrage was a fearsome sight. Its means were two-fold: to prevent dive-bombing, and to keep the aircraft high enough up for the ack-ack to reach them.

Fitted to the cable were two Dual Parachute Links (DPLs) one 20 ft. from the top, and the other 20 ft. from the bottom. These carried an explosive charge. Anything hitting the cable would jar these DPLs, which were fired by the inertia, breaking the cable in both places, and the two together exerting a pressure of 120 pounds upon whatever had hit it. If it was an aircraft wing, then that would be cut off like a wire through cheese. Needless to say, the winch driver must never jar the gears. When hauling in, we had to stop at each DPL, switch off the firing mechanism, dismantle it.

The first lessons were in recognising cordage (no such

thing as string in the Airforce), 2oz [ounce] cordage, 4oz cordage etc, also ropes – ½ in[ch] hemp, 1 in cotton and so on. Then wire cables; solid drawn flying cable, hemp-cored wire cables of various thicknesses for various purposes, 4¼ ton breaking strain and 3¼ ton BS. Next came the study of an amazing no. of knots and all their purposes. It was necessary to know and recognise all these things in the dark by touch since a good deal of our work took place in darkness. So we were able to undo any knot even if it had just come down frozen from 6,000 ft.

A balloon in a strong and variable wind was like a thing alive. The last 100 ft. or so of the hauling in could be precarious as the balloon could sweep right down to the ground – perhaps in the next street! The winch driver needed all her skill and concentration in these circumstances.

It was more dangerous for no. 1 who was directly under the belly of the balloon waiting to take hold of the 'piano' wires of which there were twelve, 6 from each side, shackled together where they joined the main cable. These she laid neatly down on the bed [of canvas], then slung a 1 yd square cushion full of straw over all the wires and flying cable, and then – bent double – she dashed out from under the balloon, dancing over the moving ropes.

These cables could break a leg with ease as they snaked about. Breaking two legs was not uncommon. When barrage balloons were scaled down and once again run by men-only teams, Irene was retrained as an instrument repairer. She was allowed to keep her kit but not the lace-up boots 'which had saved my leg on many occasions'.*

---

* Irene is featured in the painting *A Balloon Site (Coventry) 1943*, by Dame Laura Knight, Newport Museum and Art Gallery, Newport, Wales.

MAUREEN BOLSTER
WRNS*

By June 1943 Wrens were being trained as stokers on ships, work that could include assembling and servicing torpedoes and depth charges and climbing rigging to repair a minesweeping light. Until then they had simply crewed ships. For the select few who knew how to ride a motorcyle there was also the tantalizing option of becoming a dispatch rider. Maureen Bolster from Bedfordshire had been working in a factory until July 1942. Bored by the work, parted from her fiancé, Eric, who was serving with the RAF in the Middle East, she decided to become a Wren. And since she rode a 250cc bike, she began to wonder if she might become a dispatch rider, and relayed her progress in letters to Eric.

Friday 23 October – **WRNS Training Depot, Bowlands, Southsea** – Life is one rush here – squad drill, lectures, musters etc. Yesterday we marched in squad to the naval barracks to have our bosoms radio-grabbed for TB. Much booing from sailors but we'd been instructed before to take <u>NO</u> notice!

Am dying to begin DR Training but am afraid it'll be a few days before I know what's going to happen to me. I'm <u>desperate</u> to be a DR!

Wednesday 28 October – Dearest, Dearest. Do please come rescue me! I'm wondering if I've bitten off more than I can chew! It's only by the Grace of God I'm here, writing to you. Monday, was called for by the CO. 'Bolster, you are being allowed the privilege of training as Despatch Rider if you pass a test. You will be the last allowed to do this (too many accidents!) in the Command.' Was no end bucked!!! Yester-

---

*   E. M. Bolster, private papers (some published as *Entertaining Eric*, Imperial War Museum, 1988), Imperial War Museum, 661.

day, I tootled round to an enormous garage, to meet my instructor & have a test (feeling scared stiff). Man is a garage hand & very decent. He gave me a crash helmet (!) & a DR coat, and took me pillion on the front. Of course the first thing I had to do was something I've never done – turn round on the spot!! God! Up and down I had to go, backwards & forwards – in a high gale!

He's passed me. This a.m. had to go to the barracks for a vision test – sailors all drilling etc. Eyes are A1. Came back to garage & went out again on front. But, Eric, this afternoon was given helmet, breeches, coat and gloves. 'That's your bike, Miss – you'll get on & follow me!' It was a Triumph 350 (am only used to 250) with a completely new gear box! On I got, praying like mad, wobbled along into town behind man. Had to stop for traffic & the damned thing conked out! Policeman was waving me on – people stared. I got hot & bothered & little boy said – 'Cor, look at 'er! She's one of them Wren Despatch Riders.' Eventually got going, then the fun began. Miles we went – miles & miles. Had to follow the man. All sorts of antics he did, slowing down – darting forward, shooting round corners – and he made me speed so! Honestly, I've never had such an afternoon in my life – he made me do 50 m.p.h. on my first tour.

By early November she was stationed with other dispatch riders at Haslemere.

Thursday 5 November – Am miles out in the blue. Am in a cabin with 14 others – all couriers. Except for this other girl who's 25 none are under 30!!! 6 are over 40! They're tough, & strong & ugly. They've taken no notice of me at all, bar to ask me what on earth I think I'm doing here at my age. Some of them are ladies, but queer types. Their conversation is dreadful – lots of them apparently use their job as a means to another end – if you get me! Repressed women & all that!

They all hate each other & are fighting among themselves like a lot of cats.

The cabin is revoltingly untidy – greasy hairnets hanging on bedposts, drawers bulging, clothes on the floor.

In addition to the services there was the Women's Land Army (WLA), a First World War institution which was re-formed in June 1939. From being less than a tenth of the agricultural labour force, the female component rose to well over a quarter, 90,000 of whom belonged to the WLA, one third of them from the cities. Some received training, but many, particularly in the early days of the war, were put to work on their first day. They were generally poorly paid and often felt exploited by farmers who previously had paid men significantly more for the same work.

8. PREPARATIONS FOR A CROSS-CHANNEL ATTACK

AUTUMN 1943

The Battle of the Atlantic was the longest continuous campaign of the war, lasting from the day Britain declared war in September 1939 until the day Germany surrendered in May 1945. For Churchill the consequences of failure were catastrophic: Britain would starve; there would be no American troops for an invasion of Europe; supplies to Russia would cease – in short, Hitler would have won.

The commander of Germany's submarine fleet, and from 1943 head of the German navy, Admiral Dönitz, was convinced that U-boats could win the war, exactly as Churchill feared, and saturated the Atlantic with over 200 submarines to sink as many merchant ships as possible. The major problem the Allies faced was the 600-mile gap in the middle of the ocean, outside the range of planes based in North America and Britain. Here Dönitz spread out his U-boats and waited. When a convoy was spotted, the nearest fifteen or twenty submarines were alerted to gather and hunt as a 'wolf pack'. In 1942 1,662 Allied ships were lost in this fashion.

The Admiralty realized that to defeat the U-boats they needed more training, more aircraft, better radar and purpose-built anti-submarine ships. When all these conditions were met, as they were in the spring of 1943, the results were spectacular. In May – dubbed 'black May' by the Germans – Dönitz lost forty-one U-boats, an unsustainable rate of loss. He ordered his remaining submarines to back off and sent a message to Hitler that 'for the moment' the battle was lost. After that, with German submarine production failing to keep up with losses, it became clear that the battle was in fact over.

Battles on other fronts were more clear cut. In North Africa Rommel was driven back. His supply situation worsened and his forces pushed into the northern tip of Tunisia. Rommel himself was recalled before his army surrendered. In the Pacific the islands and archipelagos most recently overrun by Japan – Guadalcanal, Papua New Guinea, the Solomon and Gilbert Islands – were gradually retaken by the Allies.

At Casablanca Churchill and Roosevelt had agreed to increase Allied bombing raids on Germany, a decision heartily supported by most of the British public. In May Wing Commander Guy Gibson led a series of raids on the heavily industrialized Ruhr Valley, attacking dams with the newly developed 'bouncing bombs', giving war-weary Britons some good news and making a hero of both Gibson and Barnes Wallis, the scientist who had developed the bombs. Between January and November 1943 Allied bombs rained down on seventy-two different German cities. In July the week-long bombing of Hamburg created a firestorm. An inferno of 800 degrees centigrade or more raged for two hours sucking in air at hurricane speeds. Of the 36,000 killed and 950,000 bombed out in the city, most were civilians.

Though the Red Army continued to advance west, the Germans still controlled vast swathes of Russian territory, including the area around Smolensk. There, in April 1943, in the forest of Katyn, the Nazi authorities made a gruesome discovery. Mass graves were unearthed revealing the bodies of 14,500 Polish army officers, doctors, lawyers, professors, engineers, policemen, priests and one woman – all executed on Stalin's direct orders. The Germans quickly released newsreel evidence of this Soviet crime.* For the British government this was a huge embarrassment since Britain was allied to both Poland, whose government in exile was based in London, and to Soviet Russia. Stalin of course denied any responsibility for the massacre and Britain did nothing to challenge him. Secret files noted, 'The official line in the UK has been to pretend the whole affair was a fake . . . Any other view would have been distasteful to the public, since it could be inferred that we were allied to a power guilty of the same sort of atrocities as the Germans.'†

At dawn on 10 July Operation Husky, the invasion of Sicily, began. With heavy naval and air support two armies landed on the island's southern and eastern beaches. American General Patton took the west of the island and Montgomery the more difficult mountainous east. It took little over a month to conquer the island. One immediate effect was the overthrow of Mussolini by Italy's Fascist Grand Council. His replacement, Marshal Badoglio, reassured Hitler that Italy would fight on but simultaneously entered into secret negotiations with Eisenhower, and on 3 September 1943 signed an armistice with the Allies. The invasion of Sicily had been a success and was followed by landings on the Italian mainland in September, but the Allies' main priority was now Operation Overlord, the proposed invasion of north-west Europe scheduled for May 1944. At long last the war seemed to be going well for the Allies.

In autumn 1943 Oswald Mosley, leader of the British Union of Fascists, was released from internment because he had become seriously unwell. He and his wife Diana would spend the rest of the war under house arrest. Unsurprisingly there were questions in the House and much news coverage

---

* Norman Davies, *Europe, A History*, Oxford University Press, 1996.
† Quoted in Davies, *Europe*, and sourced 'as reported in *The Times* 10th June 1995'.

was devoted to Home Secretary Herbert Morrison's controversial decision.

THE DIARISTS

NAOMI MITCHISON

On 15 July Naomi made her first radio broadcast – a talk for the BBC about education – and was also featured on the front page of the *Radio Times* – 'a triumph for Scotland'. The house was full of visitors over the summer, the three youngest children were home from school and there were other guests camping on the Mitchisons' land, including members of the Young Communist League. There was plenty of company, but entertaining them also meant plenty of hard work. Later, in the autumn, Naomi spent five weeks in England, visiting family and friends.

Friday 3 September – Ian MacLaren rang up. I forgot it was six [time of the early evening news], but Rosemary went to speak to him and dashed back, saying he was listening at the same time and said Italy had capitulated. I turned on the radio but it took some time and we'd missed it and it wasn't in the summary. We were awfully excited, and told everyone.

I felt frightfully pleased at tea and got out a pot of raspberry jam. We had the venison steak, but various people took enormous helpings before the shooters, who had got two hares, came in, and I was jumped on for not 'as usual' providing enough. It is so bloody difficult catering, and I felt upset and hated them all, sitting around drinking, I just couldn't join [in] or be pleased any longer. It's all very unreasonable, but they are all having holidays and I'm not. I feel like a hotel manager. I shall always be sympathetic with them [*sic*] after this.

Then the various dancers turned up. We did a couple of dances and then went in for the news. Everyone crowded round the rather faint radio; there was a general feeling, I think, of slight scorn of the Italians, and several people saying 'a stab in the back' when it came to their remarks about the Germans . . . We also felt a kind of mixture of irritation and scorn against the Americans and Eisenhower, but hoped that all atrocities would be put down to them. We felt they would probably manage to push down the tower of Pisa and so on.

We none of us recognised the second national anthem but supposed it to be American. The dancers went back after the Italian news. I stayed for the Russian and the playing of the 'International' [*sic*]. I was so glad they had played it after all. I went back and told Dougie* they had played it; we were dancing a waltz, he kept on squeezing me tight with happiness and solidarity. I said Now we can really begin to plan, and to think of after the war. He said Aye, it will be our fight.

Monday 15 November – I got the feeling that London morale is worse than the tail of the blitz, worse even than last time, a lot of bad work with the Americans, and general depressions about possibilities of real change. Went to see the London plan, everyone there pointing out their own street and what was to happen to it. Don't see what can be done without a revolutionary change. More anti-Churchill feeling and general hope among the left that the Russians will win the war in time to chase the Americans out of Piccadilly.

Wednesday 24 November – One begins to feel no need to bother about anti-semitism, as the Americans have completely taken the place of the Jews – stories about rape, etc.

---

* A fisherman and piper who shared Naomi's politics.

It will end by making one quite pro-American. Nobody has a good word for them and the ones one sees about look mostly pretty awful. Ruth* takes the orthodox CP point of view about Mosley; I say it's rather nonsense, and some day one of them will be kept in and not let out for illness; not that I mind in the least if Mosley does die in gaol, it's only a wee matter of being consistent. A lot of local feeling about it at the Doves.† But I'm bored with the CP. They support the government on all the wrong things.

Murdoch seems to have put through something, by way of his boss, that has saved the Min of Supply a very large sum. He is now going to drive tanks at Lulworth. It is awful, all this saying goodbye, I can't bear it.

Sunday 5 December – **Back in Carradale** – Stayed in bed late and did little all day but still remain devilish tired. I have a sort of buzz in my head all the time; I suppose it must be disregarded, as my blood pressure is o.k. But it is an unpleasant companion. I have still got a bit of a cough too. I cleared up a lot of letters in the morning, almost all the immediate ones. In the afternoon went to see the Jacksons, who seem much pleased with their baby. If mine had lived she would be very companionable by now.

I'm not doing at all what I want. If I can't break something soon I will break myself. And the Second Front hanging over one, and this bloody Churchill gloating over suffering like a great mediaeval devil.

---

* Her daughter-in-law.
† A riverside pub in Hammersmith now called the Dove.

ANNE GARNETT

Life at the factory was getting Anne down. Recent 'blockages in the line of supply' meant that there was no work for them to do. Though this was not her fault she was reprimanded for making the lack of work too obvious by standing about smoking or chatting to the others. 'We must not chat in little groups,' she wrote. The factory dispatched all manner of small pieces of engineering equipment: the dreaded ampoules (much sought after by the Admiralty), cylinders which required numbers being painted on them, and water-filter cases and water tanks which as yet no one had asked for. By late August Ron, the more sympathetic of her two employers, had finally found her a job: filling in process cards for previous orders safely dispatched.

Wednesday 8 September – At last! Thank God we needn't bomb Italy any longer – those lovely towns I hope to see one day. Put on the news at supper – it sounds as if the Italians are going to help us drive out the Germans. To bed, drunk with happiness.

Tuesday 21 September – Long report of Churchill's report on the war tonight (he's just back from another USA trip). Fascinating account of the Germans swooping down in parachutes over-powering the guards and carrying Mussolini off with them – in a plane I suppose – what a thrill for old Musso. I can't help being rather pleased about it, having a sneaky regard for the bombastic Benito! Besides all this brotherly love between him and Hitler is very piquant and intriguing I find. How will it end? We'd best put them both on Elba, to bore one another to death.

Wednesday 6 October – Scandalous story of fire-watching at Burnett's. Under the Compulsory order 2 of the staff have to sleep on the premises each night – last night Griffins* were woken by D. 'There's men running round at Burnett's Mr Griffin': So poor Bobby groped over and in at the back door. The first thing he saw was 2 men's bikes in the hall! He banged on the fire-watcher's room and one of the girls [on duty] stood in the doorway and fended him off with a tale of 2 soldiers having rung at the door for permission to leave their bikes. Pushing past her, Bobby flashed his torch full on 2 UAF [US Air Force] lads who were hastily buckling on their belts. General ticking off of girls today, many tears and assurances of innocence. Both girls are married and their spouses due home on leave shortly. Anyway it's something to have a little clean sex on fire watching and not the Indoor Games indulged in by the boys at Bells!†

Thursday 21 October – Three hundred [new] Americans arrive in Wellington and the camp behind the Griffins is a-clamour once more, while groups of greenish-grey figures lope about the streets. Curious how such a slight difference in uniform gives a foreign air. I hear the officers are a nice lot – hope they'll brighten our winter for us as D and L and B and the rest did last year.

Thursday 4 November – Another story of our gallant allies! A USA soldier was in a Taunton Air Raid Shelter with fair companion (English). Exit FC and vanishes in the black-out, with his trousers and £40 in the pockets! Unfortunately he had to go back to Norton Camp in his under-pants, a lesson to all, let us trust!! Girl has not yet been traced.

Am getting quite used to biking to and from work in convoy now – long rows of USA jeeps and lorries around me, with much badinage going on that I am quite unable to

---

* Neighbours Babs and Bobby.
† The factory where she worked.

comprehend! I must say a good deal of it sounds uncompli-
mentary, but I smile and try to look as if I enjoy it!

Russians are swarming into the Crimea from which I
doubt if many Germans will escape alive.

Thursday 18 November – Two policemen in Thurston's office
[at the factory] this afternoon, closeted with one of the girls,
taking a statement from her. Walking back to Rockwell
Green last night she was followed by a US soldier (a white
one) who knocked her into the hedge, saying 'Scream and I'll
knock your head off.' She managed to get away, but lost her
brooch and was badly shaken. Old Smith [co-worker], hearing
this, said 'You ought to be in Cardiff, where I've come from
today. Murder someone every night, they do there – of
course, it's nearly always women, but they knifed a British
soldier last night, they did.'

Friday 19 November – Not a stroke of work to be found at the
factory, and poor Thurston had to invent a job or two for
me as Ron doesn't like to see me knitting. (This occurred
yesterday when he came into the office.) Nonetheless, the
sleeve of my jumper has grown another 3 inches!

HAROLD NICOLSON

Although vastly more at the centre of events than the ordinary
man, Harold felt 'out of things', in danger of being perceived as a
'dud' and becoming an 'old buffer'. He wrote to Vita in July, 'I do
feel it strange that a person of my experience is so much ignored
nowadays.'

The news from Italy at the end of the summer was initially
cheering, but as the Germans fought back Harold's hopes sank
and he became convinced that the Allies were 'heading for
another Dunkirk and grave humiliation'. In October he spent four

weeks in Sweden lecturing for the Ministry of Information – a 'potty little lecture tour'.

Wednesday 15 September – I have recovered from my shattering disappointment over the Italian misfortunes. I had, I suppose, felt underneath that the surrender of Italy really meant the shortening of the war. I was angry and mortified that the Germans could exploit the situation so rapidly whereas we seemed to have lost every trick. But after four days of real distress, my old easy confidence has returned. I imagine that my feelings were typical of the mass of the people, although the ordinary citizen probably does not realise to the same extent as I do what a fillip the release of Mussolini will have given to German opinion. They will again feel themselves to be invincible.

Sunday 7 November – **Letter to Ben and Nigel** – At Halsingborg, in the intervals of more speeches, I went to see the refugee camp. Since Hitler established his New Order in Denmark, some eight thousand refugees have slipped across the Sund, which is no wider than from Ryde to Portsmouth. There they all were with their babies and their bundles, looking exactly like caricatures in Der Sturmer.* When I entered the room briskly with the Mayor and the Chief of Police, the sentries leapt to attention. I saw a spasm of real panic pass over the faces of the refugees. They thought for a second that the Gestapo had arrived. So I shouted something out in English and they all relaxed immediately and grinned at each other. I was delighted to see that one word of English can change expressions of terror into expressions of delight. They crowded round me. Among them were some Danish officers who had also escaped. 'Can you take us to England,' they said, 'we wish to fight those devils,' pointing to where

---

* A Nazi newspaper.

the hills of Denmark glimmered in the sun. They seemed lost, stranded and bemused.

The Swedes of course fear the Russians, and are anxious lest we shall be too late to share Russian victories in Europe. I must have met some twenty different types of Swedes who have been in Germany lately. They were all unanimous in saying that collapse is very close. 'The whole thing,' they said, 'is like a rotten pear, only kept together by its rind.' When I said to them, 'But we don't believe in an early collapse. It will only be in July next year that we shall be able to strike with our full force,' they merely smiled. 'We know', they said, 'the true state of Germany and the real despair that has seized the German people. You don't.' The corruption among the Nazis and the SS is something terrible. The whole feeling is one of utter disillusionment and defeatism. 'Who can save us?' is what they all cry. I have come back immensely optimistic and cheered. You cannot conceive how high our prestige is.

Wednesday 10 November – I went down to the House where I had a Leicester deputation about the relief of famine in Europe. The old Peace Pledge Union people have concentrated on the slogan 'Feed the starving men and women of Europe.' This is a great pity, since there is really something to be said for relaxing the blockade in so far as Greece and Belgium are concerned. The advocacy of these people compromises what is an excellent cause. I was very cold with them and pointed out all the difficulties. But I promised to speak the next day when the matter came up on Adjournment. I did speak. I made the best House of Commons speech that I have made since my Italian speech.* The House filled up and I was warmly cheered. But of course the whole thing was spoiled by the pacifists coming in and backing me.

* In 1938, against negotiating with Italy.

I think I did a little good, and we got promises out of the Government that they would send more food, and of a different quality, to Greece.*

Friday 3 December – A workers' deputation from Leicester factories came to see me about Mosley. They were not in any way hostile or impolite. But I could see that anything I might say in defence of Morrison was 'propaganda' and untrue. I feel that it is most dangerous that the working-classes should have lost all confidence in their leaders.

I don't think I have a chance of keeping my seat in the next Election. Nobody in a constituency where the majority are working-class will keep his seat. I still have to stand, of course, but it will be an unpleasant ordeal and the end will be defeat. I am lucky to have had the seat for nine years and to have sat in one of the most important Parliaments there has ever been. But, as I said, I have no chance of remaining the Member for West Leicester.

VERA BRITTAIN

In March, as the mass bombing of Germany continued, Vera wrote, 'World has gone mad, felt sick at thought of civilian suffering behind the gleeful communiqués.'

At the end of April she and George, with Amy Burnett and her baby girl Marian, reoccupied the house in Cheyne Walk in preparation for the return of Vera's children.

A berth was found for John on a ship leaving early in July.

---

* Vera Brittain, who called on Nicolson shortly afterwards, recalled in *Testament of Experience* (Fontana, 1981, first published in 1957): 'Greek relief . . . was to be extended by 1,000 tons of food each month. It was not much – in the light of Europe's needs it was almost nothing – but the small concession enabled a number of young Greeks to survive the war.'

His parents' anxiety about the risk was heightened by news of
the loss of a plane from Lisbon to Bristol, shot down by the
Germans. All were killed, including several children and the actor
Leslie Howard. But John had an uninterrupted safe journey
home, arriving on 18 July. John, as he writes in his memoir
Family Quartet, missed America and the 'wide-open spaces of
the Mid-West'. He had an American accent, was taller than his
mother and 'had acquired a certain youthful sangfroid which she
must have found unexpected if not disturbing'. He rejected Eton
but agreed to Harrow, where 'I was virtually the only boy in
the school not to be in the Army Corps, out of deference to
my mother's pacifism. I was never bullied or given a hard time
because of this.'

Shirley left New York for Portugal early in September, but did
not arrive when expected. Vera was anxious enough, but would
have been even more worried had she known the ship had been
blown off course by a cyclone. Safe at last in Lisbon, Shirley was
further delayed by a shortage of planes and the backlog of British
children waiting to return home, so there was more waiting to
endure.

October came with no news of Shirley's homecoming and
Vera decided to keep her engagements, speaking on famine relief
in Leicester, Swindon and, on the 7th, in London.

Sunday 3 October – PPU Council in the morning. Carried
Famine Relief Fast proposal through the Council by 20–5
(6 abstentions).

Immediately following lunch went to Harrow to spend
the afternoon with John. He met me at the top of the hill
in his Gilbert & Sullivan Harrow tails (looking very nice); I
was glad to learn he seemed far more happily settled than
his letters suggested, and is doing a good deal of music. We
walked about the playing fields together & then had tea at
the School Stores, where J. most uncharacteristically ate three
large cakes.

Thursday 7 October – Hard work catching up on letters. Evening, spoke Walthamstow (Famine Relief). Left the meeting about 9 p.m. to go home. The Mayor's car carried me to Manor House Station two or three miles away, & during the drive it was quiet though I could see shells bursting far to the right & the searchlights were vivid. I quite thought the All Clear would go during the half hr. tube run, but the raid was still on when I got out at Knightsbridge Stn to get the 19 bus. Several people were waiting at the bus stop, but I had hardly got into the bus when pandemonium began; our own 'planes going to Germany (which quietened our guns) had now stopped going over. The noise of the guns increased as we went down Sloane St. & just beyond Sloane Sq. the bus stopped. Several passengers pulled down the windows to stop any shattering of glass & we could see AA shells bursting just above our heads.

Couldn't decide whether to stay in the bus or get out & risk the shell splinters ('What goes up has to come down,' said the woman bus conductor) when the bus went on. I got out at Flood Street & dashed for home with the battle still overhead & the sky like a Fifth of November pageant. Had to take refuge in a Rossetti Gdns. doorway on the way; then made a dash for our house & got in to find everyone in the shelter & thankful to see me. All Clear about ½ hr. later.

Saturday 9 October – No further news of Poppy's return.
Foggy evening; no Alert.

Sunday 10 October – Very tired, spent morning in bed. Mild & foggy. Took Marian into the Park this afternoon. The leaves were falling fast & it was all rather melancholic – too sadly reminiscent of the days ten years ago when Winifred & I used to go the same walk with John & Shirley (who was then just Marian's age). But now Battersea Park looks shabby & rather neglected, though its flowers are still quite good.

Sunday 17 October – SHIRLEY RETURNED!

Came back on a very cold wet day from lecturing at Nottingham to find a tiny fair-haired creature in red jumper & plaid skirt – so pretty! – waiting for me behind the drawing room curtains!

Air raid.

Years later, Vera asked Shirley whether she had remembered her when she came back from America. '"No," Shirley said, "you weren't real to me at all. You seemed more like a person in a book." I knew then that in spite of inevitable pain for the generous Colbys and grave risks for the children themselves, we had been right to bring them home. In another year or two, those disappearing images of a father and mother would have vanished for ever.'*

GEORGE BEARDMORE

'The times are so grey and life so pared down to mere existence,' George wrote in May, two days before his thirty-fifth birthday. During the summer there was occasional news of deaths in action – an old schoolfriend of George, Jean's cousin, 'poor charming Derek'. His novel was published in July to favourable reviews and sales. There was also a pay rise, as George agreed to take on extra responsibilities in the Housing Department. But he preferred being out of the office.

Tuesday 19 October – A big gap, but then nothing has changed. I still cycle out to try to find billets for nurses, but the field is pretty well exhausted. Also billets for workers at Napier's,[†] rather easier because the pay is better.

---

*   Vera Brittain, *Testament of Experience*, Fontana, 1981.

†   Manufacturers of aero-engines in Acton.

Two bombs fell last night in Hall's fields, behind Pinner Park School. Alerts are increasing in number. Milk scarce. Meanwhile a substantial public shelter has been built outside our front gate so that we can troop into it when the evening sneak raiders arrive. When the Alert goes we get things ready, when the guns go off we bring Victoria down to sleep behind the settee, although occasionally we take ourselves and our bundles into the surface shelter. Victoria is growing aware of the war and mentioned the word for the first time last week. Also she asked if that aeroplane in the sky were a German. Jean attempts the impossible task of trying to explain what's happening but the child will never know the alarms we've suffered.

Wednesday 17 November – Following the huge Russian drive, now almost into Poland, bets were being laid in the office that the European war will be over by Christmas. But now the date is June of next year ('44). Threats of our invading Europe – bombings of Norway – an insurrection in Denmark. The first years of peace are going to be difficult. I know for myself that once I have left this job I shall never again seek employment. And how many hundreds like me, weary of uniform, are saying the same!

Oranges are back again in the shops. The biggest crop of tomatoes this year that I've ever had. The green and pink ones alone – i.e. those not ripened – filled a barrow. We couldn't have got this far without the garden to give us green stuff.

Saturday 18 December – On Monday the 6th I came home with a slight cough and sat down in the fireside chair. Two hours later I was so weak and wretched that I couldn't undo my buttons and Jean had to help me and lift me upstairs. This was the onset of the prevalent 'flu that has decimated the office. Jean and Victoria, thank God, have so far escaped.

Particularly Jean! She is booked at the Nursing Home at the bottom of the road for about 25 July next. We aren't afraid that the fifth year of the war will have any permanent effect upon the baby.* We are glad, and that's all there is to it.

CLARA MILBURN

Clara fought off depression by keeping busy: 'the only panacea is to work and work and work'. There were times of celebration – Jack hoisted his Union Jack to mark the victory in North Africa and later the surrender of Italy; the arrival of 'four nice big cobby Light Sussex' hens made a 'thrilling day and a lovely day'; Alan passed his exam; Clara celebrated her sixtieth birthday on 24 June; there was a bumper harvest of apples, pears and tomatoes; and a Captain Keens, repatriated from Oflag VIIB, brought first-hand news of Alan, who was 'now marvellously fit and has now broadened out and looks quite different'.

Clara was implacable in her antipathy to Germany and unrelenting in her support for the 'retribution' of the bombing raids. She was sure everyone needed to sustain the war effort.

Sunday 7 November – A good day to begin what one hopes will be the last volume in this fifth year of devastating war. With the Russians forging ahead, the masses of equipment they take as well as prisoners, and the huge number of killed and wounded, the enemy must surely feel the Allies' might. According to the repatriated men, and other sources, the Germans realize they are not going to win. If our – and the American – people could put aside private differences and keep off strikes it would be another step nearer the end. In Italy we are now advancing at a quicker rate, but going is

---

* This is George's first mention of the baby.

necessarily slow in a mountainous peninsula and the Germans are adept at laying mines and placing booby-traps. They also carry off natives for slave labour and have no pity on civilians or women and children. A nasty race indeed!

Monday 8 November – Sir Walter Citrine* seems to think so much Home Guard work and fire-watching is unnecessary, and said so. He thinks people are getting weary of it! Of course they are weary, but that is no reason for slacking off – how foolish it would be to let up now. What a fool the man is! Typical Labour Party mentality!

Tuesday 9 November – Lord Mayor's Day and Churchill makes an excellent, gripping speech. As usual, he takes the long view. Our efforts are not for this generation alone, but for the happiness and peace of mankind in future. No-one should talk, or think, as if the war were already almost finished, for the Germans are still powerful. Nor should the fire-watchers and the Home Guard be discouraged in any of the work they do, which is still wholly and entirely necessary, and anyone who thinks this too hard and says so is doing a grave disservice to the nation. In fact, one in the eye for that idiot of a blatherer Walter Citrine!

Saturday 27 November – A cold, damp, murky November day. I pondered whether to go out or stay in, as I suspected I had a cold (only too certainly confirmed by evening), but in the end I went out to do the hens. Changing the birds over to the new hen house, with all the attendant jobs of clearing up the runs, making new nests, burning the old chaff and putting in fresh chaff and oak leaves, took us until 1 p.m.

Then we came in to lunch – lunch!! Perhaps I was per-

* TUC general secretary.

nickety today, but toad-in-the-hole is not what it was. That lovely pork sausage in a yellow batter, shining with fat, has given place to a beef beast, flavourless and tough-skinned, in a heavy khaki batter made with milk powder. Mine went down slowly and reluctantly. Later the situation was saved by an excellent steamed pudding with an overcoat of sweet jam.

Just now everything seems scarce. What is a pint of milk a day for three people! Kate visited her friends yesterday – mother, father, a little boy and a babe a month or so old. They can have seven pints a day! This because of the nursing mother and the children, but they do not want so much. The husband can also have extra cheese, which they do not want, so Kate came home with cheese, a tin of dried milk and four boxes of matches – and how glad we were of them all. Well, well, times change.

HERMIONE RANFURLY

In July Abercrombie telephoned Hermione's office in Cairo 'out of the blue'. With Cairo so near the front line he was planning on teaching close-quarter fighting suitable for urban warfare. He was inviting senior officers, and she was billed as Exhibit A. Two days later, with his Silver Lady revolver in her hands, she was ordered to shoot the pips out of all the playing cards she saw. ' "Right hand. Left hand. Both hands together," he bawled. By the grace of God I missed nothing.'

At the end of September Hermione's youngest sister Daphne, whom she had not seen for three and a half years, arrived to work as a secretary at Hermione's old SOE office. And in November there were preparations for a conference between Churchill, Roosevelt and China's Chiang Kai-shek to discuss the Allies' strategy against Japan.

Friday 3 September – We have landed on the toe of Italy. I am in a fever of excitement – perhaps I shall see Dan this week.

Today Whitaker, who now works for the NAAFI, came to tell me he has been made a sergeant; he was wearing three of the largest stripes I ever saw.

Friday 17 September – Every day I expect to hear that Dan is free. I have had a yellow fever inoculation so that I can fly to meet him when he gets out.

The great Russian advance continues; we are bombing Germany on a tremendous scale; the Balkans are rustling with rebellion; surely this must be the last winter of the war.

Monday 18 October – There was a big meeting in the Map Room today; Mr Oliver Stanley, Secretary of State for the Colonies, is here, and General Monty. While they were at the meeting we tried on the famous beret. It was too big for me. We gummed the lining of it with sticking paste and felt very sad that we will not be there the next time Monty doffs it. Amongst all the VIPs we take care of we find him the least attractive.

Tuesday 26 October – General Carton de Wiart arrived from England this evening and dined with Daphne and me. He is tall, slim and elegant – very direct and amusing.* He told us all he could of Dan, that he was fit and well when he last saw him and that there was a good chance of his escape though it might take a long time because they are so far north. He described their previous attempts to escape: on one occasion they dug a tunnel many yards under the chapel and battlements of the castle.

Dan was not allowed to make that attempt because he

---

* The general had been in prison with Dan and released by the Italians on 9 September to coincide with the announcement of the armistice.

ran their Mess and stores and his absence would have been noticed immediately by the Italians.

This afternoon I watched the New Zealand v South Africa rugger match. I stood with a group of wounded prisoners of war who had just been repatriated from Germany. A one-legged Australian told me that the Germans are terrified of the Russians and that our air raids on Germany are stagger-ing; he said he had read a book for two hours by the light of Kassel burning twenty miles away. These prisoners came out via France and Spain.

Friday 12 November – Tomorrow is my birthday. I shall be thirty.

Friday 19 November – Arrangements are being hurried on for the big conference at Mena. Mr Churchill will stay at the Caseys' villa, Mr Roosevelt and Generalissimo and Madame Chiang Kai Chek will have two villas nearby and so will the Chiefs of Staff. Many houses along the Mena road are being requisitioned for the enormous staffs that are coming. A wire fence has been put up round the conference zone and precautions against land and air attack have been taken.

I went to the Map Room to get the latest news. In Italy our troops are fighting their way slowly north through rain and snow. The Russian advance is so fast that the Map Room Sergeant quite resents it; 'I never stop moving them pins,' he said. He showed me a picture he has painted from memory of his wife. It was a very large water colour of a completely nude brunette.

I went to bed early. Coco ate two bananas; he is an incredibly greedy bird. I am really tired. We're almost over-whelmed with work at the office.

Wednesday 24 November – Air Marshal Tedder brought me good news this morning. He is almost certain that Dan and the Generals are hiding in the mountains in North Italy.

Friday 26 November – The story goes that Randolph Churchill woke his father yesterday morning saying, 'Twinkle, twinkle little star, how I wonder where you are.' Anyhow the Prime Minister suddenly demanded to know why some of our soldiers were not wearing the Desert Star Medal. Churchill had taken trouble over this medal: the yellow on it is for sand, the blue for sea, and so on. Few have yet been issued – hence the dilemma. Now all the ribbon in existence has been made up and any desert soldier who sees Churchill will wear it but will have to return it at the gate on departure for others to wear.

Jimmy Gault, now English Aide to General Eisenhower, invited me to dine last night to meet the General and his staff. Being the only outside guest I was placed at dinner next to the General.

For the first two courses the General sat with his back turned to me. When the sweet was served and the General had to turn a little in my direction I asked him if he knew Bonner Fellers, the American Attaché we all liked. Eisenhower replied tersely: 'Any friend of Bonner Fellers is no friend of mine',* and smartly turned his back on me.

Early this morning Jimmy Gault telephoned me to say General Eisenhower thought he'd been rude to me last night and would be pleased if I would dine with him tonight. I asked Jimmy to thank the General for his invitation and say I was sorry I have a previous engagement. An awful lie: I have no date tonight.

---

* Unknown to Hermione, Fellers had been swiftly recalled when it was discovered that the Italians had de-coded his radio messages to Washington and passed vital information to Rommel.

ALAN BROOKE

In June Churchill promised Brooke supreme command of the Allied invasion of France, for the time being remaining as CIGS until January or February of 1944, depending on the date of the invasion. Two months later in Quebec Churchill informed him that he had given way to Roosevelt's insistence that the post go to Marshall. Brooke was hugely disappointed – and disappointed too in Churchill, who 'dealt with the matter as if it were one of minor importance'.

When the Allies invaded Sicily, Brooke was pessimistic, though the attack was successful. His strategy was progressing as planned, but he remained doubtful that Marshall had fully grasped the importance of the Italian campaign. The Americans, for their part, were doubtful about Brooke's commitment to Overlord and felt he had no interest beyond the Mediterranean.

By the beginning of November Brooke was at a very low ebb, brought down by a persistent heavy cold and convinced that the Americans were sabotaging his strategy, that Churchill was 'unbalanced' and that the majority of his commanders were not up to the job. On the 20th he arrived in Cairo for a preliminary meeting with the Americans prior to meeting the Russians in Tehran. He feared the worst. Things went badly. He was especially critical of Marshall, with whom he 'had the father and mother of a row'. Two days later Brooke flew to Tehran for the first Allied conference at which Stalin would be present with Churchill and Roosevelt, and which would establish the Allies' strategy for the invasion of Europe and the timing of Overlord next year.

Monday 25 October – It is becoming more and more evident that our operations in Italy are coming to a standstill and that owing to a lack of resources we shall not only come to a standstill but also find ourselves in a very dangerous position unless the Russians go on from one success to another. Our build up in Italy is much slower than the German, and far slower than I had expected. We shall have an almighty row with the Americans who have put us in this position with their insistence to abandon the Mediterranean operations for the very problematical cross Channel operations. We are now beginning to see the full beauty of the Marshall strategy!! It is quite heartbreaking when we see what we might have done this year if our strategy had not been distorted by the Americans.

Saturday 20 November – I am at present writing in the air flying along the edge of the African coast east of Tripoli. We struck due south on leaving Malta so as to avoid Crete and any possible contacts with Germans from that island. Start of journey was a bit bumpy but has now smoothed down. We are flying over the edge of that sea of yellow and brown sand looking out over the deep blue of the Mediterranean which gradually shades into the light blue of the horizon and leaves the horizon ill defined. Below us is the black bootlace of the tarmacked desert road. Last time I was over it on my way to Tripoli it was alive with lice-like lorries spaced out every hundred yards, busy building up our forces for the invasion of Tunisia. Now it is desolate and deserted without a vestige of life to be seen on it!

I wish our conference was over. It will be an unpleasant one, the most unpleasant one we have had yet, and that is saying a good deal. I despair of ever getting our American friends to have any sort of strategic vision. Their drag on us has seriously affected our Mediterranean strategy and the whole conduct of the war.

Monday 29 November – At 3.30 p.m. we went over to the Russian Embassy to see Winston present the Stalingrad Sword to Stalin. Bands, Guards of Honour, national anthems etc. Speech by Winston after which he handed sword over in

name of King to Stalin. Stalin kissed sword and handed it
over to Voroshilov, who promptly dropped sword out of its
scabbard!

I have little hope of any form of agreement in discussions.
After listening to the arguments put forward during the last
2 days I feel more like entering a lunatic asylum or a nursing
home than continuing with my present job. I am absolutely
disgusted with the politicians' methods of waging a war! Why
will they imagine they are experts at a job they know nothing
about! It is lamentable to listen to them! May God help us in
the future prosecution of this war, we have every hope of
making an unholy mess of it and of being defeated yet!

When Brooke published his diaries in 1957, he added a commentary. To the entry above, he added that Stalin 'had a military brain
of the very highest calibre. Never once in any of his statements
did he make any strategic error, nor did he ever fail to appreciate
all the implications of a situation with a quick and unerring eye.'
According to Brooke, Stalin had no qualms about possible American and British errors in Western Europe – 'his political and
military requirements could now be best met by the greatest
squandering of British and American lives in the French theatre'.
Brooke suspected that the Americans had been briefing against
him, and that Stalin might have the impression that Brooke was
blocking the invasion of France.

Tuesday 30 November – We finished the day with a banquet in
the Legation building to celebrate Winston's 69th birthday.
We had not been seated long when the PM said that we
should dine in the Russian manner, and that anybody that
liked could propose a toast at any time during the meal. We
had not been going long when the President made a nice
speech alluding to our fathers having known each other when
he and I were boys and proposing my health. Stalin then
chipped in and said that as a result of this meeting and of

having come to such unanimous agreement he hoped that I would no longer look upon Russians with such suspicion and that if I really got to know them I should find that they were quite good chaps! This was a most unexpected and uncalled for attack and I am certain that Averell Harriman, the new USA Ambassador, must have been making mischief as he is very busy at the moment trying to improve his USA position at our expense.

I could not let this accusation pass, so I waited for a propitious moment to get up. It was rather nervous work, considering what the audience was! I thanked the President for his very kind words which I assured him I had deeply appreciated. I then turned to Stalin and reminded him that in the afternoon's conference the PM had said that 'in war truth must be accompanied by an escort of lies to ensure its security'. After four years of war and the continual cultivation of false appearances for the enemy was it not possible that one's outward appearance might even deceive one's friends? I felt convinced that he must have been looking at the dummy aeroplanes and guns and had failed to observe the real and true offensive in the shape of real friendship and comradeship which I felt towards him and all the Soviet forces! This went very well and met with some success. After dinner I returned to the attack and we finished the best of friends with long hand shakes and almost with our arms round each other's necks. He said that he liked the bold and soldierlike way in which I had spoken and the military strength of my voice! These were true military qualities that he liked and admired, and that we were now on the best of terms; furthermore that it must be remembered that some of the best friendships of this world were founded on original misunderstandings!

Brooke returned to London in December satisfied that he had 'secured the main points I was after'. These included putting back the date of the cross-Channel invasion to June 1944 and securing his preferred choice of command of the invasion land forces, Montgomery – not popular with the Americans, but the one general, despite his lack of tact, that Brooke trusted to do the job.

Marshall, however, was destined not to command Overlord; President Roosevelt wanted him in Washington, and Eisenhower was appointed supreme Allied commander in his stead.

BRITISH PRISONERS OF WAR IN GERMANY AND ITALY

Over 60,000 British POWs were held in German Oflags (for officers) and Stalags (for non-commissioned ranks). The majority had been 'put in the bag', to use a POW phrase, in France and Norway in the spring of 1940 and been moved several times. For example, by the autumn of 1943 one group of officers captured in 1940 had been moved from the fifteenth-century castle of Laufen in Upper Bavaria (their first camp, VII C) to the town of Warburg in north-west Germany (VI B) and finally to Eichstätt in Upper Bavaria (VII B camp).

Andrew Biggar, who had surrendered at Dunkirk, recalled their ' "secret-weapon" against barbed-wire-itis' – a 'university without books' with a curriculum which offered courses in first aid, metaphysics, land agency, music, stockbroking, Roman history and countless other subjects, including no fewer than nineteen languages. 'It was more than slightly amusing to see a brace of brigadiers assiduously taking notes, perhaps on an old envelope, on such a subject as Hotel Management.'

Escaping was 'the duty of every prisoner of war'. Around 35,000 British and American servicemen escaped from German or Italian prisons. Hermione Ranfurly's husband, Dan, was one of them. Imprisoned in Campo Concentramento PC No. 12, in the formidable Castello di Vincigliati in the mountains above Florence, he escaped for the first time through a tunnel dug over seven months with little more than broken kitchen knives. He was soon recaptured with all but two of his fellow escapees. His second escape was somewhat easier. After Italy signed the armistice in September 1943 the Italian guards released all their Allied prisoners hours before the Germans arrived.

ANDREW BIGGAR*

Oflag VII C, Laufen Castle, Upper Bavaria – We weren't prepared for it. We didn't in the least expect it. But without even a quick curtain-drop our whole stage was changed.

On our 200-mile trek to the Rhine we learned a lot. Herded like so many thousand cattle along unknown roads to unknown pastures, turned for the night into open fields or rough sheds, we had to look after ourselves.

Warm seed-bed though it was for greed and selfishness, this opportunity to forage and bargain did at least put us all in the right gear. We simply had to use our own initiative to exist at all sanely. It was interesting to notice that success in this respect could not be correlated to any degree with rank, profession, education, or class.

Sophistication and position were wiped out, and, as it were, we had to start from scratch and develop anew. Old dogs simply had to learn new tricks. Commanding officers and junior subalterns alike were starting level. The respect of the junior officers had to be won afresh by the seniors. Discipline followed reason rather than tradition.

The highest achievement in the cooking equipment line was a self-contained kitchen stove with two boiling rings,

*   Andrew Biggar, MC, 'Post-Graduate', *Journal of the Edinburgh Agricultural College Former Students' Association*, No. 21, October 1946.

two ovens and a hot-water boiler, all made from empty tins and the end of a German bed, and made by one who, prior to captivity, had probably never done much more of a practical nature than sharpen a pencil.

Necessity was indeed the father [*sic*] of invention. There were no needles and no wool, but it was soon discovered that needles could be made from wood and that wool could be had for the unpicking, from the tops of worn-out socks. So new feet were knitted on to old socks. A very bright lad appeared on parade one very cold day with a jersey the envy of all. Within a few weeks 50 per cent of the camp were either knitting or scouring the camp for wool. It was hardly safe to put a pair of socks on the drying-line – the next time you saw them was probably incorporated in your arch-enemy's new spring jumper. Eventually 90 per cent of the camp were in possession of a thick hand-knitted sweater.

So it was with lots of things. Something was needed; that thing had to be made.

RAYMOND GRACE*
Captain, the Buffs (Royal East Kent Regiment)

Grace had been captured on 28 May 1940, the day after his twenty-ninth birthday, whilst guarding the northern flank of the corridor leading to Dunkirk. His young wife, Christine, did not hear until mid-August that he was alive; their son Charles was then only eleven months old. In Oflag VII B, Eichstätt, Upper Bavaria, Raymond prepared a lengthy essay to give to his wife on his release, short extracts from which appear here.†

---

* H. R. Grace, private papers, Oflag VII B, Eichstätt, Upper Bavaria, from family archives.

† For paper he used a recent gift from the YMCA in Geneva, an attractive notebook headed 'A Wartime Log for British Prisoners'.

I must confess to a nervousness where that meeting [with Charles] is concerned, for it seems to me that it will be a moment of tremendous importance, in both his life and mine. First impressions, in a child's mind, are so apt to stick for such a long time. I have the feeling that I shall be tremendously shy of him.

Shall we find, I wonder that there's been much change in either or both of us, during these last years? I like to think that, if I've learnt nothing else during my Captivity, I've learnt patience. There's no doubt at all that I'm an entirely different individual, in captivity, from the person you know. I've acquired the habits of keeping more or less to myself, of keeping my mouth shut, and of not laughing a great deal.

There are one or two things that I dread may have happened to me. One of these is that I shall have become dreadfully 'petty-minded'. It's desperately easy to start magnifying the small incidents until they assume gigantic proportions. I suppose it's due to the confined space one lives in, and the confined view, which together go to confine one's mental outlook.

Another is that I shall have lost all sense of responsibility, and that I shall shrink from taking decisions when they come my way. I dread the thought that I may have become 'spineless', and a 'follower' rather than a 'leader'.

I wonder what your innermost, private feelings have been about my failure to do anything at all in the matter of 'escaping'? or did you hope and pray, at the time, that I shouldn't do anything rash? Were you hoping that one day I should suddenly walk in on you, quite unexpectedly, having made a sensational 'get-away'? or were you being continually thankful that I was content to wait quietly until the end,

without making any effort to do what the Army is pleased to
call 'the duty of every Prisoner of War'?

DAN RANFURLY

By November 1943 Dan and his fellow escapees had got as far as
Rio Salso, high up in the Apennines (approximately 125 miles
from Florence), before waist-high snow made further progress
impossible and kept them there for four months. Dan slept either
in a barn or in Theresa's humble house. Theresa, a widow, gave
him double helpings of food because he was 'twice as large as
they'. On one occasion she killed a cat for them to eat and sold
its skin for a hundred lire.

Saturday 29 January – I was asleep in the widow's house when
she woke me saying there was a crowd of people outside her
door. I got out of bed, dressed and tiptoed downstairs.
German officers were in the kitchen, their maps spread out
on the table. I crept to the back door; Germans were smoking
on the step. I went back to my room and opened the window.
More Germans were lolling against the wall beneath. I was
terrified for the widow and her daughters. If I was found
I would be retaken prisoner but they would be shot. There
was nowhere to hide so I got back into bed where my tallness
would be less noticed.

The women were wonderfully brave. They talked to the
Germans and every now and then one of them came upstairs
to tell me what was happening. After what seemed an
eternity I heard sharp German words of command, the shuffle
of soldiers' feet and the metallic clanking of equipment and
weapons. I lay stiff wondering whether they would come
upstairs. They went out into the street and started to move
off in single file. There were about three hundred of them.

For the next two or three weeks I stayed in a lonely barn

on the hillside two miles away. The nights seemed very long, and were exceedingly uncomfortable until Nereo managed to buy me some poison to kill the rats and mice that swarmed there.

All our plans waited on the weather. It was not until the beginning of March when the thaw came that [we] set out on our long trek south. Two young officers who had been with the Partisans during the last few months came with us – a big burly Irish sapper, and an American air force officer who had baled out of his plane over Foggia and dislocated both his thighs on landing. Before his legs had properly mended he escaped from an Italian prison hospital because there was talk of his being moved to Germany. He had managed to get fairly fit but his thighs were still partly dislocated. We had to walk 250 miles across high mountains before 18 March to keep our rendezvous with the agents on the coast. We made very slow progress: there were main roads and rivers to cross and poor Rudolph V fell every few hundred yards, his game leg went through the snow like a snow-plough.

On the third morning we split up into a fit party and an unfit party, hoping that the former would be able to contact the agents and get them to wait for others. I went with the unfit party. With my long legs I could eliminate many delays by going forward to find out the lie of the land. It was a point of honour that we should arrive not far behind the others. I will pass briefly over the next four days. We had a terrible journey. Suffice to say that on one day we walked thirty-three miles and on the eighteenth we arrived at the rendezvous two hours before the fit ones.

During the next six weeks, in the dark periods of the moon, we made eight or nine rendezvous on the beach. Italian Partisans who had wireless sets in the mountains informed us when to go. We would lie down on the narrow strip between the railway and the sea while one of the agents went forward to do the necessary signalling. We whistled the German song 'Lili Marlene' to recognise each other in the dark. Each time we were disappointed and had to make the whole risky journey back again.

We decided to purchase or steal a sailing boat. On the evening of 10 May we slipped across the road and collected various pieces for the ship. The moon had not yet risen but we felt remarkably conspicuous standing there a couple of hundred yards away from the German convoys.

We got the sails up but then we discovered the boat was as waterproof as a sieve. If one put one's foot on the bottom it went through. We began to bale.

When dawn came we saw the tops of the Miella mountains above the horizon and knew we had travelled seventy miles. Flights of RAF came over. Two kittyhawks roared down to investigate us. We waved our shirts and prayed they would not strafe us. After circling three or four times at water level they left us alone. All through the day we rowed. We could see the shells falling on either side of the line. It seemed endless. In the early afternoon we saw some fishing boats and made towards them. By now we were almost waterlogged. One of them took us in tow. Somehow we reached Ortona harbour. It was wonderful to go ashore and feel safe.

9. D-DAY LANDINGS

SUMMER 1944

In December Rommel, now stationed in France, began a tour of inspection of the Atlantic Wall, the German defences against the expected Allied invasion. He drew up plans for a six-mile-wide strip of land along the coast studded with bunkers and minefields. Thirty miles or so inland, between Calais and Dieppe, he was shown a network of rocket-launching sites waiting for a soon-to-be-completed secret weapon.

For Churchill, the months leading up to the invasion of Europe were a great strain. Sir Alexander Cadogan of the Foreign Office noted in his diary on 19 April, 'PM, I fear, is breaking down . . . I really don't know if he can carry on.'[*] Churchill was particularly exercised by the plans to bomb the French railway system in the run-up to Overlord. He admitted, '[I] had not fully realized that our use of air power . . . would assume so cruel and remorseless a form. It was clear that great slaughter would inevitably result.'[†]

In late April and throughout May, Montgomery, com-

---

[*] David Dilks (ed.), *The Diaries of Sir Alexander Cadogan*, London, 1971, quoted in Roger Parkinson, *A Day's March Nearer Home. Alamein to VE Day Based on the War Cabinet Papers*, Hart-Davies MacGibbon, 1974.

[†] Quoted by Roger Parkinson, *A Day's March Nearer Home*, utilizing CAB 65 (War Cab) '44, Public Record Office.

mander of the ground forces for D-Day, visited troops in every conceivable location. He told them that though they faced scores of enemy divisions, many were weak and under strength: the Germans had put 'Everything in the shop window. There is nothing "in the kitty".'* He was talking to men who were about to embark on one of the most hazardous military missions ever devised, but 'Monty' was an inspirational speaker and left them feeling full of confidence that they would succeed. The Allies were given a further reason for confidence two days before D-Day. In the early hours of 4 June Rome had been liberated, the first Axis capital to be captured. It was a hugely symbolic victory.

It has been said that Tuesday 6 June 1944 marked the apogee of British military effort. And, as a brilliant combination of logistics, ingenuity, discipline, security and cooperation between the armed services, Overlord was indeed a triumph. In the first eighteen hours of D-Day 200,000 men were landed in Normandy, followed immediately by three more divisions and 19,000 vehicles. Assault ships numbered 5,000; 1,200 warships bombarded the coast and protected the landings; over 10,000 planes were deployed. Through the hole they punched in the Atlantic Wall four million men and women would eventually flow. D-Day was a colossal undertaking, and other operations – Anvil, Tarzan, Buccaneer and Shingle, covering the south of France, Burma, the Andaman Islands and Anzio in Italy – took second place to Overlord for resources, particularly landing craft.

Weather delayed the operation by a day. Eisenhower, as supreme Allied commander, gave the go-ahead early on the morning of the 5th partly because the forecast was slightly better for the following morning but also because another delay would have meant a two-week postponement waiting for favourable tides. With that would have come a score of

---

* Max Hastings, *Overlord*, Pan Books, 1999.

morale, organizational and security problems and the very real danger that the enemy would discover the Allies' plans. But when the invasion did begin, the Germans had been so comprehensively deceived into believing that it would happen later and elsewhere that initial operations – even the sound of bombardments and the sight of gliders landing – were thought to be diversions.

The BBC had seventeen war correspondents deployed alongside Allied troops. One of them, Howard Marshall, was in a landing craft that hit a mine on a French beach. He waded ashore, assessed the scene, then found a returning ship and made his way to a studio near Portsmouth. 'I'm sitting here in my soaked-through clothes with no notes at all . . . They're at the bottom of the sea.' It was irresistible radio and the first of 235 reports on the progress of the war broadcast between D-Day and VE Day, almost a year later. Every night ten to fifteen million listeners in Britain learned of the war's progress this way, as did many millions in other countries.

Sixty miles of French coastline were taken, troops and equipment poured across the Channel and there had been no German ground counter-offensive, but a week after D-Day the Germans responded with their deadly new secret weapon. The 'pilotless plane' that landed on London on 13 June was known to its German inventors as the Fi103. To the Britons who first became aware of them as a low hum in the distance, then a great rattling before the sound stopped completely, they were doodlebugs or buzz bombs. The silence meant its engine had stopped and the doodlebug was falling from the sky. One ton of high explosive would detonate in about fifteen seconds.

It was Goebbels who named them *Vergeltungswaffen* – weapons of vengeance – adding a number to hint that there would be more deadly versions to come. Between June and September 7,500 V1s reached England, 2,500 of which fell on London. The death toll was over 6,000, proportionately higher than during the Blitz. Thousands of fighter aircraft were diverted from operations over the Continent to deal with the threat and a massive anti-aircraft defence belt was created south of London.

At the Tehran Conference in late 1943 Stalin had agreed to a Russian offensive to coincide with Overlord in order to prevent German forces being transferred from the east, and on 22 June the Red Army attacked. When Stalin's forces reached the outskirts of Warsaw at the end of July, they halted on the banks of the River Vistula, east of the city. As around 37,000 poorly armed members of the Polish underground attempted to wrest control of the city from the Germans, Hitler put Himmler in charge of crushing the uprising. The Russians sat and watched. Around 250,000 civilians died and the survivors were forced to leave the city. German demolition squads then destroyed Warsaw block by block. Only then did the Soviets cross the Vistula and continue their advance.

In Normandy the long-awaited breakthrough came at the end of July. Caen was captured and six US divisions surged through to take Brittany, swinging east to the south of the German forces around Falaise. Approximately 50,000 German troops were trapped as Montgomery pushed down from the north and Patton pushed up to cut them off. The brutal reality of the Battle for Normandy was captured by the young Kingsley Amis, then serving near Falaise with a British signals unit: 'The stench of rotting human and animal bodies was so overpowering that the pilots of the spotter planes flying above the scene . . . vomited.'[*] By contrast, Frank Gillard's curiously bloodless BBC bulletin broadcast on 21 August concentrated on the mechanical carnage, leaving it to listeners

---

[*] Kingsley Amis, *Memoirs*, Hutchinson, 1991, quoted in Paul Fussell, *The Boys' Crusade. American G.I.s in Europe: Chaos and Fear in World War Two*, Phoenix, 2005.

to supply the missing ingredient: 'Some of the most frightful slaughter of the whole of the war must have taken place up and down this road a few days ago.'

THE DIARISTS

CLARA MILBURN

The flag that Clara bought for Jack in 1942 – 'very optimistic I was to buy it then' – was flown for the first time on 23 April, St George's Day. It soon had a second outing – on 5 June to mark the fall of Rome. The next day Clara and Jack heard on the eight o'clock news that the D-Day invasion had begun.

Tuesday 6 June, evening – The broadcast at this time is simply wonderful. We are now hearing the sound of the aeroplanes which took the parachutists over to France, and then the recorded voice of an R.A.F. pilot who took a glider over, and the little chats on the inter-com: 'O.K., pilot?' 'O.K., Skipper.' Bless them, they're fine chaps. Now we are listening to the Navy's work by a man who earned the George Cross. Howard Marshall went along with the troops and landed, and is now back again telling us what happened. He has been twice in the sea . . . so he is just telling us – all impromptu – how his barge arrived. The Germans had prepared pronged obstacles with a mine on the prong, one of which blew up his barge, but the men waded out and the Bren-gun carrier went through five feet of water and on to the beach! Somehow or another he got to another barge and, after that had sunk, he got on to an ML and came back, having 'done his stuff' in time to get home and broadcast.

At 9 p.m. His Gracious Majesty broadcast to his people, and his talk was heard in the United States as well as the Empire. He called us all to prayer on this most historic occasion. His little impediment of speech endears him to us, I think. We grow anxious for him if he falters and rejoice when he overcomes his difficulty of enunciation. He went along very well on the whole tonight. The news lasted until 9.40 p.m., and then we had a service of dedication with the Bishop of London taking the prayers and reading the lesson and the Archbishop of Canterbury giving the address. Three hymns were beautifully sung, too.

I hate to feel Alan is out of all this. It's such a moving thing to be listening to the wireless and seeing in one's mind all that our brave fellows are going through, though really we cannot know what they are doing from such scraps of news. I write this last bit in bed at the end of this day of days – D. Day . . . At last the invasion has started. May God defend the right and bring us to victory and real peace.

Friday 9 June – We seem to be gaining a little ground in Normandy, but this is a stiff job, I am sure. We had records tonight of all kinds of things, the landing of gliders and the Germans shelling of them. Somehow I don't like this much. It makes it into a 'show', and it is much too grave a business for that. What we are having to suffer because of these bullying, arrogant Germans! And an escaped prisoner said: 'The Germans are like ourselves'! They are the absolute opposite, never satisfied unless they are preparing for a war or over-running their neighbours, pillaging, murdering, dominating, pretending and persecuting. We are just too slack and stupid between wars, only too glad to be at peace again and never looking ahead or being prepared. We don't like war and so don't want to think about it unless we are obliged to – with what dire and terrible results! I hope this nation will always keep fully armed and trained and then there will

be none; or, if belligerents do arise, we shall have the means
to settle them quickly.

CHARLES RITCHIE

Approximately 14,000 Canadians landed in Normandy on D-Day.
Charles's brother Roley was to follow in a second wave a few
days later. On 6 June the Canadians were responsible for taking
Juno Beach in the centre of the British front. The plan was for
the two British divisions to their left and right to take Caen and
Bayeux with the Canadians covering the road and railway linking
the two towns.

Tuesday 6 June – D-Day has come. It had become an hallu-
cination – something like the Second Coming or the End of
the World. Roley has not yet gone. He rang me on the
telephone yesterday.

The soldiers who have been left behind in London look
forlorn and subdued. The town seems empty. The gaiety and
sense of pressure and excitement have gone. There is a
morning-after feeling abroad. The taxis have become plentiful
again and the drivers are beginning to be quite polite now
that the American debauch is over.

Friday 9 June to Wednesday 14 June – At this point I became
unendurably restless and determined by hook or crook to get
to the Normandy beachhead. This was strictly forbidden to
all civilians, as the landing had only taken place on 6 June
and troops were still landing. However, I had the inspiration
to sell Mr. Massey the idea that a message of good wishes
should be sent to the Canadian troops in Normandy from
Mr. Mackenzie King. I then drafted the message in Mr.
King's name and induced Mr. Massey to get the Prime Minister's approval. Admiral Nelles of the Royal Canadian Navy

arranged a passage for me on a troopship, but said that I would have to arrange my own landing in Normandy as it was impossible to obtain permission for a civilian to land.

Thursday 15 June to Saturday 17 June – Thursday was fine – we started off to join our troopship *Prince William*. It was at this point that I first became conscious of my civilian clothes. I was eyed with curiosity and – not quite – hostility. It was apparent to all that I must be some sort of bloody nuisance, most probably a journalist.

The next day, Friday the 16th, I got word to transfer at once to the *Prince Henry* our sister ship as she was sailing forthwith for France. We took on troops that night – infantry-men – four hundred and sixty of them – one after another coming up the ship's ladder until watching them coming made you dizzy. Stolid, cheerful, English faces – about half of them looked like boys in their teens. All were top-heavy with the weight of their equipment, staggering as they slid down the incline from the gangplank leading on to the ship's deck, blundering about helplessly like cows caught in a too narrow lane.

The troops were very quiet as we steamed out of South-ampton Water.

Saturday 17 June. About 11 a.m. we sighted the coast of Normandy and anchored about five miles off the coast opposite the port of Arromanches.

It was my first experience of the machine-like precision of the landing arrangements about which we read in the news-papers. The troops in the end were landed but there was nothing very machine-like in the process. By hollering from the bridge at every passing small craft asking for aid and by an exchange of insults with those who refused it, some craft which should no doubt have been taking troops off another landing craft was pressed into service.

There is no natural harbour at Arromanches. The artificial

harbour which has been constructed is known as the Mulberry and was full of small shipping – the bigger ships ride at anchor outside. It was crowded with troopships, a variety of landing craft, tankers, munition and supply ships, and small tugs in which are seated majors with megaphones who are supposed to have some control. They dash about like sheepdogs. The captains and crews of the hounded small craft curse and protest but in the end they do as they are told.

Monday 19 June – John* and I departed by Jeep for the headquarters of the Third Canadian Division. This represented a considerable achievement on his part. He had bluffed the local brigadier into appreciating the importance of my mission.

It was another day of wind and rain and low cloud.

The German warning signs still left beside the roads, the skull and crossbones and the word *Minen*. There was hardly a field in which there were not either tents or supply dumps – soldiers naked to the waist washing in a wet field, hospitals marked with red crosses, petrol dumps and stores staked in rows – one of 'our' airstrips thick with planes grounded by bad weather.

The main street [of Bayeux] was decorated with tricolours, but the demonstrative period, if there ever was one here, was over.

General Keller's headquarters were only a couple of miles from the German lines and at one point we nearly took a wrong turning in our Jeep which would have brought us out behind the German lines.

The Headquarters are in the grounds of a château. The General, who was living in a camouflaged truck concealed in a mound in the park, emerged on my arrival. He talked like

---

*   A military acquaintance Ritchie had met in Southampton whom he had
    persuaded to accompany him ashore.

a General saying that his men were 'in good heart'. He summoned a circle of officers and some men standing in the damp park. I read them the Prime Minister's message of goodwill as drafted by me. The General expressed gratification and sent a message to our people at home. I thought his enthusiasm rather muted, and I do not think that the name of Mackenzie King makes the military heart beat faster.

I asked the officer whether I could go along the line to see my cousins who were with the regiment a mile or two away. He said that a moving vehicle on that road might attract enemy fire to their position and wondered sarcastically whether they would want to see me in these conditions. I said probably not.

A day or two later after my return to the beachhead at Arromanches B. W. told me that Roley had been very badly wounded. He had last seen him swathed in bandages from head to foot on a stretcher. He had been returned to England as an emergency case.

GEORGE BEARDMORE

George was now senior billeting officer, cycling to the most recent bomb incidents as part of an emergency team, gathering information about those who had died or about survivors and assisting the homeless to find accommodation. 'This was the work I had wanted since the war began. A stream of the slightly injured, the bereaved, the indignant, the homeless, the bewildered passed through the office. Let's hope to God I was able to satisfy if not comfort them.' George's workload increased when he was made information officer for the sites of rocket attacks, and he was also busy organizing the evacuation of children. After initial doubts, he found himself pleased at the responsibility: 'I had been a clerk for so many years and it was nice to find authority in my make-up.' There were other responsibilities at home: Jean gave birth to their second child, Anthea, on Friday 28 July at 1.30 in the morning.

Wednesday 7 June – While cycling through the quiet streets yesterday – only prams and buses, bicycles and tradesmen's vans (very old, with their place-names half-obliterated, relic of the 1940 anti-invasion precautions) – I found it difficult to believe that not two hundred miles away blood and thunder is in progress. Even then, having a stuffy head-cold which keeps my head ringing, I shall never be able to put the events of 6 June 1944 into their proper perspective.

Monday 12 June – That word 'invasion' only touches the surface of the mind. We don't really <u>think</u> about it, I suppose because it's been on our lips these last eighteen months – 'When is the Second Front taking place?' and so on. We won't ever understand what must have been the long-distance planning, the decisions of detail that had to be made, the final assembling, co-ordination of forces, the order to go. And in man-made things details are always going wrong, failing, or being lost. And in a huge enterprise like this! Even to describe it, supposing I were omniscient, wouldn't convey a hundredth part. Words are so limited, and movies not much better.

Well, whatever's going on over there, my sympathies as usual are with the unknown, the forgotten, the buried alive, the mutilated and disfigured who won't ever appear except as a name in a paper, or perhaps as a photograph on a piano in a town in Indiana or Alberta or Yorkshire, 'Bugles calling for them in sad shires', anonymously.

Sunday 18 June – The latest development to affect our lives is the 'Bumble Bomb', which is a pilotless aeroplane carrying a cargo of high explosive let loose on the continent and pointed in our direction in the hope that it will land where it will do most harm. Our first intimation of this menace was a noise like a motor-boat fifty feet above our heads first thing last Thursday morning, the 15th. I sprang out of bed to find out what on earth it was but it had passed out of sight by the time I had reached the window. I said: 'A plane out of control, I should think,' but Jean, sitting up in bed and leaning on one arm, said after a while: 'Georgie, you don't think it's something new, do you?' Since then we have heard two or three of the damned things, in the distance. Amos had heard what they really were from somewhere. Sparing of comment, as usual, he said: 'See you in the Shelter, then.' However, we haven't yet taken to the Surface Shelter because Jean is now pretty heavy and uncomfortable. She sleeps downstairs behind the 1940 barricades while I sleep with Victoria in the big bed upstairs in case she grows frightened, which she was last night. Heaven knows what permanent effect all these bumps in the night and other strange noises are going to have on her.

Sunday 25 June – Jean is determined to remain calm and she succeeds even though I have noticed sturdy WVS women flinch and tremble as the bumps resound in the distance. There is a frightening quality in these bumbles not associated with the piloted bombers. Ted P.* suggests that women in particular find their non-human element more terrifying than the bomb itself. One recognises the buzz as one lies awake and immediately begins to tense up – I have felt my muscles brace themselves – for the engine to cut out and the thing to drop. And when it does, one waits for the bump, and when that's come, one wonders whether or not it has landed in Harrow. I mean I do. But then noises at night have always been deceptive.

At Gayton Road about six hundred houses were seriously

---

* A family friend.

affected – ceilings down, doors off, roofs ripped open, apart
from the house and four flats which were so completely
destroyed as to be non-existent. Only four killed and twenty-
one in hospital. At Parkside Way six were killed and only
three in hospital, with perhaps five hundred houses affected
of which about sixty were made uninhabitable. My first
intimation of the Parkside Way incident, after cycling through
Headstone Park, was seeing a boy of 10 in a dressing-gown
crossing the street with a jug of water in his hand drawn
from a street stand-pipe.

The dawn armadas continue, especially on clear days.
Long processions of four-engined bombers in formations of
thirty-four, a cross-stitch against the blue.

Writing all this is perfectly useless except that it serves as
an outlet for a mind oppressed with too many vivid images.

Saturday 19 August – The baby is prospering although she has
an extra large pimple on her head which we don't know
what to do with. She is pretty quiet even though fly-bombs
shake the house and her first siren went off three hours after
her birth. After the 6 p.m. feed she is put down in the sling-
cot in the downstairs back room with Victoria, windows
wide-open and chicken-wire and curtains drawn. After the
10 p.m. feed she is transferred to the shelter of a chair within
the chimney-breast recess. All the same, a neighbour with a
new baby four doors away takes it into the Surface Shelter
and if it cries, it cries.

First reports this morning of the Americans in Paris after
their snaring and annihilation of that section of the German
front facing them. Something to remember – at the movies
last night, the expression on the face of the old lady of
Chartres as she smashed a picture of Hitler to the ground.

Sunday 27 August – Last Wednesday I took the family to
Wharfedale, Yorkshire, to give them a holiday at my brother

Alan's house, near Wetherby. I shan't easily forget waiting at 4 a.m. on the platform of Doncaster Station for a crowded train to come in, full of troops. Victoria sat on a suitcase and counted the number of stars she could see – interesting, really, because necessarily she had never seen stars before, except while on the run between the house and the Shelter. The baby howled her tiny head off, and who can blame her. They are safe for a time and Jean is rested, although the experience would seem to underline the maxim that one should never, in wartime at least, leave one's home.

Yesterday I was swimming with a jolly party of people in the Wharfe and today I am home again and not liking the loneliness, another Bomb Bachelor.

Up there they know nothing of fly-bombs and the threat of rockets. To them it was a story, something you hear before passing on to matters of real interest, like the Roses' match at Leeds. Only Freda kept on asking: 'But weren't you frightened, weren't you frightened?' leaving Jean and me to wonder whether we had been frightened or not. I suppose we had, but in moments of crisis one is too busy racing to pick up Victoria and find shelter for ourselves.

Since Wednesday Paris has been liberated, Bulgaria has asked for an armistice, and Roumania has been granted one. But let us get control of the fly-bomb and rocket sites before we rejoice. The Alert sounded as I was walking down the platform at St. Pancras, and one of the abominable things passed dead overhead as I was waiting in Euston for the train to pull out.

HAROLD NICOLSON

Following tours in French North Africa and then in the Orkneys visiting the fleet at Scapa Flow, giving lectures to both troops and civilians, Harold was back in London on 6 June, caught the 9 a.m.

news, and was in the House of Commons at midday to hear
Churchill briefly announce 'the first of a series of landings in force
upon the Continent of Europe'.

The following weekend he wrote to his sons:

Sunday 11 June – You will want to know the general atmosphere during invasion week. First, at Sissinghurst. It is literally
dominated by aeroplanes. All night they howl and rage above
us. It is like sleeping in Piccadilly Underground – trains roar
past at different levels and going in different directions all the
night. Then in daytime there is also much activity: great
fleets of bombers floating slowly above us in the empyrean,
their drone being a throb all round us and not a definite noise
coming from a definite object. And then the fighters at a
lower level swishing along at enormous speeds. So far that is
all that Sissinghurst has seen of the invasion. Otherwise the
trains run the same, the papers come the same, everything is
the same. We listen intently to the wireless at all hours.

In London it is different. There are people who ring up
under the illusion (a) that I have inside knowledge, and (b)
that if I had it, I should repeat it over the telephone. There is
a continual crowd around the ticker-tape in the House of
Commons corridor. There are all sorts of rumours buzzing
through the smoking-room. And there is the hourly expectation that Winston may make another statement. Apart from
this, and the fact that the newspapers are snapped up the
moment they appear on the streets, there is nothing much
to notice. People are relieved it has begun. They scan the
weather a little more acutely than usual, and notice the
direction of the wind. But on the whole we are all amazingly
calm.

Wednesday 14 June – There have been mysterious rocket
planes falling in Kent. The thing is very hush at the moment.

Friday 16 June – Viti has been kept up and rendered sleepless by the robot 'planes. They come over after we have gone to bed. I can see them clearly, since they are illuminated like little launches at a regatta. They fly slowly and low, and it is a mystery how any of them get through at all. They make a terrific noise like an express train with a curious hidden undertone. In a week or so we shall have learnt how to deal with them. The Germans, of course, have boosted the thing immeasurably and tried to raise the spirits of their people by claiming that this secret weapon can really destroy London. In fact Goebbels says that London is 'paralysed'. This is absurd. There was not a sign of anything yesterday and the traffic continued just as usual.

Thursday 6 July – Winston makes his statement about the flying bomb. I had feared that he might dismiss the thing as a mere nuisance and thus offend the many people who are really frightened of it. But he took the opposite line and, if anything, exaggerated its danger. This was most effective and the House felt generally there was nothing more to be said.

Monday 24 July – At 4.45 this morning I am suddenly awakened by the sound of a flying bomb zooming over my head. I do not wake up with any start, but quite calmly and completely. As I hear it (a few seconds only), it cuts out and I know that it is about to descend. I bury my head in my pillow and then comes quite a small crash and no sense of blast through the room. But a second later I hear things falling and splintering in my sitting-room and I get up to look. The shutters have been thrown open and the iron bars smashed out. Only one pane is broken. My lovely apothecary pot with lilies in it is destroyed. I put on a greatcoat and go out into the court. There are points of torches everywhere and the wardens running about to see if anyone is hurt. They tell me it has fallen in Essex Street. I notice a thick soup-like haze in the air and all today my eyes have been red and smarting. I go back to bed and sleep.

VERA BRITTAIN

At the end of January, after another heavy air raid on Berlin, Vera wrote, 'The people who invented "saturation raids" are nothing but homicidal maniacs who ought to be shut up in a criminal lunatic asylum'. *Seed of Chaos*, her attack on mass bombing, was published in April. It was barely noticed in Britain, but the American edition, which had already appeared, caused outrage and led to a spate of abusive letters.

In February Harrow was bombed, and John's school house was set on fire and the tuck shop gutted, but John was safe in the shelter at the time. Given the increased danger in London, Vera asked her tenants to give up the cottage in the New Forest so she could move back in. However, she still needed to be in London from time to time, both for her work and to visit her mother.

Friday 23 June – Came to London, arriving Waterloo just after 12.0 – two hours after part of the station, York Rd & County Hall got a direct hit from a crashing robot 'plane. Saw no signs of this but soon heard the robots, as it was an ideal day for them, with heavy clouds. They sound like a mixture of an angry bee & a broken-down tug on the Thames, wh. keeps you in suspense as it gradually nears. The engine stops – a light flashes, & someone is 'for' it; the explosion follows immediately, causing its own cloud of smoke – but there is no smoke-pall over London. Again not much sleep amid the intermittent explosions.

Saturday 24 June – John rang up this morning, but was very reticent in reply to my questions. A letter to G. picked up later from Mother's flat said that they are spending the nights in the shelter & diving under desks by day when the robots come over. J. told G. not to tell me – wh. knowing me better he promptly did. I wrote later to tell John that it was suspense about those I loved, rather than danger for them, which got me down – & to Shirley explaining that the War had settled that she must go to boarding school, as work is impossible in town.

Friday 30 June – One of the worst flying bomb days we have yet had, & of course we had chosen to have John over from Harrow as it was the Training Corps day from which he is free.

After tea took a taxi to Mother's flat so that she could see John; we had only been there a few minutes when we heard a doodlebug making straight for us; the engine cut out just above us & we rushed into the passage as the bomb screamed down. It shook the whole place & gave us all a shock but nothing was broken in the flat. We went out to see whether our house was still there & found everything covered with smoke & dust & crowds rushing down to the Embankment. Bomb had fallen just opposite on the other side of the river by the Hovis building but house seemed all right. Hurried John back to S. Ken. & put him on the train for Harrow.

In Lyndhurst a VI landed half a mile from the cottage. Vera and Shirley went in search of the spot where it had fallen:

We soon discovered that the bomb had devastated the uninhabited loveliness of a woodland glade. The place appeared as though a mathematical circle of blight had descended from heaven. Everything within was burnt and brown, the leaves stripped from their boughs and the grass consumed by a sweeping flame. The explosion had blown off the tops of the nearer trees, leaving only the shattered trunks and split branches to raise protesting arms to the sky.

We seemed to have walked from the sunlit forest into some strange island of desolation. This time there were no human casualties; the beautiful oaks and beeches, some hundreds of years old, had been the only victims.*

ALAN BROOKE

Brooke had been promoted to field marshal at the beginning of the year, but he was feeling increasingly tired and exasperated. He had to persist in arguing the need to keep up the pressure on the Germans in Italy and to resist the Americans' plan to open another front in the south of France. Although the landing at Anzio had stalled after the initial impetus, by the last week of May the Italian campaign was making good headway, even though the Americans 'nearly succeeded in ruining our strategy'.

Brooke was concerned about Churchill's health, and also by the endless meetings – which he felt were often a waste of time – and the frequent changes of plan. There was a protracted dispute about the strategy in the Pacific, which reached, but thankfully passed, the point of the chiefs of staff thinking they would have to resign – not the best situation just prior to the invasion of Europe. After a meeting with the PM in March Brooke wrote, 'I began to wonder whether I was Alice in Wonderland, or whether I was really fit for a lunatic asylum! I am honestly getting very doubtful about his balance of mind . . .'

Saturday 27 May – Just longing for a rest of a few hours from continual war responsibility. The hardest part of bearing such responsibility is pretending that you are absolutely confident of success when you are really torn to shreds with doubts and misgivings!

I never want again to go through a time like the present

---

* Vera Brittain, *Testament of Experience*, Fontana, 1981.

one. The cross Channel operation is just eating into my heart.
I wish to God we could start and have done with it!!

Went home for the weekend.

Monday 5 June – I am very uneasy about the whole operation.
At the best, it will fall so very very far short of the expectation
of the bulk of the people, namely all those who know nothing
of its difficulties. At the worst it may well be the most ghastly
disaster of the whole war. I wish to God it were safely over.

Six days after D-Day Brooke went to Normandy with Churchill
and General Smuts for a day's tour. 'It was a wonderful moment
to find myself re-entering France', though he noted that 'the
French population did not seem in any way pleased to see us
arrive as a victorious country to liberate France'.

Monday 19 June – Arrived up early [in London, from Ferney
Close] to find that a pilotless plane had struck the Guards
Chapel, Wellington Barracks during Sunday Service and had
killed about 60 people!! Amongst them to my great grief
Ivan Cobbold! And on my writing table was a letter from
him written Saturday, sending me on a wire asking me to
lunch this week. It all gave me a very nasty turn, and I
cannot get him and poor Blanche out of my mind.

Long Cabinet at which Winston was in very good form,
quite 10 years younger, all due to the fact that the flying
bombs have again put us in the front line! We shall have
to stop them and find some efficient counter or they will
become troublesome.

Thursday 27 July – Back to WO [War Office] to have an hour
with S of S [secretary of state] discussing post war policy and
our policy in Europe. Should Germany be dismembered or
gradually converted to an ally to meet Russian threat of 20
years hence? I suggested the latter and feel certain that we

must from now on regard Germany in a very different light. Germany is no longer the dominating power of Europe, Russia is. Unfortunately Russia is not entirely European. She has however vast resources and cannot fail to become the main threat in 15 years from now. Therefore foster Germany, gradually build her up, and bring her into a federation of Western Europe.

Then dinner with PM, Ike and Bedell Smith,* intended to bring me closer to Ike and assist in easy running between Ike and Monty. It did a lot of good.

There is no doubt that Ike is all out to do all he can to maintain the best of relations between British and Americans, but it is equally clear that Ike knows nothing about strategy and is quite unsuited to the post of Supreme Commander as far as running the strategy of the war is concerned! Bedell Smith on the other hand has brains, no military education in the true sense, and unfortunately suffers from a swollen head. He is certainly one of the best American officers, but still falls far short when it comes to strategic outlook. With that Supreme Command set up it is no wonder that Monty's real high ability is not always realized . . .

Monday 28 August – Attended Thanksgiving Service in the Crypt of St Paul's Cathedral for the liberation of Paris at 12 noon. Hearing the 'Marseillaise, boom out gave me a deep thrill which stirred me inwardly. France seemed to wake again after being knocked out for 5 years.

NAOMI MITCHISON

During the spring, as troops based nearby mounted exercises, Naomi's days passed in constant expectation of the invasion –

---

*   Eisenhower's chief of staff.

'this awful ache about the Second Front, the thing one wants and fears so terribly, that is at the back of one's thought all the time, like a wave, a tidal wave coming in from the horizon blotting out everything. In ten years nobody will know, one won't know oneself, what the word meant emotionally, to all of us'.

As well as running the farm, Naomi had been giving lectures on politics to the troops based locally, taking on more community and committee work and providing accommodation for members of the Free French. During the course of the summer Murdoch, now 22, came home on leave from his weapons research work.

Tuesday 6 June – Got the news from Angus as soon as I went over about 8.30. All the men talking about it, more or less, especially Fred Brownie who was a volunteer in the last war.

We listened at 1, but no great excitement among the females. Hugh [gardener] talking gloomily about how many would be killed. Angus had said that as soon as the shelling stopped here we would know the thing was on, and there has been none for more than a week.

I went about all day in three layers of consciousness, partly fidgeting about this, and being so remote and out of it.

Listened to the King's rather revolting broadcast, felt awfully ashamed of that kind of bilge. Listened to all the rest. Very exciting stuff by the correspondents.

Friday 16 June – All day I was worrying a bit about the pilotless planes. One feels one should be there, somewhere nearer than this anyway. Not that anyone is very likely to get involved. But it must be beastly having them in the day. I also keep wondering how much ordinary people in Normandy want to be liberated. I mean, having their farms burnt and cattle killed and everything. I wish I really knew what they thought, not just what the papers and radio say. One is kind of conditioned not to believe anything from correspondents. Or would one be so excited? No doubt I would want it myself, as it were, but would Duncan? Yes probably. But would the MacLeans and MacKinnons?*

Thursday 3 August – I took the day kind of partly off, to be with Murdoch. He is going to Italy, which is a good idea, I think, and will no doubt not be exactly front line, but interesting and with interesting possibilities. Otherwise he might get whizzed off to the far east for years. Obviously he ought to do something. He may go on to investigate German factories before they smash them. I talked to him about the future. I just feel I can't go back. I have a mass of things I desperately want to do, whereas Dick really hasn't, is tired, but mentally, not physically like I am. We get on one another's nerves just now, at least I suppose I do on his as well as he on mine. I sometimes get so angry I have to go out of the room. He doesn't think my farming worth while, well it probably isn't in most senses, but he does think I ought to be about for his times and conveniences. Probably this is quite unfair but I am writing in fury, and it isn't the first time I've been in the same state today.

Tuesday 15 August – Murdoch went off by plane and one feels for an indefinite time. Of course an excellent thing and he must be looking forward to it, but these constant partings pull the heart out of one's breast. One has to be cheerful about it and goodness knows it's not like the far east. But one has to avoid asking too many questions. Every now and then I get a glimpse of what he's been doing.

Thursday 31 August – I find myself arguing with Lachie and Angus for not destroying Germany, which they want to do, because of the atrocities. I try and recall to Angus that it is not right for a socialist to think in a purely nationalist way,

---

* All local farmers.

that we have our socialist comrades in Germany who must do the remaking, and I even try to persuade him that a Christian must forgive, but he never seems to apply his violent Christianity to this kind of thing!

I keep on wondering, myself, how the ordinary people in Germany are taking all this. One can't imagine that they can go on believing in victory . . .

ANNE GARNETT

Since 29 March an American soldier, Bill Virgil Swans, had been billeted with Anne and Frank. Bill was a 'nice young lad' with fair hair and blue eyes who was 'thrilled with home comforts and a big bed, his first for 2 years'. To Anne he looked far too young to be married with twin boys aged two, whom he'd only seen once, and to have lost his first daughter at the age of four months.

With talk of the second front imminent, Bill had asked Anne and Frank to look after his trunk 'in case anything happens' and given them addresses for his family.

Monday 15 May – O, if only this awful 2nd Front would begin and we could get it over. It's like a millstone of anxiety and horror hung round our necks. The lorries, barges, tanks and guns are still streaming through the town, and we bomb, bomb, bomb the whole of Europe and every day it looks as if it must start, and yet it doesn't.

Tuesday 6 June – THE DAY or, as it's called, D DAY. We've done it at last! And in style. Skies and seas black with planes and ships. Sick with excitement all day – hoping and praying. Impressive call to prayer by the King tonight. Churchill says all goes to plan so far. Went and planted leeks and pushed manure home this afternoon – no work too hard.

Thursday 8 June – Sensation caused when we got to bed last night by Frank discovering a hard knob in my left breast! To sleep with dark premonitions of my young life cut short by cancer.

Tuesday 13 June – **London** – Sirens wailed in the night, and though I tried to keep awake to hear London's famous barrage, I turned over and knew nothing till the All Clear woke me. Pleasant stroll along the wide crusty streets – the emptiness gives Georgian and Early V. London back its dignity in spite of lack of paint and bomb-wounds. To Jimmy's (75 Harley St) by 1. He was charming and most reassuring – sure it's nothing urgent (i.e. cancer) but wants a frozen section done and then he'll do the op. and may have to remove the breast. This puts me back just where I was, but he's done wonders for Frank who seems greatly cheered and that's the great thing. Trouble = No beds, everything cleared out for 2nd Front. I may have to wait 6 weeks.

Friday 23 June – Can't seem to concentrate on anything nowadays and am very bad at amusing conversation, fear I have cancer on the brain! Think it's effort of trying to adjust myself to idea of possible life of pain and operations. When I've come to terms with it hope to feel more normal. The uncertainty is the most difficult part – I'm neither fish, fowl nor red herring at present.

Saturday 1 July – Griffins and Frank were drinking in the lounge to celebrate arrival of four large geese on our farm. My dark forebodings realised when we went to bed, Frank v. queer, and I got him to eat 3 lumps of sugar, he seemed OK and I went to sleep. Later woke to hear queer grunts and to my horror he was quite unconscious. Felt I must have given him too much sugar, and fled down in pitchy dark, grappling

frantically with bolts and bars and across street to Johnny.*
He was an angel and came over at once. Night of horror –
Frank 'out' for nearly 2 hours, in the end Doc. went and
phoned Bob and got a stomach tube and we poured glucose
down him. Was nearly out myself and collapsed in Doc's
arms from relief when F. began to stir.

Thursday 6 July – Priceless letter from Gert. this a.m. written at
Redhill as the doodle-bugs sailed by 'Not many fall near and
I'm quite alright – had to wait under my umbrella for my
train at Victoria as the roof is off.' What a way to spend a
holiday! Also letter from AVS saying that dear old No 3,
St Edmund's Terrace has had a hit – Miss Rossetti half buried
in debris but not badly injured, and Helen who was on the
stairs, unhurt. Feel very sad at this. Have always had affection
for No 3, for long home of the Garnetts (Father born there,
before the Rossettis moved in).

Sad morning trying to billet a woman from E. Ham for
Mrs Williams, alas, she has four in family and no one will
have her. Came home deeply depressed – never thought
we'd have to go through this billeting again.

Thurs. – night. Long awaited statement on Flying Bombs
by P.M. in House. Pretty grim, though so far they've killed
1 person each save 2. Deep shelters to be opened and
evacuation of mothers and kids begins tomorrow. To bed
with slight attack of the horrors after this.

Saturday 15 July – **London** – Marvellous depot, everything bright
and shining, run by two young WVS who've lived in Shoreditch Town hall 4 years. Soon got the hang of it and was
bustling round fitting people up with clothes – huge fun and
the folk were *grand* . . . My first doodle came while I was doing

---

* Their GP.

the forms by the door – nasty moment when engine of bug and my heart seemed to stop together. Lady V.* and I came off at 5 and strolled through the borough to see the ruins of our new friends' homes. Lovely sun made it more cruel and then sirens wailed again and at once streets emptied and we were left to watch a bug buzz over and wonder where we'd fling ourselves. Both sick with fright but Lady V. merely looked interested! A beer in a nice pub after this and bus ride home, past where our first bug fell in Broad St – people still raking in rubble, past St Paul's and its gallant surroundings.

Monday 17 July – At 4 a.m. they came over thick and fast. I counted 11, and 8 later on. Lady V. and I met in the passage having bolted from our rooms for one or 2 of the nearest [sic]. We found mutual comfort in each other's company. Have formed strong attachment to this spirited woman. Lady V., another, and I were station-marshals, at St Pancras. Not very auspicious as one child evacuee was lost, the water and biscuits were late arriving and I had to keep phoning from the station master's office, and as I raced down the train with a precious spoon for the babies' food I lost my pants: loud cheers from all beholders!!

Sad farewell to Lady V., and taxied to Hosp. where it's been bliss to be bathed and de-loused by kind nurse and put in spotless bed.

Tuesday 18 July – Heavenly peace! I lie in bed, with dappled shadows from the plane-tree outside the window shifting over me, and my feet don't hurt any more because Nurse has pricked my blisters.

Wednesday 19 July – About 2 p.m. I woke up to find a beaming nurse beside me, eager to tell me that the frozen section

---

* Fellow WVS worker Lady Vyvyan.

showed negative and that all that had to be done was the removal of the cyst. Heavenly gratitude and bliss! Even the soreness and being sick were pleasures – and best of all, Frank's beaming face when he came to see me in the evening.

Sunday 23 July – Turning my Amazing Adventures over in my mind as I lie in bed and thinking how I've been delivered from a very dark slough, I feel sad that the comfort I craved didn't come from my church, but from the various people I've met and from Lady V. who as far as I know, has no particular religious convictions. Feeling as I do, the very real presence of God in the Sacraments, I should have liked to find personal comfort through the church – but it didn't happen that way. It came (none the less God Given) lying under a tree in Hyde Park, and cheering E.enders in Shoreditch.

On 29 July the Lee-Michells took Joan – the wife of an Australian surgeon with the Army Medical Corps – and her two small children into their home. Joan and Anne had met in hospital where their beds had been next to each other.

HERMIONE RANFURLY

On 21 December 1943 Hermione had learnt that the generals last seen with Dan had reached Allied lines. Dan, however, was not with them. The disappointment was crushing. 'I kept thinking of all the things that could still happen to Dan, he might get recaptured or shot or drowned or meet a Mona Lisa. Oh, bloody hell.'

General Jumbo Wilson had succeeded General Eisenhower as supreme Allied commander in the Mediterranean, and Hermione, Coco the parrot and her sister Daphne had moved to Tunis.

Daphne was now secretary to Dudley Clarke, the man who 'thinks up all the misleading things for our enemies'.*

In April Hermione was offered a flight home to England but was determined to wait for Dan. On 13 May she arrived for work to find a signal on her desk from General Alexander marked 'For General Wilson's Eyes Only'. Dan was on his way.

Saturday 13 May – **Algiers** – I ran all the way up 'Bond Street' and in at the door of the cottage to tell Whitaker. He burst into tears.

At five o'clock I was on the airfield. Some officers from head quarters came over: 'Meeting a VIP?' they asked. 'Yes,' I said, 'I am meeting a VIP.' They wandered off.

Dakota 328 made a perfect landing, blew clouds of dust and came to a standstill. I'd waited three years and one month for this arrival.

The doors were opened. Steps were run up. People began to walk down into the sunshine. I stood there transfixed and seconds turned into hours. I waved. I stood and waited but I began to sway and my eyes misted up. I did not see Dan getting out of the plane but, suddenly, his arms were around me . . . Heaven – is being together.

Monday 15 May – When he arrived his clothes were almost rags. Even in rags Dan looks elegant.

Today I returned to the office and felt surprised to find the war is still going on. General Jumbo was very kind. He said that I could have indefinite leave to go to England with Dan and that I could come back to my job afterwards.

They travelled back to England on the SS *Arundel Castle*.

---

* Perhaps best known for Operation Mincemeat, in which false documents were put on a drowned British officer's body in order to mislead the Germans about landings planned for Sicily.

Tuesday 30 May – **On the train to London** – After being away from England for four and a quarter years it was exciting to sail up the Firth of Clyde on a fine summer evening. Seagulls escorted us home. After seeing Immigration and Customs officers we hauled our luggage along the decks and over the gangway down to a dirty quay. No porter, no taxis – only groups of dock-hands slouching about in their lunch break with hands in pockets. We asked a group of them if taxis came to the docks but none of them answered and one spat at us. Maybe they thought we'd been on a Mediterranean cruise. We moved away and sat down on our baggage and waited – happy as grigs.

Wednesday 31 May – Early this morning we reached London and went straight to Claridge's Hotel. The concierge, the hall porter and the liftman gave us a marvellous welcome; we were surprised they should remember us. We have a lovely room on the eighth floor from where we can see plenty of sky, which is going to be important.

Tuesday 6 June – Last night we set our alarm to wake us before dawn. This morning it was dark when we climbed out of bed, drew back the curtains and leaned out on the smutty ledge of our windowsill. Quite soon it seemed as if the whole vault of heaven was vibrating with the roar of aeroplanes. As it grew light we began to see them – great formations of bombers heading for Europe. It was a magnificent and moving sight and we watched – fascinated – with thoughts flashing through our heads: how terrible what they must do; pray god they may return safely; can this be the beginning of the end of the war; so Overlord has started, it's not a secret any more; when the sun comes up every plane will be a target; in a few minutes they'll be over enemy territory.

At eight o'clock the waiter wheeled in our breakfast.

'Kippers for breakfast and the Invasion's on,' he said, and gently closed the door.

Hermione took four weeks' leave before returning to Cairo, and was able to spend a considerable amount of it with her sister Cynthia, who had just been told that she had TB of the stomach lining and that it was likely to be incurable. Since Hermione and Dan were not allowed to serve in the same country, he opted to join Fitzroy Maclean and the mission to Yugoslavia. They would be with Tito, the leader of the Yugoslav partisans.

Tuesday 27 June – I went to say goodbye to Cynthia. Because of children being taken away from London and the buzz-bombs the train was alarmingly full. I found Cynthia a bit better but not out of danger. On my way back, at Oxford, I watched wounded being unloaded from a train – they'd been flown in from France this morning. So sad.

Our leave in England has been wonderful because we are together. But it has also been a rather sad time. The courage of the people in England is amazing but so many look weary and sorrowful.

So many of our friends in Dan's Yeomanry are dead. Most people seemed to be looking backwards rather than forwards, but what can they look forward to except peace and that is still far away and the price of reaching it will surely be devastating?

Wednesday 28 June – **London** – I was woken by air-raid sirens. The sound of a buzz-bomb approaching at roof level came nearer and nearer till it seemed to fill our room. I put my head under the pillow. I thought, 'This cannot happen to us – not before breakfast – not on our last day in London.'

Things on the dressing table began to rattle. A window slammed. Dan woke up. Now the noise was deafening – I couldn't hear what he said. When it passed over us I counted up to eighteen and then it exploded. 'That must have hit Oxford Street,' I thought complacently and got up and was violently sick in the loo. Ten minutes later another drone started. Without drawing the curtains I knew it was a rainy day because in fine weather most of them got shot down nearer the coast.

Thursday 29 June – **Algiers** – Whitaker was full of news. Several of the General's guests had stayed in the cottage when I was away. 'Some queer types,' said Whitaker and showed me a photo of Monty.

'Was he nice to you?' I asked.

'He's a phoney,' declared Whitaker with distaste, 'no more General Montgomery than Ginger Rogers.' Afterwards Mark explained that it was Monty's double – he was part of a deception plan for Overlord.

On 21 July General Jumbo and the entire staff of Allied Forces Headquarters, numbering 25,000, moved from North Africa to Caserta in Italy, where the preparations were being made for the invasion of southern France.

Wednesday 9 August – I was given a day off so I took my luggage and Coco to Villa Pina and spent the morning cleaning. Our new ADC telephoned me at lunchtime: 'Marshal Tito has a free afternoon and we do not know what to do with him, so we are bringing him down to tea with you.' My heart sank. This was typical of my job, I thought, as I dusted angrily. Apart from office work you might be sent anywhere at any moment, be asked to meet aeroplanes, do hostess at official dinner parties, comfort lonely officers, give tea to Partisan dictators when you don't even own a teapot.

Tito drank beer, carefully covered by tommy guns which his guards would not put away at any price. Coco crawled on to the Marshal's knee while I wondered nervously whether he would be shot if he pecked my guest or dirtied his elegant uniform. The Yugoslavs lost a little of their shyness when I showed them my Mauser pistol which they carefully took to bits and put together again. I walked them round the garden and showed them Capri through the haze. We caught a field mouse. They asked about the shipping lying below us like an Armada, and told me of their desperate need for hospitals and medicine.

SOLDIERS, SAILORS AND SPECIAL OPERATIONS IN NORMANDY

The Germans expected an invasion but could not be sure exactly where on the French coast the attack would come. The one thing they were certain of, however, was that it wouldn't come on 6 June – the forecast high winds and rough seas would make it impossible. But the Allies, gambling everything on the promise of a thirty-six-hour window of marginally improved conditions, decided to go.

The invading forces were unloaded from troopships into landing craft which took them to the beaches. There they had to wade ashore through a five-foot swell. Landings took place on five beaches across fifty miles of coast. The Americans landed at Omaha and Utah, the Canadians at Juno and the British at Gold and Sword. At Sword, in spite of heavy casualties, units succeeded in getting ashore within an hour.

H. T. BONE
Lieutenant, 2nd Battalion, East Yorkshire Regiment,
8th Brigade*

Sword Beach – Apart from our ordinary equipment we were loaded down with heavy packs, a pick or shovel each, 24 hours rations, ammunition and maps. Under our arm-pits were large bulges of the inflated Mae-Wests [life-jackets]. In the Mess decks we blacked our faces with black Palm Olive cream and listened to the naval orders over the loud-hailer. Most of us had taken communion on the Sunday, but the padre had a few words to say to us. Then the actual loading into the craft – swinging on davits – the boat lowering and finally, 'Away boats.' While this was going on, all around could be seen the rest of the convoy, with battleships and cruisers firing their big guns every few minutes and destroyers rushing round. One had been hit by something and only the up-ended part of its bows remained in view. As our flotilla swung into line behind its leader we raised our flag, a black silk square with the white rose of Yorkshire in the centre. It was some distance to the beaches and it was a wet trip.

The Colonel and the flotilla leader were piloting us in, and for a few brief minutes nothing happened except the music of the guns and the whang of occasional bullets overhead, with the sporadic explosions of mortar bombs and the background of our own heavy machine-gun fire. The doors opened as we grounded and the Colonel was out. The sea was choppy and the boat swung a good bit as one by one we followed him. Several fell in and got soaked through. I was lucky. I stopped for a few seconds to help my men with their heavy wireless sets and to ensure they kept them dry.

---

*   Lieutenant H. T. Bone, private papers, Imperial War Museum, 87311.

PATRICK PORTEOUS
Major, No. 4 Commando, 4th Special Service Brigade*

Sword Beach – There was a lot of stuff flying about from some big German pillboxes just to our left. I saw the troop commander in the landing craft next to mine shot dead on the spot – he just dashed out and keeled over.

At the edge of the water we found a hell of a lot of chaps from the previous unit to have landed, I think it was the East Yorks. They were all dead or wounded, just swilling about in the water.

I ordered all my chaps to throw their smoke grenades which created a big belt of smoke down our left-hand side and protected us from the pillbox.

We got across the beach and into some sand dunes. At that point I think I had lost about a quarter of my troop, either killed or wounded. Our job was to make our way to a coastal battery about a mile-and-a-half away, and destroy the guns with special charges made of plastic explosive.

The invasion force was to be supplied with ammunition, stores and back-up personnel via two artificial harbours (Mulberries), as favoured by Churchill.† By the afternoon of 6 June the Mulberries had been given the word to sail. Seven miles of piers and jetties created from sections of concrete plus steel pontoons were towed across the Channel. Mulberry A was allocated to the American sector at Omaha, and Mulberry B (nicknamed Port

---

* Quoted in Russell Miller, *Nothing Less Than Victory, The Oral History of D-Day*, Penguin, 1994.

† In a memorandum to Mountbatten on 30 May 1942 he enumerated the advantages of a floating pier that 'must float up and down with the tide'. He concluded, 'Don't argue the matter. The difficulties will argue for themselves.'

Winston) to the British and Canadian Gold and Juno Beaches. Those in charge of code names had a field day. Each Mulberry consisted of floating piers, floating outer breakwaters and pierheads called, respectively, whales, bombardons and spuds, while swiss rolls (or roly-polys) were floating canvas roadways carried on steel wires. There were also 'bubble harbours', which created areas of calm water by forcing bubbles below the surface of the sea to suppress waves.

For the use of smaller craft there were five Gooseberry harbours – formed by sinking merchant ships in a semicircle (often with the assistance of German guns), from which pontoons were laid enabling troops to land without getting wet. And finally there were amphibious trucks for ship-to-shore transport called DUKWs (or ducks).

CHARLES WILSON
Trooper, regimental survey party, 147th (Essex Yeomanry) Field Regiment, 56th Infantry Brigade*

Gold Beach – I was one of the 'roly-poly team', whose job it was to drag out to the shore a huge roll of matting and wire mesh, which was intended to prevent following vehicles getting bogged down in the sand. The 'roly-poly' was about eight feet in diameter, with an axle to which ropes were attached. Most of us stripped down to vest, pants and gym shoes.

The 'roly-poly' was quite unmanageable in the rough water and dragged us away, towards some mines. We let go the ropes and swam and scrambled ashore.

The Bren carrier was the first vehicle off the LCT [landing craft, tank]. It floated for a moment, drifted on to a mine and

* Charles Wilson, *Essex Yeomanry Journal*, 1969, quoted in Russell Miller, *Nothing Less Than Victory*, Penguin, 1994.

sank. The battery CP [command post] half-track got off along
the beach, with me running behind.

Our survey jeep came off the LCT and went down like a
stone, being so overloaded. Our MO's jeep followed and met
a similar fate and the driver was just pulled out in time, half-
drowned. The rising tide helped the LCT lift off the sand
bank and it moved inshore, squashing the two jeeps flat.

Eventually a way was cleared off the beach and the
battery half-track moved inland. I walked along behind it
with the rest of the command post staff, as it crawled along
a narrow lane which the engineers were sweeping for mines.
In we came to fields and hedges, two poor stone cottages
and our first Frenchmen, two grey-stubbled old men who
kissed us on both cheeks. The road was crowded with
vehicles and infantry moving inland.

Quite apart from the regular troops landing in Normandy, at
the time of the invasion the Allies had more than forty Special
Operations Executive-run circuits active in France. Additional
paramilitary 'Jedburgh' teams, of three men each, were tasked
with supervising local resistance members to defend the newly
established Allied bridgeheads by slowing down German attempts
to regroup.

THOMAS MACPHERSON
Major, SOE, Jedburgh team 'Quinine'*

A messenger came over that told us about the northward
movement of the Das Reich Armoured Division and the Second Motorised Division, heading up towards the beaches and

---

*   Major Thomas Macpherson, sound archive, Imperial War Museum, 17912;
   Roderick Bailey, *Forgotten Voices of the Secret War, an inside history of Special
   Operations during the Second World War*, Ebury, 2008.

coming through the edge of my territory on two roads. There was almost a continuous stream of tanks, armoured cars, trucks and so on going up that road and what one had to do was stop them from time to time, make them de-bus, make them waste time. Now there were various ways of doing that and this was possible because it was quite heavily wooded and there were tracks through the wood almost parallel to the road itself, so we could move people. We dropped off two people here, two people there, with instructions to wait until there was a non-armoured vehicle and then simply empty their Sten magazines into it once and depart. That stopped the column. They had to get out and go and see what was happening. I myself, with two, went up the road further and started felling trees across it, brutally by explosive. Just a bang and the tree would fall down. They were not major obstacles but the southernmost two or three of them we booby-trapped, so that would delay them further. They had to look at each tree. The first one, I'm glad to say, was booby-trapped. They tried to push it aside with an armoured car and blew the front off the car. After that they were suitably cautious.

10. GERMAN SURRENDER

SPRING 1945

As Montgomery's army swept up the north coast of France in the summer of 1944 they overran the V1 launch sites, but on 8 September a new menace appeared: V2 rockets* aimed at London and newly liberated Antwerp from mobile launchers in Holland and Germany. The rockets were fired into suborbital space and descended faster than the speed of sound. If you heard them, they'd missed you. Since they flew so high there was no way of intercepting them. They would continue to terrorize and inflict damage until well into March 1945.

Throughout March and into April Allied progress in Europe was marked by the crossing of rivers: the Rhine and Main in the west, the Oder and Elbe in the east. For every British soldier in north-west Europe there were now three Americans, and Montgomery's influence and importance diminished proportionately.

When he became supreme Allied commander, Eisenhower was tasked with undertaking 'operations aimed at the heart of Germany and the destruction of her armed forces'.†

---

* Over 10,000 slave workers died in the manufacture of V2 rockets in 1944 from ammonia dust and paint fumes. One survivor recorded, 'It was [there] that I realised how the pyramids were built.'

† Directive to Eisenhower from combined chiefs of staff, Washington, 12 February 1944.

He pursued his task vigorously but his understanding of European power politics was perhaps limited. On 28 March, without contacting either London or Washington, Eisenhower contacted Stalin to suggest that US forces should meet the Red Army in Dresden. Berlin would be left to the Russians.

In the Far East the Japanese were being forced out of Manila in the Philippines, and in Burma British and Commonwealth troops were heading for Mandalay. As the Japanese were pushed back, they resorted to kamikaze tactics – suicide missions in which pilots deliberately crashed their planes into Allied ships. And when American bombers attacked Tokyo, the city's high proportion of wooden houses produced firestorms perhaps even more devastating than the bombing of Dresden.

Roosevelt had coined the phrase 'United Nations' to describe the Allied countries, and it was first used publicly when the North Atlantic Treaty was signed in January 1942. In the autumn of 1944, at the Dumbarton Oaks Conference in Washington, America, Britain, Russia and China put forward draft proposals for a formal organization. There were further discussions at Yalta and it was agreed that fifty Allied nations would meet in San Francisco in April 1945 to review the proposals.

Late on Thursday 12 April Churchill learned that Roosevelt had died. The British premier had been aware for some time that Roosevelt's health was rapidly failing, but nonetheless he was shocked: 'I felt as if I had been struck a physical blow'.* A four-year mutually supportive relationship in pursuit of victory was over within sight of the prize. The same day, Generals Eisenhower, Bradley and Patton arrived at Ohrdruf, a sub-camp of Buchenwald, which the Americans

* W. S. Churchill, *The Second World War*, Volume 6: *Triumph and Tragedy*, Cassell, 1948.

had liberated a few days previously. It wasn't the first of the concentration camps to be freed, nor was its existence a surprise. Allied Intelligence had known about them as early as 1942, and the horrors revealed by the Russian liberation of Majdanek, near Lublin in Poland, in July 1944 had been widely publicized. But the grotesque enormity of what the Nazis had done was a profound shock for all those who saw it.

In January 1945 the SS began the evacuation of Auschwitz, and attempts were made to destroy the evidence of what had taken place there. Pits full of ashes and bones were emptied and covered with turf and vegetation. Crematorium 1 was transformed into an air-raid shelter. On 17 January 58,000 inmates began a forced march to other camps, leaving behind those who were too ill or weak to move. Ten days later the Russians reached the camp and liberated over 7,000 prisoners.

On 15 April British troops entered Bergen-Belsen in northern Germany. Many of those evacuated from the camps in the east who had not been shot or died from exhaustion and disease on the marches were here. The camp now held 60,000 prisoners. There was no water, no sanitation; dysentery and typhus were rampant and the corpses of those who had recently perished lay in piles around the camp.

In Italy, with the Allies advancing, Mussolini was recognized by a partisan unit while trying to escape to Switzerland and on 25 April summarily executed. Five days later, in his Berlin bunker, where he had been living since January that year, Adolf Hitler and his new wife Eva Braun committed suicide. Their bodies were wrapped in blankets, taken out to a shell crater, doused with petrol and burnt.

THE DIARISTS

ANNE GARNETT

Anne's convalescence had gone well, although she was finding work at the factory unusually dangerous: ampoules 'popped' with alarming regularity as she checked them and showered her with acid that ate into her clothes. On one occasion she got acid in both eyes and was off work for a week. The doctor advised wearing goggles.

Her lodger Joan had left with her little girls in October, and Frank had attended a Home Guard farewell parade in December. Gertie's departure in January, to look after her mother, meant Anne had to fit in housework between the factory, the mobile canteen and tending to her new vegetable garden on the former tennis court. She was shocked by the way Britain was 'giving in to the Russians' over the Poles, adding, 'Should be heartbroken if I ever had cherished any illusions or ideals about the outcome of this war.'

Saturday 21 April – Black-out restrictions to end on Monday! Thus, bit by bit, normal life returns and Peace day will be shorn of some of its glamour because we shall have grown used to lights again and no bombs. News all of the fearful prison-camps now being unearthed in Germany, fresh grue-some horrors turn up every day and the Yanks publish it all with a truly Hollywood 'eye to the box office'. But I suppose we ought to hear it all. The name of Germany is going to stink for some years after all this.

Friday 27 April – News tonight of link-up between Russians and USA which took place at last on Wed. in the Elbe.

More camps liberated – the prisoners leap to lose their chains!

Saturday 28 April – News tonight of Germany asking for un-conditional surrender from us and USA, but not Russia – so we ignore it. Also that Musso. has been arrested trying to escape in German uniform and carrying bags of *spicci* [loose change].

I think the war will be over in the next day or two. Churchill says 'there may be some celebration if certain events occur' . . . I'll say!!

Tuesday 1 May – Everything white and thick ice on puddles. Even the lilac hangs its blooms. Rumours rife as to Hitler. Germans say he suffered from cerebral haemorrhage but that may well be caused by a bullet!

Welcome news that we are dropping supplies of food over occupied Holland. Ghastly account of Dachau concentration camp.

Wednesday 2 May – 8 a.m. news announces Hitler's death: a hero's, according to the Germans, and he died in defence of his country, fighting to the last. We all take this with much salt.

Thursday 3 May – We now hear Hitler killed himself.

Frank has bought a lovely big [Union] Jack to fly on armistice day. Terrific news. The whole of the German army in N. Germany and the S. except for a bit round Munich has surrendered. This only leaves Denmark and Norway, to which havens hundreds of Huns are fleeing in every kind of available craft, while we bomb and strafe them. Dunkirk over again.

Saturday 5 May – More great news – all the Germans in Holland and Denmark have surrendered. Thank God the

Dutch are free of their tormentors at last, and the Danes spared battles over their land.

Sunday 6 May – All on tenterhooks expecting the Armistice. It may come any minute now – Germans surrendering everywhere. Awkward domestic complications however as the [chimney] sweep is supposed to be coming tomorrow.

Monday 7 May – Sweep arrived at 7.15 – chaos unspeakable, I sat helplessly and looked at the soot and wondered how ever I'd get the kitchen clean! No hot water of course.

Frank phoned to say V. day is to be tomorrow! Grand thrill, we hung out our flags and got Snows [friends] and Griffins up to drink our bottle of fizz.

Tuesday 8 May – Glorious day! The sunshine and the flags and the happy crowds, and the marvellous joy and feeling of relief! Mad holiday all day, apart from meals and washing up, and ended by grand party next door – lots of champagne and frolics. Came in here to light bonfire and dance around it. Frank and I went to church at 7.30. Immense congregation, people standing in the churchyard, wonderful singing.

Wednesday 9 May – Another holiday. Wellington very much *en fete*, it has risen well to the occasion, with dancing in streets at night and happy crowds all day.

Friday 11 May – Best news yet – basic petrol allowance to be resumed within a month, and petrol for lawn mowers! This is sheer joy – what a difference it will make to us!

ALAN BROOKE

Brooke continued to use his diary as 'the only safety valve' for his irritation with Churchill, recording what he later described as 'continued abuse' – although he also recorded his affection and admiration for the prime minister. He had been with Churchill to see first hand the crossing of the Rhine by the 9th American and 2nd British Armies in the last week of March and was 'certain that the end of the Germans is very near indeed'.

The last months of the war brought cruel personal losses for Brooke. His old friend and comrade Field Marshal Dill died in November 1944. Brooke had been with Dill the previous September in Quebec and been very concerned about his health but had not been able to see him again before his death. 'Another of the prominent landmarks of my life was gone.' Then, in February 1945, his ADC and constant companion Captain Barney Charlesworth was killed in an air crash – a 'frightful blow' – and in April, in the final days of the Italian campaign, he heard of the death of a great-nephew.

Wednesday 2 May – Last night on the midnight news, Hitler was reported as dead. After longing for this news for the last 6 years, and wondering whether I should ever be privileged to hear it, when I finally listened to it I remained completely unmoved. Why? I do not know. I fully realized that it was the real full stop to the many and long chapters of this war, but I think that I have become so war weary with the continual strain of the war that my brain is numbed, and incapable of feeling intensely.

Tuesday 8 May – VE Day. The Chiefs of Staff held their usual meeting in the morning, and then went to Buckingham Palace to meet the King with the War Cabinet.

The King made a very nice little speech of congratulation, finishing up with a reference to the Chiefs of Staff as that organization which probably only those present in the room had any idea what their real part had been in securing the success of this war. We were then photographed, first of all together, and then only the King, PM, and COS.

We then left for the Home Office where a balcony had been prepared on which the PM, Cabinet and COS were to come to see the crowd in Whitehall and to be cheered by them. A vast crowd stretching from near the WO to Parliament Square. Then back to the WO to finish off work. I had to go and see PJ [Grigg, secretary of state] and on coming out Lady Grigg collared me and brought me into the passage. She said, 'I watched you getting into your car this morning from the window with a crowd looking at you, and none of them realizing that beside them was the man who had probably done most to win the war against Germany!' She said it was all wrong that they should not realize it, 'I do, and lots of people do, tell Lady Brookie from me.' It was very nice of her, she said it so nicely and I wish you had been able to hear her.

There is no doubt the public has never understood what the Chiefs of Staff have been doing in the running of this war. On the whole the PM has never enlightened them much, and has never once in all his speeches referred to the Chiefs of Staff or what they have been doing in the direction of the war on the highest plane. It may be inevitable, but I do feel that it is time that this country was educated as to how wars are run and how strategy is controlled.

At times the work and difficulties to be faced have been almost beyond powers of endurance. The difficulties with Winston have been of almost unbearable proportions, at times I have felt I could not possibly face a single other day. And yet I would not have missed the last 3½ years of struggle and endeavour for anything on earth.

The suffering and agony of war in my mind must exist to gradually educate us to the fundamental law of 'loving our neighbour as ourselves'. When that lesson has been learned, then war will cease to exist. We are however many centuries from such a state of affairs. Many more wars, and much suffering is required before we finally learn our lesson. However humanity in this world is still young, there are still many millions of years to run during which high perfection will be attained. For the present we can do no more than go on striving to improve more friendly relations towards those that surround us.

With these reflections I must leave behind the German war and now turn my energies during my few remaining days [as CIGS] towards the final defeat of Japan.

Saturday 12 May – Spent the morning in complete peace mending an old rabbit hutch! After lunch went to Turgis Green where I met Mussens [Fisher's gamekeeper] and Bertie Fisher.* Mussens had nests of hawfinch, not ready to photograph, and nightingale, bullfinch, black cap. I spent 1½ hours photographing the bullfinches, light not very good and heat oppressive. Came home for late tea and more work at the rabbit hutch.

HAROLD NICOLSON

Harold followed the Italian campaign closely, as his son Nigel was serving there with the Grenadier Guards. He felt that this 'miraculous campaign' – and in particular the taking of Rome – had been overshadowed by the Normandy invasion. His younger son Ben, badly injured in an air crash, was now recovering at home. On the day before VE Day, Harold, Vita and Ben hoisted the flag on the tower at Sissinghurst.

The following is taken from a letter to Nigel written in London.

Tuesday 8 May – I attended a meeting of the Institut Français and lunched at the Beefsteak. By that time things began to liven up. There was some cheering in the streets and crowds in Leicester Square. But when I had finished my luncheon, I

---

* A general, who had retired in 1940, and a neighbour.

found a very different scene. The whole of Trafalgar Square and Whitehall was packed with people. Somebody had made a corner in rosettes, flags, streamers, paper whisks and, above all, paper caps. The latter were horrible, being of the comic variety. I also regret to say that I observed three Guardsmen in full uniform wearing such hats: they were <u>not</u> Grenadiers; they belonged to the Coldstream. And through this cheerful, but not exuberant, crowd I pushed my way to the House of Commons. The last few yards were very difficult, as the crowd was packed against the railings. I tore my trousers in trying to squeeze past a stranded car. But at length the police saw me and backed a horse into the crowd, making a gap through which, amid cheers, I was squirted into Palace Yard. There I paused to recover myself, and seeing that it was approaching the hour of 3 p.m., I decided to remain there and hear Winston's broadcast which was to be relayed through loud-speakers. As Big Ben struck three, there was an extraordinary hush over the assembled multitude, and then came Winston's voice. He was short and effective, merely announcing that unconditional surrender had been signed, and naming the signatories.

'The evil-doers', he intoned, 'now lie prostrate before us.' The crowd gasped at this phrase. 'Advance Britannia!' he shouted at the end, and there followed the Last Post and God Save the King which we all sang very loud indeed. And then cheer upon cheer.

I dashed back into the House and into the Chamber. After the roar and heat outside, it was like suddenly entering an Oxford quadrangle on Eights Week night. Cool and hushed the Chamber was, with P J Grigg answering questions as if nothing unusual were impending. The clock reached 3.15, which is the moment when Questions automatically close. We knew that it would take Winston some time to get to the House from Downing Street in such a crowd. We therefore made conversation by asking supplementary questions until

3.23. Then a slight stir was observed behind the Speaker's chair, and Winston, looking coy and cheerful, came in. The House rose as a man, and yelled and yelled and waved their Order Papers. He responded, not with a bow exactly, but with an odd shy jerk of the head and with a wide grin. Then he started to read to us the statement that he had just made on the wireless. When he had finished reading, he put his manuscript aside and with wide gestures thanked and blessed the House for all its noble support of him throughout these years.

Then he proposed that 'this House do now attend at the Church of St Margaret's, Westminster, to give humble and reverend thanks to Almighty God for our deliverance from the threat of German domination'. The motion was carried, and the Serjeant at Arms put the mace on his shoulder and, following the Speaker, we all strode out. Through the Central Lobby we streamed, through St Stephen's Chapel, and out into the sunshine of Parliament Square. We entered St Margaret's by the West door which was furthest away from us, and that meant a long sinuous procession through a lane kept open for us through the crowd. I had expected some jeers or tittering, since politicians are not popular and in the mass they seem absurd. But not at all. Cheers were what we received, and adulation. The service itself was very short and simple, and beautifully sung. Then the Chaplain to the Speaker read in a loud voice the names of those who had laid down their lives: 'Ronald Cartland; Hubert Duggan; Victor Cazalet; John Macnamara; Robert Bernays' – only the names of my particular friends registered on my consciousness. I was moved. The tears came into my eyes. Furtively I wiped them away. 'Men are so emotional,' sniffed Nancy Astor, who was sitting next to me. Damn her.

After leaving the service at St Margaret's Harold went to give a lecture at a police course in west London, returning for dinner in Pall Mall, where he listened to the King's broadcast.

I went on to a party at Chips Channon's.* Why did I go to that party? I should have been much happier seeing all the flood-lighting and the crowds outside Buckingham Palace. But I went and I loathed it. There in his room, copied from the Amalienburg,† under the lights of many candles, were gathered the Nurembergers and the Munichois celebrating <u>our</u> victory over <u>their</u> friend Herr von Ribbentrop. I left early and in haste, leaving my coat behind me. A voice hailed me in Belgrave Square. It was Charles, seventh Marquess of Londonderry, Hitler's friend.‡ As we walked towards his mansion in Park Lane, he explained to me how he had warned the Government about Hitler; how they would not listen to him; how, but for him, we should not have had Spitfires and 'all this', waving a thin arm at the glow above a floodlit Buckingham Palace, at the sound of cheering in the park, and at the cone of searchlights which joined each other like a maypole above our heads.

Enraged by this, I left him in Park Lane and walked back through the happy but quite sober crowds to Trafalgar Square. The National Gallery was alive with every stone outlined in flood-lighting, and down there was Big Ben with a grin upon his illumined face. The statue of Nelson was picked out by a searchlight, and there was the smell of distant bonfires in the air. I walked to the Temple and beyond. Looking down Fleet Street one saw the best sight of all – the dome of St Paul's rather dim-lit, and then above it a concentration of searchlights upon the huge golden cross. So I went to bed.

That was my victory day.

---

* Conservative MP, supporter of Chamberlain and the Munich agreement.
† The eighteenth-century hunting lodge in the grounds of the Nymphenburg Palace in Munich.
‡ Londonderry had been secretary of state for air in the 1931 National Government and had supported rearmament in parallel with appeasement.

GEORGE BEARDMORE

For George the winter of 1944–5 had been the 'worst period of the war'. The intense cold and the explosions of the V2s created for George the illusion of being at the Russian Front. Everyone was 'weary of war and its effects'.

Friday 30 March – Another rocket, and worst of the lot, landed at the top of Uppingham Avenue. The rocket had landed at 3.40 in the morning, killing nine people among whom was a 9-year-old boy who had been flung out of bed, through the rafters, and into a back garden ten houses away – at first, nobody had been able to find him.

As I watched the mass funeral (Union Jack, Bishop of Willesden, Civil Defence, WVS, and the Controllers' cars lined up for three hundred yards) tears came to my eyes not with the grief and distress caused to survivors but with the incalculable trouble to which they will be put, months and years of it, before they can resume any sort of normal life and the incident becomes only a tale to tell to the grand-children. Even obtaining an everyday thing like soap has its problems, let alone the replacement of identity-cards, ration-books, personal papers, with which I can give some help. In fact, I suggested to the WVS that they leave some bars of soap in my office for dispensation; it duly arrived, and within a day it had all gone. Also here for the first time I had an official from Public Assistance sitting at my side, giving away money – not loaning, giving.

This incident was also made memorable by the office I had set up suddenly catching fire, provisionally put down to a short in the electricity supply creating a spark that set alight a small gas-leak. Luckily only seven or eight of us were inside the house, and we managed to get out in a mad scramble without casualty. A moment later, in the street and

watching the blaze, which had started at the back, I remembered the infinite pains with which the WVS had gathered
and collated information about the inhabitants of the
affected houses before and after. Without thinking twice
about it I threw myself inside, swept the papers up in my
left arm and while shielding my face with my right arm
bolted outside again. The only damage resulted from the
right side of my head catching fire. At least, there was a
strong smell of burning and I found the hair singed off. No
medals for rescuing papers. Now if they had been a baby
instead.

Thursday 26 April – I have the billeting of nurses on the brain.
Canvassing for voluntary billets, always a degrading business,
has produced nothing so now I am faced with compulsory
billeting, which is worse.

Took a Luminal [sleeping pill] last night but the eyes are
still tired. The ceilings are now distributed over the garden
and I have made several sowings, but apart from the main
crops like runner-beans, tomatoes, and Brussels, I shan't
spend much energy there.

In the foregoing there is no hint that this morning's paper
told us that the Russians had now completely encircled
Berlin and occupied one third of it, nor that the full horror
of the Concentration Camps at Belsen and Buchenwald was
the chief topic in press and radio. Only confirms my general
finding that people are impossible but individuals unique
and precious. Rockets came to a halt about a month ago, on
Monday we were given permission to leave our blackouts
undrawn, and enamel saucepans have returned to the shops.
The late evenings are quite wonderful, so quiet, with the
lights from windows slanting across the street and shining on
the almond-trees' new foliage, and neighbours coming out in
the mild air to gossip over their front gates and fences.

I am laying in all the coal I can find, at whatever price,

because although the war may be in its closing stages we have yet to pay for it.

Monday 21 May – I remember that in the past – how long ago! – Coronation Day was ruined for me by lack of sleep. Now our two Victory Days were almost ruined by bronchitis, very fittingly if one bears in mind the attacks I had during the war, but all the same I made myself join in the bonfires, the staying-up when I wanted to be in bed, and the fireworks. Jean made a really lovely supper (to which friends came) and for which Victoria was allowed to stay up. The curtains were left undrawn because a community spirit is abroad and everyone wants to share in every one else's rejoicings. All the searchlights shone in the sky, the office-girls and Gates [work colleague] went up to Town to join the vast crowds in front of Buckingham Palace, and the whole business was clouded by impending trouble with Russia over the future of Poland.

I must be anti-social because I find that rejoicing with a hundred thousand others isn't my idea of fun, or even of celebration. We have come to the end of it with only the loss of Jean's mother. Our home is intact, our children have been safely born and raised without (so far as we can see) impairment, and our purpose in this, our unique life, has not been lessened. On the contrary it has been advanced.

VERA BRITTAIN

Even though the Allied forces were closing on Berlin and victory seemed certain, for those in London, like Vera, the V2s falling on the capital were a vivid reminder that the war was far from over. In April George left to cover the San Francisco Conference as a correspondent and so reported on the establishment of the United Nations Organization. On VE Day Vera was alone in her London flat, both the children being at school, although her mother was living nearby. She had spent the previous day with Josefine von Reitzenstein, a refugee from Germany who had written a book of letters to her daughter for which Vera had provided an introduction.

Tuesday 6 March – Six or seven rockets during night – one very loud, with a huge flash due south. No sirens during darkness. Got up at 7.0 & caught 10.0 train from Liverpool St. to Holt, Norfolk, for lecture at Gresham's School. Papers all full of descriptions of the American entry into Cologne, showing that the city we knew is a heap of ruins, tho' the Cathedral spires look unchanged & the Cathedral itself is repairable. The Cathedral Square, the museums & medieval buildings, the wide ring streets in the outskirts – all are gone.

Monday 26 March – Several rockets during night; two at 10.30 & 11.30, shortly after I got into the flat from Bangor. Also a flying bomb Alert.

Went down to Lyndhurst for Easter. Another rocket fell heavily (I was told by a naval man in the train that it was near Euston, where he had just been) as I was waiting at Waterloo. G. who came with me to help me with my luggage, said it was only an engine, but I knew better.

Tuesday 8 May – Felt disinclined to hear a 'Victory' service so went to the little meeting of the London Mission at Kingsway Hall to hear Donald Soper give a really inspiring address on thanksgiving, penitence and dedication. After lunch went back to Whitehall determined to end this War near Westminster as I ended the last. Flags now everywhere; 'planes flying over crowds; bells ringing; mounted policemen moving back a throng which grew immense between 2.0 & 3.0; yet sense of anti-climax persisted in contrast with spontaneity of Armistice Day 1918; it was all so formal & 'arranged'.

At 3.0 Churchill's voice duly announced the end of the War & after silence the crowds cheered. Typically he ended with the words 'Advance Britannia!' & introduced no phrase of constructive hope for a better society which renounces war. Caught a glimpse of him standing in his car as he went from Downing St. to the H. of Commons surrounded by cheering crowds, waving his hat, with the usual cigar & self-satisfied expression.

Walked half the way home for tea with Mother, thinking how strange it was that, though this time I have kept (so far) all my private world which last time I had totally lost, not one of them is here, & again I experience the end of a European war half-exasperated & half-saddened by the triviality of her preoccupations in contrast to the immensity of world events.

Dined at Rembrandt with J. von R., talked to her till past 11 p.m., when we walked to Sloane Avenue & looked at partially flood-lit buildings & a display of searchlights half-obscured by a cloudy sky; saw it from the roof of the flat. Left her at S. Kensington station & walked home with the War officially (at 1 minute past midnight) as well as actually over in Europe. Bonfires in St Luke's Churchyard & elsewhere; Chelsea Town Hall floodlit; people in streets, but everything orderly & controlled.

On 30 May Vera was one of the speakers at a peace meeting at Central Hall, Westminster. The Hall (capacity almost 3,000) was packed, and another 2,000 were accommodated in two overflow meetings or in Hyde Park, where late at night Vera made a fourth speech. She later wrote in *Testament of Experience*:

When Victor Gollancz, in a vehement and uncompromising speech, demanded the return of the Left parties in the forthcoming election, the response was a waterfall roar such as I had heard only at a stadium. Hardly less impressive was the answer to my own appeal for the end of the 'non-fraternisation' order now imposed on the British troops occupying Germany.

The meeting, spectacularly successful though it had been, was virtually boycotted by the ordinary Press. This policy was not only unimaginative, but completely stupid from the standpoint of the Press itself. A perspicacious reporter at that meeting could have forecast the result of the General Election.

CHARLES RITCHIE

Charles' brother Roley recovered from his injuries and Ritchie himself was to be posted back to Ottawa to the Department of External Affairs at the end of January 1945. He used his remaining leave to visit friends in Paris.

Wednesday 3 January – **Paris** – At last I got an opportunity to get out alone into the streets and to look for Paris. It was like a dream in which you see the woman you love but cannot speak to her and cannot touch her. The untouched beauty of the city lying about me in burnished splendour under the winter sun made the emptiness more sinister. Paris is dead – there is no movement, no life, no crowds of talking, gesticulating people, no hum of assurance, no noisy erratic traffic of people and vehicles. Nothing but a spacious emptiness of the streets and the shabby, silent passers-by with drawn faces and hunched shoulders, grim, cold, hungry people. You look at their faces, and pity and nostalgia for the past seem out of place. The irony of the heroic arches and spectacular perspectives – the backdrop for their humiliation and their bitter unresigned endurance.

Saturday 3 February – Ottawa – I am in for an intensive bout of re-education. In the Department I feel like a new boy at school. They all seem to know so much more than I do. I asked myself what I can have been doing in these years when they were informing themselves so fully. Living through the war must be the answer.

Saturday 3 March – Dinner last night for the Soviet Ambassador, Zarubin. Sat next to the Soviet Ambassadress and asked her how she liked Ottawa after Moscow. She replied with animation, 'Moscow wonderful, concerts wonderful, ballet wonderful, opera wonderful, Moscow big city – Ottawa nothing (*nichevo*) – cinema, cinema, cinema.'

Ritchie was staying with a favourite relation, Aunt Elsie, a fellow Anglophile, whose sons were still 'at the war'. His diary entries are few and sparse, picking up again in April, when he travelled to the United States for the San Francisco Conference, which he was attending as an adviser to the Canadian delegation. On the way he shared a train with the Canadian prime minister, Mackenzie King, and found himself charmed by 'the fat little conjurer with his flickering shifty eyes'.

Saturday 21 April – **On the train** – Talking of Mussolini he [Mackenzie King] said, 'A remarkable finely-shaped head – the head of a Caesar – deep-set eyes full of intelligence. He did a lot of good – cleaned up a lot of corruption, but he had too much power for too long. They worship false gods in Europe – that is the trouble. Europe is too full of pictures of Napoleon and statues of Caesars.'

Thursday 26 April – **San Francisco** – No one can resist the attraction of the town and the cheerfulness of the inhabitants. Nowhere could have been found in the world which is more of a contrast to the battered cities and tired people of Europe.

The Bay is a beautiful background, the sun shines perpetually, the streets are thronged, there are American sailors everywhere with their girls and this somehow adds to the musical-comedy atmosphere. You expect them at any moment to break into song and dance.

The town is full of stories about the Russians – that they have a warship laden with caviare in the harbour, etc., etc.

Meanwhile the local Hearst press conducts an unceasing campaign of anti-Russian mischief-making – doing their damnedest to start a new world war before this one is finished.

Wednesday 23 May – The British Delegation seems pretty thin and undistinguished now that Eden and the other senior Cabinet ministers have gone. The delegation is weak on the economic and social side.

There is a grave lack of authority – of men of solid experience, wisdom and moderation, who inform a committee – not so much by what they say as by what they are. Then there is the lack of any representation of the English internationalists or those who have devoted themselves to oppressed peoples and to social causes – that whole humanitarian and social side of English activity goes unrepresented. There were representatives of it, but they have gone home – the brunt of the British representation is borne by a little group thinking in terms of political and military power and with not much feeling for public opinion. They produce no ideas which can attract other nations and are not much fitted to deal with Commonwealth countries.

The United States delegation as a whole is no more impressive than the British.

The USSR have achieved a most unfavourable reputation

in the Committees. Their reputation is one of solid stone-walling and refusal to compromise. On the other hand, they are continually blackmailing other governments by posing as the protectors of the masses against reactionary influence. The insincerity of these tactics is patent to those who see them at close quarters, but will not be so to the public for whom they are designed.

The Chinese are an endearing delegation, polite and humorous – but then are they really a Great Power?

The French are among the disappointments of this Conference. The Big Power representatives, however undistinguished individually, *do* represent Power and so carry weight. The French delegation here reinforce the painful impression that I formed in Paris. You do not feel that they have France, *La grande nation*, behind them. They are full of schemes and combinations and suspicions. But there is no steadiness or clarity in their policy. They have no one who is a connecting link with the past and who still retains faith and vitality. The national continuity has been broken.

You can see the effects of fatigue in the drained faces of almost all the European delegates. Europe (I do not count Russia) is not making much of a showing at this Conference.

Back in Ottawa he wrote about the final, public sessions of the conference.

Thursday 28 June – The Opera House was packed with a pleased, excited, well-fed people. There was a feeling of a gala performance. On the floodlit stage ranged in front of the flags of the United Nations were standing hand-picked specimens of each branch of the United States Armed Forces.

One after another the speakers mounted the rostrum and addressed us – most of them in their native languages. The text of the speeches in English had been circulated to the audience, but this was hardly necessary as we knew what they would say, and they all said it – in Chinese, Arabic, French, and Russian we were told that mankind was embarking on another effort to organize the world so that peace should reign. We were told that the success of the Conference showed that this ideal could be attained if unity was preserved – that we owed it to the living and to the dead to devote all our efforts to this end.

CLARA MILBURN

The Germans were 'detestable', Clara wrote, and was especially savage about the Gestapo. Reluctantly she accepted the need to provide them with food – 'common humanity . . . will not allow one's enemies to starve' – but was appalled by the news of thousands starved to death in the camps 'while outside the wire were fields and farms and well-fed Germans'. The prospect of Alan returning drew closer, although there were setbacks and alarming news of POWs suffering in bombing attacks. Clara 'scrounged' cooking chocolate, sherry, bacon, ready for the home-coming.

On VE Day Jack was ill and had to stay in bed. Clara hoisted the flag she had given him, following instructions he had written for her. She had been using Alan's room as a study, but now made it ready for him, though she still did not know when to expect him.

Wednesday 9 May – A Day of Days!

This morning at 9.15 the telephone rang and a voice said: 'I've got a very nice telegram for you. You are Milburn, Burleigh, Balsall Common 29?'

'Yes,' I said.

The voice said: 'This is the telegram. "Arrived safely. Coming soon. Alan."'

I nearly leapt to the ceiling and rushed to the bottom of the stairs. 'We've got the right telegram at last!' I cried.

And then all three of us, Jack in bed, Kate nearby and myself all choky, shed a tear or two. We were living again, after five-and-a-half years!

At 11.15 a.m. the telephone rang again and it was a long-distance call. 'Is that Burleigh, Balsall Common?'

'Yes! Is that Alan?' I said.

'Yes.'

And then I said: 'Oh, bless you, my darling.' And off went Alan into a description of his leaving Germany and arriving here, ending by saying he might arrive late tonight or early tomorrow and would ring up again later, and so we said 'Goodbye.'

I wrote 19 postcards and one letter, had three or four long-distance telephone calls and about two dozen others during the day. I made two long-distance calls, and when I asked for a third the operator said: 'You're keeping me busy.'

'Yes,' I said, 'this is a thrilling day.'

'Something special?'

'Yes, my son has arrived in England after five years as a prisoner of war.'

'Exeter,' said the operator's voice, and then to me: 'Was he in Germany?'

'Yes.'

'He'll be glad to get home – there you are, call out, please. They're waiting.'

Such mateyness, it is amusing.

And here we are at 7.15 p.m., and so far no other word from Alan.

Thursday 10 May – <u>He came!</u>

All evening we waited and hoped, myself scarcely daring to move from the house, though I did take Twink to post.

Biggs, who saw me on the way back, said the last train from London came in at 9.20 p.m., so we hoped and waited. I hung out of the window looking, looking . . . and then, tired with the day's exertions and happenings, I went to bed and presently to sleep.

The next thing I knew Jack was saying: 'Can't you hear the telephone? It's ringing.' I shook myself into wakefulness and went into Alan's room, picked up the receiver, declared myself and heard: 'This is Alan.' He was at Leamington station and it was getting on for 12 p.m.

I soon dressed, went down, got out the car and drove off into the warm, clear night – meeting few people or vehicles until I got into Leamington. There crowds thronged the Parade and I blew the horn at intervals to clear a passage for the car. At the station I saw the trellised metal gates closed at the entrance and in front of them were two figures, one in khaki in a beret and a figure in blue.

The khaki beret wouldn't be Alan, I thought, but it detached itself, came to the car and said: 'Is it Ma?', and so out I flung myself and, as the blue figure drew discreetly away, we had a good hug and a kiss and then soon were speeding home, talking hard. At home we found Jack up and dressed, and Kate, too. Soon Alan was disposing of two boiled eggs with bread and butter, and we all drank chocolate while we talked and talked. At last we got to bed at 2.30 a.m. and today have not felt quite as energetic as usual, as may be imagined.

Saturday 12 May – Still warm and sunny and the MG went roaring out, taking one to the butcher's and grocer's. I managed to thread myself in and out of the weird little seat and enjoyed being driven. We met quite a lot of people and Alan was shaking hands here and there, 'telling the tale' at the baker's while a crowd stood around. All Balsall Common knows that I drove to Leamington at midnight to fetch him home! I find there is a bit of mending to be done for Alan (and how I have longed to have the little toffee tin of grey trouser buttons out again all these long five years) and a few things to store and put away.

Alan, still enjoying the garden, sat in a deckchair for a time after lunch and then did a bit of work on his car. Jack got into his overall coat and there they were just as they were six years ago, working together in the garage. A rest for Jack after tea and Alan and I did a bit of gardening. They were all 'bits' today, nothing serious. It was too hot. The telephone rang at intervals all day with messages, all full of kindness and congratulations. Many letters arrived too – I shall be busy tomorrow.

I walk about in a half-dream and the long, bad years of war begin to fade a little as Alan's voice is heard, the MG's voice, too, and the house is once more a real home.

HERMIONE RANFURLY

In January Hermione became senior civil assistant (PA) to Air Marshal Slessor in Naples. Her separation from General Jumbo in December had been sudden. His request that she accompany him to Washington – where he was to be the new head of the British Joint Staff Mission – had provoked Lady Wilson (who had always described Hermione as 'unsuitable') to insist that he sack her 'with no notice, no pay, no reference'. She had spent Christmas in London, with 'no job, no billet and no luggage', yet she wrote that it was nothing compared to the horrors being suffered under quislings and fascists in Yugoslavia and under both Germans and Russians in Poland.

In early April Slessor informed her that he would be returning to London to be Air Member for Personnel at the Air Ministry and wanted her to go with him. Dan was also being sent home after five years' overseas service. The coincidence was 'miraculous'. On her way home, she visited her mother in her nursing home in Switzerland. After six and a half years, she was as 'young and pretty as ever'. Hermione then boarded a train for Lyons, where she was collected by a staff car and driven to Paris. She had hoped to leave her parrot, Coco, with Arthur Forbes (whom she had first met piloting the Caseys' plane) before flying to England. But Arthur was away and General Wood, who shared an office with him, accompanied her and Coco to Arthur's house – to the undoubted surprise of the housekeeper. Wood took her back to his flat, where he told her about his recent visit to two concentration camps in Germany.

Monday 9 April – **On the train from Vevey, Switzerland, to Lyons** – I looked out of the window and thought of peace. I have almost forgotten what it was like. The taxi driver who took me to the frontier told me that he will get drunk when Hitler is dead. He had bought two bottles of whisky for this purpose long ago – they cost him seventy francs each.

Monday 30 April – Sitting in his [General Wood's] luxury flat, with the sun shining outside on the Champs Elysées and the gramophone playing dance tunes, I looked at the appalling photographs he had taken with his Leica camera and listened to his description of piles of corpses, 'like busted sawdust dolls', and torture implements.

Wednesday 2 May – **London** – Late last night it was announced that Hitler is dead. Reinforced by this wonderful news early today I continued my search for somewhere for Dan and me to live. This is proving difficult: London is overcrowded. Agents have nothing to offer at a price we could afford; hotels are booked solid for months.

I contacted Arthur Forbes, who was as kind and amusing as ever. He was undaunted when I told him I'd left Coco in his Paris flat and said he could send him back to me easily via his air transport network. 'I always presumed you had named him after me so it's the least I can do,' he said. Arthur was called Coco as a child – but I can't remember why.

This evening I learned that Berlin surrendered to the Russians at 3 p.m. today – and the German armies in Italy signed their unconditional surrender in our old office in Caserta.

Saturday 5 May – I dined with David Stirling who is just back from Colditz prison in Germany. He looks thinner but fit. He talked about going to the Far East war. After dinner we were joined by Peter Stirling and Fitzroy. They were all in high spirits and made me laugh. They brought the news that the Fourteenth Army has captured Rangoon and that Hitler and Goebbels are thought to have committed suicide but no bodies were found. 'Not surprising,' said Peter. 'There is no food in Berlin so probably Himmler ate them.'

Tuesday 8 May – Today the people of London and their children and thousands of visitors took to the streets and parks to celebrate victory in Europe.

There was no traffic because people filled the streets and pavements. I walked to the office and found only Air Marshal Slessor there. 'It's a National Holiday – you shouldn't have come,' he said. 'Supposing I stay and help till lunchtime,' I said and added, 'besides it's a brilliant time to throw some of your more boring papers out of our windows.' Before I left I peeled the canvas off one window and emptied the contents of five waste paper baskets on to Kingsway. I longed to be more generous but did not dare.

Thursday 10 May – Marvellous. Coco has arrived. I collected him from a young pilot in Chelsea who had flown him over in a smart metal box with 'Explosive' painted on the lid. He was touchingly pleased to see me and I am overjoyed to get him back.

Monday 14 May – Our thoughts and prayers are beamed on the Far East where terrible fighting continues.

Saturday 26 May – On Thursday I put on my prettiest clothes and arrived at King's Cross Station an hour early for Dan's train. 'When the train glides in,' I thought, 'it will be the end of all our misery – the beginning of living happily ever after . . .'

I saw him a long way down the platform. I stood and watched him, just like I did a long time ago, on sand, at Rehovoth. Heaven . . . is being together.

NAOMI MITCHISON

As usual Naomi had gone down to London in the early part of the year but was back in Carradale as the war entered its final months. Dick was with her, as were her younger children and several friends including Margaret Cole. But Murdoch was still fighting in Italy.

Sunday 15 April – In the evening we were listening to Ed Murrow's broadcast on a concentration camp (the one, I think where Ossietzky* was, and no doubt a lot of others one knew) and that made us talk and talk about what was wrong with the German soul, what could be done, and how such catastrophes could be avoided in the future.

---

* A pacifist who had been imprisoned by the Nazis in 1933 and awarded the Nobel Peace Prize in 1935. He had died in 1938.

Monday 23 April – My fellow blood transfusers talking about the prison camps. That really seems to have got under the skin of even Carradale. I keep on saying that when some of us talked about concentration camps three years before the war the people who talk about them now, wouldn't listen. One just can't imagine the quality of hell it must be in Berlin. I suppose Hitler and Goering will either get themselves killed or commit suicide. I hope they won't be martyrs anyhow!

Wednesday 2 May – One feels Hitler's death is just rather pointless now. He should have died some time ago. I wonder how many people comfort themselves with thinking he's frizzling. The Italian news is grand, I wonder if they'll go on over the Brenner. I know this part of Austria where the fighting is, pretty well, the Voralberg Pass, the Innthal, all so magic and lovely.

Naomi travelled to London with her youngest daughter Val, arriving early in the morning at River Court. They had lunch and dinner in town with Dick, watched the celebrations in Piccadilly Circus, then joined in some dancing with the crowds at Hammersmith, ending the day on the roof at their house watching the searchlights 'whirling round and reflected beautifully in the river'.

Monday 14 May – **Edinburgh** – Then I came back [from an education committee], talked farming with Uncle Willie who feels himself rather old, and finds in a way that he is already missing the sense of urgency and common purpose of the war and can scarcely face the added energy that is wanted for post war problems which he realises will be so much more difficult. It was a relief, all the same, to talk to someone who wasn't bitterly anti-German nor screaming for a 'hard' peace. He was very tentative with me, obviously feeling that I, as one of the younger generation, must want a 'hard' peace. And of course I don't. I think it's all nonsense, and I believe I would think the same if I had, personally, suffered more.

Naomi's great sadness during the war was the loss of her baby girl Clemency in the summer of 1940, buried at sea in July. Some time after that she began work on her novel *The Bull Calves*, continuing throughout the war. It was published in 1947, and is prefaced by a poem in memory of Clemency. The final section of the poem looks ahead one hundred years:

> But the trees I planted in the heavy months, carrying
>   you,
> Thinking you would see them grown, they will be tall
>   and lovely:
> Red oak and beech and tsuga, grey alder and douglas:
> But not for you or your children. What will it matter
>   then, forgotten daughter,
> Forgotten as I shall be forgotten in the running of time,
> As I alone remember, with what tears yet, the first kiss,
>   the faint warmth and stirring?
> The waves will cover us all diving into darkness out of
>   the bodies of death,
> Vanishing as the wake of a boat in a strong current.
> The hot tears will be cooled and the despair of the
>   middle-aged, rolling up their map,
> Will be forgotten, with other evil things, will be
>   interpreted,
> Will be forgiven at last.*

* Naomi Mitchison, *The Bull Calves*, Jonathan Cape, 1947.

THE LIBERATION OF EUROPE

In the last few weeks of the war thousands of French and Belgian civilians died as the Allies pursued the Germans east. Many scores were settled, by individuals and by resistance groups. In France the number of civilian deaths, sometimes put as high as 40,000, exceeded those attributed to the four-year occupation by German forces.* In Holland the population starved waiting for airborne food drops. There were millions of refugees. Many inmates of Nazi forced-labour and extermination camps remained for months where they had been held prisoner, now as 'displaced persons', waiting to return home. Since the liberation of Belsen on 15 April the camp had been sealed off on account of a typhus epidemic which had been deliberately engineered by the Nazi camp authorities.

MEA ALLAN†

Mea Allan of the *Daily Herald* was the only woman journalist accredited to the British army. Her journals and letters home from Europe reveal her particular interest in post-war recovery, as does her unpublished memoir, now in the archives of the Imperial War Museum. In 1943 Mea had given her editor on the *Herald*, Percy Cudlipp, a copy of her second novel, *Change of Heart*, in which she'd imagined what might happen after the war, and she'd asked him whether, if Britain won, 'he would let her go

---

* Norman Davies, *Europe at War 1939–45: No Simple Victory*, Macmillan, 2006.
† M. E. Allan, private papers including unpublished ms. 'Reporting for Duty', Imperial War Museum, 9581.

to the Continent to see how people were rebuilding their cities, their lives and their governments. He gave his promise – and kept it'.

On 4 May, the day Hitler's death was announced, Mea was in Kevelaer in Germany, just across the Dutch border. Since 19 April the town had been a displaced-persons transit camp efficiently run by the Allied Military Government. Within the space of a fortnight nearly 50,000 men, women and children had been repatriated at a rate of 2,000 a day.

The camp was a fantastic place with its crowds in transit. It could all have been a frightening muddle, but Mil Gov was handling the situation superbly in a routine as meticulous as any tactical battle plan. No displaced person unless sick spent more than twenty-four hours here. Each in turn was issued with a ration card and a registration card, and there was plenty of bread and good thick soup made of meat and vegetables being served to the queue steadily filing past to receive bowlful and spoon. Russian women, themselves dis-placed persons, had volunteered their services as cooks, nurses and helpers. They are husky young women whose colourful red and flowered headscarves add cheerfulness to the bare rooms of the monastery where the meals are served. Nearby a huge church formed a sleeping room for some of the men and the whole floor is a sea of bedding-straw, brilliant gold in the shafts of sunlight streaming through the windows, on which sit and lounge the still-dazed refugees who never expected to see their homes again.

Sunday 6 May – **Letter to her parents from Kevelaer** – The hotel we slept in had been bombed slightly and was full of that beastly bombed smell. It was bare but for beds and mattresses and a few of the heavier pieces of furniture. Cold water, no electric light and it was very queer being in Germany and not being able to smile at people – and not wanting to. The Belsen and Buchenwald revelations have shaken us all. I saw the newsreel films of the 2 camps last night. I do beg you to go and see them for the sake of seeing what the Germans are capable of and for telling other people.

I am going to Belsen, to do the story of the clearing up. You will have read of the striped uniform the prisoners wore. I have seen many of them in the streets of Paris and Brussels. Sometimes it is the striped jacket with a pair of tattered trousers. Or the striped trousers with an old jacket and odds and ends of any clothes bundled round them. It is terrible to see on their faces the stamp of all the suffering they have endured. And these are the fittest cases who have already been sent home. The rest are in hospital or dying in the sickbay at the cleaned up section of the camp.

[7 May] My second German town [Suchteln] – in another requisitioned hotel. Today is Sunday and all day the church bells have been ding-donging. The Germans around here are very 'religious' – this is the Catholic Rhineland and every room almost has its crucifix on the wall. A pity the people couldn't have placed their religion more among the people of the world instead of allowing a Gestapo to rise up among them. All the people are well-fed and there seem to be dozens of children everywhere. The girls all have silk stockings . . . Don't pity the Germans. The war correspondents here – there are about 7 of us plus our conducting officers – are a nice crowd.

My conducting officer has told me we definitely start tomorrow a.m. at 9.30.

Mea recorded her experiences in Belsen in her memoir.

To pass by the camp would give no indication of what was behind the innocent-looking concrete posts and deer-netting, fences of a type common in Germany and about ten foot high. Behind the fences were little pine trees and stretches of grass, and at the main gates a swimming pool.

I was taken to the guard room and soused from head to foot with DDT powder: my hair, inside my cap, back and front of my battle blouse, back and front of my slacks and inside sleeves and boots, and handed over to an RAMC captain who was a Czech by the name of I. Gluck.

I got there in time to see the last barbed wire barricade being removed from around the last hut. Captain Gluck told me that the operation had begun early that morning and that a sort of smile had spread throughout the camp. A vision was born then, he said, of freedom. Like most Czechs he was small and sturdy, and every fibre of him radiated confidence. For him each passing hour saw some improvement, some amelioration of the filth and starvation.

'Let me,' he said, 'show you some very good huts. Here is one . . .'

I was appalled. It was a woman's hut, but you could hardly tell to which sex they belonged.

'And that,' I said, 'is a very good hut . . . Will any of them in there recover?'

'Perhaps. Probably not. But the other inmates of that hut are now able to walk. Like these . . .'

The Belsen walk was ghostly, a light weightless and almost bouncing step as in a slow-motion film. To me it was horrifying. To Captain Gluck it was triumph. He reeled off the statistics. Of the 35,000 people in Belsen the majority were still in the original camp, but each day saw a thousand or more sent to Camp Two where they were dusted, bathed and, as garments were available, reclothed.

I spoke to some of the hundred medical students from London hospitals, among them 21-year-old Gordon Dutton who was in his final year, Philip Kemp who was 22, both of whom were angry. A rumour had reached them that certain people in London thought they were too young and sensitive to tackle the work they were doing. This was not how Gordon and Philip felt about it. They were taking a fierce joy in their job.

'Up till today all the people wanted was food,' Philip said. 'Today they are asking if they can have a radio, tomorrow it will be newspapers. It is a miracle seeing people coming back to life.'

Three days later, Friday 11 May, Mea was in Hamburg.

In Hamburg I met Lili Marlene [sic], the famous German crooner, counterpart of our own Vera Lynn, whose song 'Underneath the lamplight'* was as familiar to British soldiers in the North African desert war as it was to the Germans of Rommel's army, for both listened to the same radio programmes. It was she who told me what had happened in Hamburg to make it the graveyard of a town I explored later that week, with eighty percent of its buildings destroyed.

In July 1943 she had returned to Hamburg to visit her parents and had been caught in what must have been the war's most horrific and terrible air raid. It had been during the night of Saturday the 24th when alternately 2,300 tons of HEs [high explosive bombs] and incendiaries rained down on the city. The ground rocked with explosions, she said, and the crash of buildings. The tarmacadamed streets ran in rivers of flame, and those who were trapped became human torches. Hamburg has many bridges, and thousands flocked under them for shelter: they were suffocated by clouds of dense black smoke rolling in from the burning tar. So intense was the heat that people's bodies swelled up and burst.

The Big Fire Raid, as the surviving Hamburgers would

---

* In fact 'Lili Marleen' was the song, not the singer. Lale Andersen, a cabaret singer, recorded it in 1939 and it was she who Mea Allan met in Hamburg.

always grimly remember it, lasted only fifty minutes, but it took a toll of 20,000 lives. In all, with the fatalities from the raids of the two succeeding nights, 50,000 people perished.

And such was the displacement of air – flames 100 yards high consuming the oxygen, the wind came in like a tornado and played skittles with the tottering buildings. And such was the shock to nature that the flowering trees broke into blossom again in the autumn.

11. JAPANESE SURRENDER

SUMMER 1945

On 2 May the remaining defenders of Berlin surrendered; on the 4th Montgomery accepted the Germans' unconditional surrender on Lüneburg Heath in northern Germany; and on 7 May the final surrender document was signed. The next day the Allies celebrated Victory in Europe (VE) Day.

The end of the war in Europe also marked the end of the coalition National Government in Britain. Churchill felt that the coalition should continue in office until Japan had been defeated, and Clement Attlee, deputy prime minister and leader of the Labour Party, concurred. However, at Labour's annual conference on 21 May the party voted to withdraw from the coalition, forcing a general election. The election, the first since 1935, was set for 5 July, but the results were to be held back until the 26th to allow the votes of servicemen and women serving abroad to be collated and counted.

The Conservative Party was confident that it would emerge victorious. Churchill's personal popularity remained high, and he was generally well received at election meetings. However, it was easy to mistake public admiration for what he had done for an endorsement of Conservative policy. While home on leave the recently promoted General Slim, commander of the British forces in Burma, gave Churchill a blunt assessment of the political climate: 'Well, Prime Minister, I know one thing. My army won't be voting for you.'* The vast majority of the civilian population also wanted change – too many sacrifices had been made for things to stay the way they were – and in the eyes of many voters the Conservatives were still the party of appeasement.

As the country geared up for the election, British, Indian and African troops under Slim in monsoon-swept Burma – and throughout the Far East – still had months of fighting ahead against an enemy whose code of honour dictated that death was preferable to surrender. Meanwhile, American forces in the Pacific were slowly reclaiming Japan's island conquests, bringing the seemingly inevitable invasion of the Japanese mainland closer.

In July the Big Three – America represented by Harry S. Truman, who had succeeded Roosevelt, Britain and Russia – met at Potsdam to decide how Nazi Germany should be punished for its crimes and to establish the post-war order. The timing of the conference was problematic for Churchill, as it coincided with the British general election. He therefore invited Attlee and Ernest Bevin to attend the sessions with him. The Potsdam Conference was a curtain-raiser for the Cold War. By July the Red Army had taken effective control of the Baltic States, Poland, Czechoslovakia, Hungary, Bulgaria and Romania. For some, the liberation of Europe was no liberation at all. Refugees fearing communist takeovers fled in their hundreds of thousands. Nazi Germany's invasion of Poland had triggered the war; now Stalin installed a communist government there. Although Britain and America protested, Stalin was adamant. He saw eastern Europe as a bulwark against future attack and a legitimate sphere of Soviet influence. Short of threatening a new war, Britain and America could only defer contentious issues to a future peace conference. Stalin was happy to accede to a free vote for the Poles, safe in the knowledge

---

* Ronald Lewin, *Slim: The Standard Bearer*, Leo Cooper, 1977.

that 'it's not who votes that matters, but who counts the votes'.*

The Allied leaders also discussed the continuing war in the Far East and issued a declaration calling for Japan's surrender. If the Japanese failed to accede, they would face 'prompt and utter destruction'. What the Japanese could not have known was that on 16 July the Americans had successfully tested an atomic bomb.

The day after this declaration was made, the results of the British general election came through: Labour had secured a majority of 146. Attlee and Bevin, now prime minister and foreign secretary respectively, returned on 3 August to an exhausted Britain. Six years of war had left the country with 75 per cent of its pre-war wealth: national income was down by 50 per cent; exports were 33 per cent of the 1938 figure; the merchant fleet was 70 per cent of its pre-war size; and about 40 per cent of overseas markets had been lost, mainly to the Americans.

Three days later, as President Truman sailed home from Potsdam on 6 August, he was still waiting for some sign that the Japanese might surrender. None had been forthcoming.

That morning Tsutomu Yamaguchi was crossing a potato field outside the city of Hiroshima. High above he saw a plane circling and two parachutes drifting down. Exactly forty-three seconds later Mr Yamaguchi was blinded by a flash of white light and engulfed in a huge booming ball of fire which threw him across the field. When he regained consciousness, his torso and half his face were burned and his

---

* This is often considered an apocryphal remark by Stalin but can be found in the memoirs of Boris Bazhanov, his former secretary, originally published in Paris in 1930 following Bazhanov's defection. Discussing voting in Communist Party meetings, Bazhanov recalled Stalin saying, 'I consider it completely unimportant who in the party will vote, or how, but what is extraordinarily important is this – who will count the votes and how.'

eardrums were ruptured. It took him over two days to make the 200-mile journey home but, conscientiously, he reported for work back in Nagasaki on 9 August.

Meanwhile, the government had released minimal information of a 'bombing incident in Hiroshima' and had suffered another blow when the Soviet Union declared war on Japan on 8 August, but still refused to surrender. Mr Yamaguchi was explaining to his incredulous boss how one bomb had destroyed the whole of Hiroshima when the same flash of light blasted through the window. He was saved by the sheltering effect of a steel stairwell. His wife and son also survived. Tsutomu Yamaguchi is the only person officially recognized by the Japanese government as having survived both nuclear explosions.*

The scale of devastation at Hiroshima was almost incomprehensible. The resulting firestorm eventually engulfed 4.4 square miles of the city, killing anyone who did not flee in the first minutes after the attack. Casualties are estimated as between 90,000 and 160,000 out of a population of 255,000. Those not immediately vaporized suffered horrendous burns, and those who seemed to have escaped injury soon began to suffer the effects of radiation poisoning, the worst affected dying within ten days. Other victims still suffer the effects today.

The Japanese cabinet had been debating surrender for an hour when the second atomic bomb fell. Even then they could not agree. At 2 a.m. on 12 August Admiral Suzuki, the prime minister, asked Emperor Hirohito to choose which course to take. At noon on 15 August Japan surrendered unconditionally. With the aid of a terrifyingly violent new

---

* Although some thirty people are known to have travelled on two trains from Hiroshima to Nagasaki and survived both atomic bombs, Yamaguchi is one of the few who were close to the hypocentre of both nuclear explosions to have survived.

weapon which would alter the stakes for all future conflicts the Second World War had come to an end.

THE DIARISTS

NAOMI MITCHISON

In the 1945 general election Dick was the Labour Party candidate for Kettering. The other candidates were the sitting Conservative, John Profumo,* and J. C. Dempsey, a local councillor standing as a pacifist independent. Naomi canvassed energetically, gradually getting the hang of the loudhailer. Their friends the Coles, Jack Haldane, their daughter Lois, Denny M from Carradale and Clement Attlee himself all visited the constituency to speak in Dick's support. The three weeks between polling day and the results were spent in Carradale, where Naomi returned to her work on the estate and, having sold River Court, dealt with the arrival of furniture and papers from Hammersmith – 'an invasion of ghosts'.

Thursday 26 July – **Kettering** – When we got to the hotel, Dick was fairly confident, from what had been seen by the locals when emptying out the ballot boxes yesterday. We had breakfast and went in. For the first half-hour it looked about even and most people said it would be narrow. But soon we were going ahead. A lot of the service votes had gone to Dempsey, no doubt because he was the man they

---

* In the early 1960s Profumo was at the centre of the scandal now known by his name, and resigned from his post as secretary of state for war in the Conservative government.

knew. Quite a lot of votes – several hundreds I think – were invalid because they hadn't been properly stamped. A few were spoiled. Gradually our people got more and more pleased and excited and the others gloomier. I became very sorry for them and tried to be nice to them. Profumo himself was being very decent and so was his mother. It was raining and the returning officer (who never managed to get Dick's name right and was obviously very upset at the turn things had taken) said he would announce it officially at 12.30.

We then heard that Tiffany* was in for the next constituency and our own majority of over six thousand made us hopeful of what might be happening all over. But it wasn't till 12 when we listened to the news that we began to realise it. There was a bowl of gladioli in the pub and I stuck two in my hair. We listened with delight at the names of the men who were out, especially Bracken and Amery and Grigg.[†] I was slightly sorry about Harold Nicolson and very about Lady Bonham Carter and Mark and somewhat about Sinclair.[‡] Beveridge[§] will do fully as well out of Parliament as in.

Almost all the country had gone left.

---

* The Labour candidate in Peterborough.
[†] Brendan Bracken, Leo Amery and P. J. Grigg were all members of the government.
[‡] Sir Archibald Sinclair, leader of the Liberal Party and secretary of state for air in the coalition government.
[§] Beveridge had joined the Liberal Party and won the seat at Berwick-upon-Tweed in 1944, which he now lost. He later became leader of the Liberals in the House of Lords.

HAROLD NICOLSON

Harold had correctly forecast his own rejection in Leicester but not the Labour landslide and the size of Churchill's defeat. He also lost his flat in Temple – receiving notice to leave by Christmas – as it was being reclaimed for the use of barristers. He had lived there for fifteen years. He felt 'as if chapter after chapter was being closed, finished, put away'.

Friday 27 July – I spend the morning analysing the Election results. It is an amazing statement of public opinion, but I am not yet quite sure what it really means.

I feel sad and hurt, as if I had some wound or lesion inside. But I cannot make out what is the centre of this sadness. Naturally I much mind leaving the House and being outside public life. I also realise that I had counted upon my friends being returned, and half hoped that they would assist me, either to get back, or else to the House of Lords, or else to some job like Chairman of the British Council. But they will want any seat that they can get for their own front bench; they will require every peerage possible; and the Labour Government will want someone far more left-wing than I am for the British Council. Therefore I see a denial of future opportunity.

But there is something else. It is not, I think, dread of the social revolution. I have expected this for a long time and do not fear it. It may be the conflict within me between the patrician and the humanitarian. I hate uneducated people having power; but I like to think the poor will be rendered happy. This is a familiar conflict.

One thing I do mind is missing the appearance of the new House. I want to see how the new people fit in. I want to see how the brilliant Harold Wilson really does.*

---

* Then twenty-nine, Wilson became Labour prime minister in 1964.

Wednesday 1 August – Robin Maugham* rings me up. He had been round to No. 10 on 26 July. Winston was in magnificent form and took his defeat with humour. He confessed that it was distressing after all these years to abandon the reins of power. Someone said, 'But at least, sir, while you held the reins, you managed to win the race.' 'Yes,' said Winston, 'I won the race – and now they have warned me off the turf.'

Somebody mentioned that I had lost the seat of West Leicester. Robin remembered the actual words which Winston used and memorised them. 'The House,' he said, 'will be a sadder place without him' – then he paused, and added, 'and smaller.' This pleases me more than anything.

Monday 6 August – The 9 o'clock news announces that we have split the atom. A long statement, drafted by Winston, is read, explaining how the discovery was made. It cost £500,000,000 and took four years. They have used it today on a Japanese town. They cannot tell exactly what damage was done. It is to be used eventually for domestic purposes.

GEORGE BEARDMORE

George voted Liberal in the general election. He was a polling clerk (in Victoria's school) and recorded an 82 per cent turnout. For the time being he continued as a housing officer, frustrated at the lack of funding to make large empty houses habitable again.

The shock of the atomic bombs left him struggling to empathize as they were so outside his own experience. 'I can't begin to imagine,' he wrote on 22 August, 'three square miles pulverised and so many thousand Japanese scorched to cinders. My instinct is to ask: "Who's the Incident Officer?"'

---

* Friend and fellow author, nephew of Somerset Maugham.

It wasn't until the first weekend in October that the end of the war was celebrated in the local park.

Sunday 7 October – Today, one of the best days of a rich season, leaves are at their most colourful under a long yellow sun, with mists about, and the faint nostalgic sweetness of autumn – log-cutting, buttered crumpets, and fairy-tales all implied by a moment of silence in a wood otherwise filled with the rustling of falling leaves.

Now then, in the last analysis, which gives me more satisfaction, the foregoing, or a Victory celebration in Headstone Park with Home Guard explosives and Fire Guard incendiaries for fireworks? Why, across the park where one of my first fly-bombs had landed, new tiles are still visible on many of the houses, while I know, because it was my job, that many of the inhabitants were either killed or have left to try to begin new lives elsewhere. Who is to speak for the elderly Browns killed by the rocket that landed behind the Embassy Cinema and of which I pocketed a gyroscope by way of souvenir? Filled with similar thoughts, I guess, Jean said: 'Let's leave 'em to it and go home,' and she turned the push-chair round while I caught Victoria's hand to bring her away.

ALAN BROOKE

At Potsdam, Brooke joined the combined chiefs of staff for the last conference of the war. He later commented that it was by far the easiest of his meetings with the Americans – 'the old battles were done and finished'. The focus was mainly upon the war with Japan: the strategy, the part to be played by British forces and issues of command in the Pacific. Brooke accepted that in this theatre of the war the Americans were the dominant partner.

Berlin was nearby. It was extraordinary to be there, with the war in Europe finally behind them, though the devastation was all too present.

Thursday 19 July – After tea we went back to Berlin to visit the stadium where Olympic Games were run, and also to see Hitler's dugout where he is supposed to have died. A sordid and unromantic spot. Absolute chaos outside of concrete mixers, iron reinforcing bars, timber, broken furniture, shell holes, clothes, etc, etc. Down below even worse chaos. It is however possible to make out one large sitting room probably used for meals, a study for Hitler, a bedroom of Hitler's opening into two separate bath and WC rooms, connecting through to Eva Braun's room. Beyond these an electric engine room, further bunks, galley and a well equipped surgery. Outside we were shown where Goebbels and his family were found, also where a body was found which was taken for Hitler. However, the Russian in charge said that he considered Hitler was now in Argentina, and that Eva Braun had never died, but a mistress of Goebbels. I wonder if the truth will ever be known. We also had a look at the Air Ministry and had a drive round Berlin. The more one sees of it the more one realizes how completely destroyed it is. Weather warming up again. Apparently tripartite talks going strong and making some headway.

Friday 27 July – A day of partings!

After lunch I had a long interview with S o S.* It was a sad one and I hate to see him go. We have worked wonderfully together, and I have grown to know him well and to appreciate his high qualities. I am genuinely fond of him, and very sad at our parting. Then at 5.30 pm had to go and see Winston at 10 Downing St, with other Chiefs of Staff. It was a very sad and very moving little meeting at which I found

---

* P. J. Grigg.

myself unable to say much for fear of breaking down. He was standing the blow wonderfully well.

Saturday 28 July – Met Hosking★ at 8.30 at the White Lion and went on to the hide at once. A huge erection 26 feet high! But within 12 feet of the nest. There are 3 young birds. By 9am I was established. At 10.45 the hen came for the first time and was at nest feeding for 10 minutes. At 12.15 she returned and was again there for close on 10 minutes. I took a lot of photographs and only hope that they may be good. It was a wonderful chance, and I believe the first time that a coloured cine picture of a hobby has been taken!

The bombing of Hiroshima passed without comment in his diary except a sentence at the start of the entry for 10 August: 'A memorable day as regards the war with Japan!'

VERA BRITTAIN

Vera's excitement at the general election result was offset by what had happened at Bilston, where George had failed to gain the party nomination by two votes, and which now returned the Labour candidate with a large majority. She 'listened all day on wireless to the incredible results coming in'.

Wednesday 15 August – V.J. Day. Last night at midnight Attlee broadcast the news of Japan's surrender. One is thankful that the awful slaughter has stopped, but the manner of its ending leaves no such feeling of relief as the end of the War in Europe – because the atomic bomb means that far from terror being over, its possibilities have only just begun.

★   Eric Hosking, bird photographer. Brooke had helped him gain permission to
    build a hide to observe a hobby hawk's nest.

Squarely upon the demoralised generation is laid the awful responsibility of deciding whether the human race is to continue or not.

She was now free to travel again, and went first to the Netherlands and Scandinavia. In Sweden she met a small elderly Polish woman who had survived the concentration camp at Ravensbrück.

Undated but some time in October – She had just discovered that her husband is still alive, & was looking forward to going back to Poland; she had been arrested in Warsaw for being in the resistance Movement. Had remarkably reasonable attitude towards the Germans; thought we should not try to repay them in kind – not, she said, out of pity for them, but because to kill was so terribly corrupting, so bad for the killer especially if he was young. She felt no special hatred for the German officials who had imprisoned her because, she said, they had their orders from above, & had no choice about fulfilling orders which damaged them in the fulfilment.

While Vera was abroad the newspapers in Britain published the list found in Berlin of those who were to be shot or imprisoned had the Nazis invaded Britain. Among the 3,000 or so names were hers, George's and other leading pacifists. She felt vindicated: it was a rebuff to the many who had accused her during the war of being unpatriotic.

HERMIONE RANFURLY

Hermione had found a flat to rent in a mews in Mayfair, where they unwrapped their wedding presents for the first time. Dan was demobbed on 15 July and, despite his fears of being too old to start back in the City where he had left off and 'puzzling what

he should do', it was less than a fortnight before he found a job –
'a good one' – starting in September. Hermione was still at the
Air Ministry and receiving first-hand information from Air Marshal
Slessor on how 'frightful' the next winter in Europe was going
to be. Rations had already been cut as a precaution against the
predicted famine.

Wednesday 8 August – After a busy morning in the office I
hurried along the Strand to meet Dan and George Jellicoe for
lunch at the Savoy Grill. I found them bent over the Midday
Standard at a nice corner table. They hardly looked up when
I arrived but moved the paper so I could read it too.

Across the front page, in huge letters, was one word –
'OBLITERATION'. In aghast silence we read that the Allies
had dropped an Atom bomb on Hiroshima last Monday at
1.30 am. Four square miles, or sixty per cent of the city, were
wiped out by the incredible pressure and heat. All living
things were destroyed. Since then, from Guam, General
Spaatz, US Air Force, has announced that reconnaissance
photos, taken as soon as the seven-and-a-half-mile high moun-
tain of dust and smoke had cleared, show the heart of the
city swept as though by a bulldozer with awful thoroughness.
It is rumoured that the bomb weighed only five hundred
pounds.

Throughout lunch we talked of this news which eclipsed
anything we had ever heard in our lives. It seemed to us that
all modern inventions, even Navies, Armies and Air Forces
are now out of date, dwarfed by this appalling weapon.

Walter Monckton* wandered over and sat down at our
table: 'This is the biggest thing which has happened since
Christ came,' he said. 'The heat, the driving power of this
thing, is vast. If one tenth of one per cent can completely

---

* Monckton became solicitor general in May 1945, having been director
   general at the Ministry of Information.

destroy four and one tenth square miles then a full dose could destroy four thousand square miles. It means we could change the weather, melt the poles – and every aspect of trade and civilisation as we know them could be altered. This discovery is so huge that there is little one can think of that it might not change.'

Friday 10 August – I lunched with John Wyndham* at Boulestins – prawns and pigeons. Suddenly the head waiter came to our table and said, 'Japan has surrendered'.

Walking back to the office, with paper cascading from office windows and swirling in gusts along the streets, and people on the roofs and balconies singing and shouting, I felt terribly sad. It is so wonderful that World War II is over, and no wonder people celebrate, but what we have all done – to defend ourselves and to win the war – is too frightful for words.

*   The author, although his best-known novels did not appear until the 1950s.

Afterword

With the war over, people naturally assumed that things could only get better. But as Anthony Heap, a local government official in London, put it, 'No sooner did we awake from the six year nightmare of war and feel free to enjoy life once more, than the means to do so immediately became scantier than they had been during the war'.

The switch from a wartime economy – five million service personnel and another four million employed supplying them – to a peacetime one was far from straightforward. In August 1945 the economist John Maynard Keynes told the new government that the country faced a 'financial Dunkirk' and would soon be 'virtually bankrupt and the economic basis for the hopes of the public non-existent'. But he felt that there might be a glimmer of hope if the lend-lease arrangement with the United States were to continue. President Truman, however, promptly terminated the agreement: all goods had to be paid for. Britain owed America $650 million. Total war had been replaced by total economic ruin.

Keynes was dispatched to America with a begging bowl, hoping for a gift of $5 billion. He returned with the outstanding $650 million written off and a loan of $3,750 million at 2 per cent interest payable from 1951. It was enough to allow the Labour government to introduce their ambitious welfare reforms, but wartime rationing would remain in place until 1954, long after the rest of western Europe.

In 1943, when her husband Dick had predicted that the war would be over 'next year', Naomi Mitchison had replied,

'It will never be over. We've all got into the habit of it; that's the way total war is'. Settling back into the rhythm of life in peacetime with no bombs raining down on them and learning to live without the friends and family killed during the war was traumatic for everyone. And though none of the nine diarists had a partner or child killed in the war, they all lost people close to them, and some had believed, even if only for a short time, that those dearest to them might be dead.

All of them experienced air raids at first hand; some had to deal with the grisly aftermath. As a driver on the Queen's Messenger Convoy, Anne saw Exeter High Street reduced to 'just a goat's track between shattered walls'. In Glasgow Naomi helped dig out the body of the son of a couple from Carradale. Clara witnessed the destruction of Coventry, noting how 'English folk clung to their homes' until they were literally bombed out of them. And George, having finally found the job he'd been looking for as a housing officer, was responsible for coping with the victims of flying bombs. 'Tears came to my eyes not with the grief and distress caused to survivors but with the incalculable trouble to which they will be put, months and years of it, before they can resume any sort of normal life and the incident becomes only a tale to tell to the grandchildren.'

For those with children, or expecting them, the anxiety was exacerbated. Vera was separated from her young children for three years with no transatlantic telephone calls and with letters taking up to six months to arrive. Naomi, expecting her seventh child in July 1940, wrote, 'I haven't made little she-plans about it as I did with the others; the future is black-fogged ahead of this one; all one can cultivate is acceptance'. George and Jean were naturally worried about the effect constant air raids at home in London or 'insufferable billets' in the country would have on their little daughter Victoria. But by the time they were expecting a second, in the fifth year of the war, at the height of the flying bombs, George could write, 'We are glad, and that's all there is to it.'

Anne Garnett's tumour could not be blamed on the war, but it certainly informed the way she reacted to the diagnosis. Instead of being angry that her operation was delayed six weeks because all hospital beds were being freed for D-Day, Anne found the resilience of Londoners in the face of the flying bombs delivered her 'from a very dark slough'. 'I should have liked to find personal comfort through the church,' she wrote, 'but it didn't happen that way. It came (none the less God Given) lying under a tree in Hyde Park, and cheering E.enders in Shoreditch.'

One of the first things Anne did in peacetime was to get a dog, Jason, a yellow Labrador. She'd had a succession of terriers in the 1930s but had gone without for the duration of the war. Though Anne stopped keeping a diary in July 1945, she kept up her voluminous correspondence, conducted at her desk after breakfast every day. Her husband Frank continued to struggle with diabetes and finally died in 1974. Anne herself died of a heart attack on 28 December 1988, seven days after her eightieth birthday and two years after the first volume of her pre-war diaries, *Caught from Time*, was published by her youngest daughter Caroline's publishing company, Tabb House. A second volume, *Fields of Young Corn*, came out in 1989, and Anne's wartime diaries, *Through Ripe Fields*, are being prepared for publication.

With Alan home again, **Clara Milburn**'s diaries also cease. Alan married Judy in 1946 and Clara happily allowed them, and eventually their two children, to become her chief focus. When Jack died in 1955, she moved to be near them in Kenilworth, although sadly Alan was killed in a car crash in 1959. Judy wrote, 'I remember a friend from his university days writing to me to say what many people felt: what a tragic waste it was after he had come through the war and all that time in prison camp. His mother felt that deeply, and, a year later, became seriously ill'. Clara died in 1961, aged 77.

Years later Judy's son-in-law came across Clara's diaries and contacted a journalist friend, Peter Donnelly, who edited them and wrote an introduction, while Judy provided a short epilogue. They were published by Harrap in 1979 as *Mrs Milburn's Diaries: An Englishwoman's Day-to-Day Reflections 1939–45*.

Charles Ritchie was sent to the Canadian embassy in Paris in August 1946. Elizabeth Bowen felt his absence keenly, writing in the first letter of hers which he kept that he'd taken with him 'my real life, my only life, everything that is meant by my heart'. Her novel *The Heat of the Day*, set in wartime London and published in 1949, was dedicated to Ritchie. Despite marrying his second cousin, actress Sylvia Smellie, in 1948, Charles remained close to Elizabeth, spending a few days every year with her at her family home in Cork. When Elizabeth's husband died in 1952 she became increasingly sad that he was married to Sylvia and not to her.

In 1967 Charles returned to London as high commissioner, the final posting of a distinguished diplomatic career. Elizabeth encouraged him to consider publication of his diaries. Her death from lung cancer, coinciding with his retirement in 1973, dealt him a savage blow. 'If she ever thought that she loved me more than I did her, she is revenged,' he wrote. Sylvia always maintained that their marriage was happy, prompting Ritchie to say that any happiness was due to Sylvia's ability to will it to be so. He died, childless, in Ottawa in 1995.

His wartime diary was published in 1974 as *The Siren Years – A Canadian Diplomat Abroad 1937–45*. This was succeeded by *An Appetite for Life: The Education of a Young Diarist 1924–27*, then *Diplomatic Passport – more undiplomatic diaries 1944–62* and finally *Storm Signals – more undiplomatic diaries 1962–71*. A family memoir, *My Grandfather's House*, was published in 1987.

When her husband Dick became an MP in 1945, **Naomi Mitchison** admitted to being somewhat jealous, but she knew that at heart she did not really want to go into Parliament. However, in December 1945 she was elected a Labour county councillor for Argyll and remained so for the next twenty years. She continued to write – novels, poetry, science fiction, children's stories, memoirs, articles and letters – as well as campaign for a wide range of progressive causes. She also travelled, in particular establishing a close relationship with the Bakgatla people in Botswana. Carradale remained her home, where the garden often took her away from her writing and where her ever-growing family visited. Her sons all became distinguished scientists, and her daughters followed her in writing and journalism.

In 1985, when she was 87, selections from her diary edited by Dorothy Sheridan (archivist at Mass Observation, the social research organization), were published by Gollancz as *Among You Taking Notes*. In her foreword Naomi wrote, 'Was I as I appear in the diary? I rather hope not as I don't like myself much. It reads sadly . . . because it is full of hope for a new kind of world, for something different, happier, more honest, for a new relationship between people. But the bright vision fades, fades, always, always.' At her hundredth birthday (her fellow Scot Neal Ascherson remembered in the *Guardian*) she 'sat like a tribal queen, a swarm of grandchildren surrounded her, a small figure hidden in the press of loving friends and relations . . . the old house at Carradale was crammed with Labour ministers and MPs, crofters and professors, editors and fishermen'.

She died in January 1999. She was 101.

Alan Brooke stayed on as CIGS until June 1946, when he was awarded the Order of Merit and handed over to Montgomery, now a field marshal. In January that year he was created Viscount Alanbrooke of Brookeborough, but despite his peerage was far from comfortable financially. He had to sell Ferney Close, moving into the former gardener's cottage on the estate, and even sold some precious volumes from his collection of bird books.

As others' memoirs of the war appeared, especially Churchill's, Brooke began to feel that the record needed to be set right. In particular he was disappointed that Churchill had given scant recognition to the contribution of his generals, including that of Brooke himself. He added a retrospective commentary to his wartime diaries, and they were published, edited by historian Arthur Bryant, in two volumes, *The Turn of the Tide* in 1957 and *The Triumph in the West* in 1959. Although Bryant cut out much of Brooke's criticism, the books offended the many people who admired Churchill unreservedly. Brooke died suddenly a month before his eightieth birthday, for which eighty friends had planned to present him with the bird books he had reluctantly sold nearly twenty years before. In 1994 a statue of Brooke was erected in Whitehall, outside the Ministry of Defence. MASTER OF STRATEGY is engraved on its base and it is flanked by statues of Slim and Montgomery.

Brooke's complete *War Diaries 1939–1945*, dedicated to Benita as 'first reader and safekeeper' and edited by Alex Danchev and Daniel Todman, were published by Weidenfeld and Nicolson in 2001.

Hermione and Dan Ranfurly bought a house in the country, at Little Pednor near Great Missenden in Buckinghamshire, within commuting distance of the City. Whitaker, who had found work in the north and never liked the country – particularly cowpats – saw little of them after that time. In 1946 Hermione and Dan returned to Italy to thank the many families who had risked their lives to help Dan survive the long winter of his escape. Their daughter Caroline was born in 1948, and in 1952 Dan became governor of the Bahamas at the age of only 40.

Between 1952 and 1956 Hermione embraced her position at Government House, raising money to build the Ranfurly Home for Children – still running today – and starting the Ranfurly Out Island Library, which delivered books to the communities on the inhabited Out Islands of the Bahamas. Upon her return to England her book-lending scheme went global with the Duke of Edinburgh as its patron. Now known as Book Aid International, it has distributed 35.5 million books to eighty-four countries in the developing world.

Dan died in 1989 and Hermione plunged into a lengthy period of illness. During her convalescence she began to edit her wartime diaries, which had been considered too sensitive for publication immediately after the war. *To War with Whitaker – the wartime diaries of the Countess of Ranfurly 1939–45* was published in 1994. In the preface Hermione wrote that the diaries 'prove how lucky I have always been'. Her childhood memoirs, *The Ugly One*, so called because her family always described her thus, were published in 1998. Hermione's death in 2001, aged 87, interrupted progress on a third work, intended to cover her life after the war; her daughter Caroline is currently preparing this for publication.

Harold Nicolson joined the Labour Party and stood in the North Croydon by-election in 1948. Once again he lost. His political life over, he continued as an author, columnist and reviewer, giving up his London life and retiring to Sissinghurst. Harold and Vita continued to write to each other every day that they were apart. His three volumes of diaries and letters were published by Collins between 1966 and 1968, and Nicolson assisted his son Nigel in editing them. In his introduction to the second volume Nigel noted, 'His diary was the only one of his possessions which V. Sackville-West was instructed to take with her should she be forced to flee Kent by the threat of a German invasion . . . He had one eye cocked on a morsel of posterity'.

When Harold died from a heart attack in 1968, aged 81, six years after Vita, their garden at Sissinghurst passed to the National Trust. It has become one of the Trust's most visited properties. As a memorial to him, his sons created the gazebo that stands in the garden, which marks one of his favourite viewpoints.

Despite having a young family to provide for, **George Beardmore** began writing full time, principally for children. His writing did not make him a fortune, and the years before retirement were especially difficult. He and Jean edited *Arnold Bennett in Love*, a collection of letters published in 1972. Jean died in 1973. George moved to Dorset four years later, discovering his wartime journals in the process of packing before the move. He began to prepare them for publication but died in 1979 aged 71. *Civilians at War: Journals 1938–1946* was published by John Murray in 1984.

After the war **Vera Brittain** continued to write campaigning articles on such issues as apartheid and independence for the colonies. She was a founder member of CND and produced another ten books, including her second volume of auto-biography *Testament of Experience* in 1957. Her daughter, by then Shirley Williams, became a Labour MP in 1964. Vera was delighted by Shirley's political success, although she did not live to see her become a member of Harold Wilson's cabinet, as she died in 1970. Her ashes were scattered on her brother's grave in Italy as she had requested. George remar-ried in 1971 and died in 1979, the same year as BBC Television broadcast an adaptation of *Testament of Youth*.

Wartime Chronicle, the third volume of her diaries, was published in 1989 by Victor Gollancz, edited by Alan Bishop and Aleksandra Bennett.

Thanks

We would like to thank Martin Lamb for his invaluable contribution to the essays providing historical context. Without our confidence in his research this book would not have been written.

We are also most grateful to the following, for illuminating the very individual stories of their parents: Adam Nicolson on his grandfather, Harold; Lady Caroline Simmonds on her mother, Hermione Ranfurly; Caroline Tabb on her mother, Anne Garnett; Eva Fox-Gál on her father, Hans Gál; Geraint Talfan Davies on his father, Aneirin ap Talfan; and Charles and Hugh Grace on their father, Raymond Grace. We acknowledge the crucial role played by Nicholas Wetton in obtaining permission to use the diary extracts and photographs. We thank our editor, Georgina Morley, and our agent, Andrew Kidd, for their guidance and advice; the Staff at the Departments of Printed Books and Documents Dept of the IWM for making their invaluable material available for research; and, finally, the editors of the published diaries themselves.

Text Acknowledgements

Every effort has been made to contact copyright holders. The publishers and the Imperial War Museum (IWM) would be grateful for any information which might help to trace those whose identities or addresses are not currently known, and the publishers will be pleased to rectify any omissions brought to their notice at the earliest opportunity.

Alanbrooke. *War Diaries 1939–1945*, edited by Alex Danchev and Daniel Todman. Phoenix. 2002. Reprinted by permission of David Higham Associates.

Allan, M. E. (Mea). (Private Papers including unpublished ms *Reporting for Duty*) IWM Ref: 9581. Published by permission of R. D. F. Allan.

ap Talfan, Aneirin. *Dyddiau'r Ceiliog Rhedyn*. Foyles Welsh Co. Ltd., London 1941–2 (English translation from Welsh by Geraint Talfan Davies).

Beardmore, George. *Civilians at War: Journals 1938–1946*. John Murray, 1984. Reprinted by permission of the publisher.

Begg, Jane. (Private Papers – lecture delivered February 1945) MacBeth, J. R., IWM Ref: 91271. Published by permission of Finella S. M. MacKinnon.

Berry, Paul and Bostridge, Mark. *Vera Brittain: A Life*. Chatto & Windus, 1995.

Biggar, Andrew, M. C., Article entitled 'Post-Graduate'. *Journal of the Edinburgh Agricultural College Former Students Association*, No. 21., October 1946.

Birchall, Barbara. From *Goodnight Children Everywhere. Memories of Evacuation in World War II*, edited by Pam Schweiter. Age Exchange, 1990.

Bone, Lieutenant H. T. (Private Papers) IWM Ref: 87311. Published by permission of Gillian Temple-Bone.

Branson, Clive. *British Soldier in India – the Letters of Clive Branson*. Communist Party, 1944.

Brittain, Vera. *Wartime Chronicle, Vera Brittain's Diary 1939–1945*, edited by Alan Bishop and Y. Aleksandra Bennett. Victor Gollancz, 1989. Extracts from the works of Vera Brittain are included by permission of Mark Bostridge and T. J. Brittain-Catlin, Literary Executors for the Estate of Vera Brittain 1970.

Brittain, Vera. *Testament of Experience*. Fontana, 1980.

Brittain, Vera. *England's Hour*. Futura, 1981.

Brittain, Vera. *One Voice*. Continuum, 2005.

de Cosson, Tony. From Ranfurly, Countess of, *To War With Whitaker, The Wartime Diaries of the Countess of Ranfurly*. William Heinemann, 1994.

Dixon, J. L. (Private Papers) IWM Ref: 87341.

Emanuel, Muriel & Gissing, Vera. *Nicholas Winton and the Rescued Generation*. Vallentine Mitchell, 2002.

Gál, Hans. *Musik hinter Stacheldraht. Tagebuchblätter aus dem Sommer 1940*. Bern: Peter Lang, 2003. Unpublished translation by Eva Fox-Gál and Anthony Fox: 'Music Behind Barbed Wire – A Diary of the Summer of 1940'. Published by permission of Eva Fox-Gál.

Garnett, Anne (Mrs A. Lee-Michell). Unpublished journal 1941–45 IWM Ref: 9281. Extracts from Anne Garnett's wartime diaries, the copyright of her daughter, publisher of her girlhood diaries *Caught from Time* and *Fields of Young Corn*, Caroline White of Tabb House, by permission.

Gissing, Vera. *Pearls of Childhood*. Robson Books, 1994.

Grace, H. R. Private Papers: *A Wartime Log for British Prisoners*, Oflag VII B, Eichstatt, Upper Bavaria.

Jesse, F. Tennyson and Harwood, H. M. *London Front – Letters written to America August 1939–July 1940*. Constable, 1940. Reprinted by permission of the publisher.

Kitching, Thomas. *Life and Death in Changi: The War and Internment Diary of Thomas Kitching – The diary of Tom Kitching who died in Japanese hands in Singapore in 1944*, edited by Brian Kitching. William Culross & Son, 1998.

Macpherson, Major Thomas. From Sound Archive IWM Ref: 17912. Also from *Forgotten Voices of the Secret War, an inside history of Special Operations during the Second World War*, edited by Roderick Bailey. Ebury, 2008. Reprinted by permission of The Random House Group Ltd.

McGinlay, Major A. O. From Robert Lyman. *The Longest Siege: Tobruk – The Battle That Saved North Africa*. Macmillan, 2009.

Milburn, Clara. *Mrs Milburn's Diaries*, edited by Peter Donnelly. Harrap, 1979. Reprinted by permission of Thomas Donnelly.

Mitchison, Naomi. *Among You Taking Notes*, edited by Dorothy Sheridan. Victor Gollancz, 1985. Reprinted by permission of David Higham Associates.

Mitchison, Naomi. *The Cleansing of the Knife*. Canongate, 1978.

Mitchison, Naomi. *The Bull Calves*. Richard Drew, 1985.

Moorehead, Alan. *African Trilogy*. Hamish Hamilton, 1944.

Morrison, A. Private Papers: Unpublished: *On the Road To – Anywhere!* IWM Ref: 75751.

Nicolson, Harold. *Diaries and Letters 1939–45*, edited by Nigel Nicolson. Collins, 1967. Courtesy of the Harold Nicolson Estate.

Nicolson, Harold. *Diaries and Letters 1930–1939*, edited by Nigel Nicolson. Collins, 1966.

Nicolson, Harold. *Why Britain is at War*. Penguin, 1939.

Nixon, Barbara. *Raiders Overhead – A Diary of the London Blitz*. Scolar Press/Gulliver Publishing, 1980 (Originally published in 1943).

Northwood, Captain Vernon. From Robert Lyman. *The Longest Siege: Tobruk – The Battle That Saved North Africa*. Macmillan, 2009.

Porteous, Major Patrick. From Russell Miller. *Nothing Less Than Victory, The Oral History of D-Day*. Penguin, 1994.

Ranfurly, Countess of. *To War With Whitaker*. William Heinemann, 1994. © Lady Ranfurly, 1994. Reproduced by permission of PFD (www.pfd.com) on behalf of The Estate of Lady Ranfurly.

Ritchie, Charles. *Undiplomatic Diaries: 1937–1971*. © 2008. Published by McClelland & Stewart Ltd. Used with permission of the publisher.

Sansom, William. *Westminster at War*. Faber & Faber, 1947.

Storer, Corporal Irene. (Private Papers) Forsdyke, I. IWM Ref: 86371. Published by permission of Mrs Joan Horton.

Truman, Anita. From *Goodnight Children Everywhere. Memories of Evacuation in World War II*, edited by Pam Schweiter. Age Exchange, 1990.

Wells (née Bolster), Esther Maureen. Private Papers, some published under *Entertaining Eric* (pub. IWM 1988) IWM Ref: 661. Published by permission of Jim Wells.

Wilson, Charles. *Essex Yeomanry Journal 1969*. Reprinted by permission of Essex Yeomanry Association.